The Works Of John
Greenleaf Whittier
Vol.- VI

by

John Greenleaf Whittier

The Works Of John
Greenleaf Whittier
Vol.- VI

by John Greenleaf Whittier

ISBN: 978-93-59957-86-9

Published by

DOUBLE 9 BOOKS

2/13-B, Ansari Road
Daryaganj, New Delhi – 110002
info@double9books.com
www.double9books.com
Tel. 011-40042856

This book is under public domain

ABOUT THE AUTHOR

John Greenleaf Whittier was an American Quaker author who lived from December 17, 1807, to September 7, 1892. He fought to end slavery in the United States. He was inspired by the Scottish poet Robert Burns and is often called one of the fireside poets. Whittier is best known for his works against slavery and his book Snow-Bound, which came out in 1866. John Whittier and Abigail (née Hussey) Whittier had a child on December 17, 1807, on their farm in Haverhill, Massachusetts. The word for his given name, feuillevert, comes from the Huguenots who came before him. The farm was where he grew up. He lived with his parents, his brother and two sisters, an aunt and uncle from his mother's side, and many guests and farm workers. As a child, Whittier was color-blind because he couldn't tell the difference between cherries that were ripe and ones that weren't. It wasn't making much money on the farm, and there was just enough to get by. Whittier himself wasn't cut out for hard farm work, and he had bad health and was weak his whole life.

CONTENTS

OLD PORTRAITS AND MODERN SKETCHES...................................7

THOMAS ELLWOOD.. 22

JAMES NAYLER... 41

ANDREW MARVELL.. 51

JOHN ROBERTS... 65

SAMUEL HOPKINS... 79

RICHARD BAXTER 88

WILLIAM LEGGETT 109

NATHANIEL PEABODY ROGERS 127

ROBERT DINSMORE 143

PLACIDO, THE SLAVE POET (1845.)................................ 154

PERSONAL SKETCHES AND TRIBUTES 161
THE FUNERAL OF TORREY 161

EDWARD EVERETT.. 163

LEWIS TAPPAN (1873.) 166

BAYARD TAYLOR 168

WILLIAM ELLERY CHANNING 169

DEATH OF PRESIDENT GARFIELD 170

LYDIA MARIA CHILD 171

OLIVER WENDELL HOLMES 185

LONGFELLOW 186

OLD NEWBURY... 187

SCHOOLDAY REMEMBRANCES.. 189

EDWIN PERCY WHIPPLE.. 190

HISTORICAL PAPERS 192
DANIEL O'CONNELL 192

ENGLAND UNDER JAMES II 207

THE BORDER WAR OF 1708 218

THE GREAT IPSWICH FRIGHT 224

POPE NIGHT 229

THE BOY CAPTIVES. AN INCIDENT OF
   THE INDIAN WAR OF 1695 233

THE BLACK MEN IN THE REVOLUTION
AND WAR OF 1812 239

THE SCOTTISH REFORMERS 245

THE PILGRIMS OF PLYMOUTH 253

GOVERNOR ENDICOTT.. 255

JOHN WINTHROP 256

OLD PORTRAITS AND MODERN SKETCHES

Inscribed as follows, when first collected in book-form:—
To Dr. G. BAILEY, of the National Era, Washington, D. C., these
sketches, many of which originally appeared in the columns of the
paper under his editorial supervision, are, in their present form,
offered as a token of the esteem and confidence which years of
political and literary communion have justified and confirmed, on
the part of his friend and associate,
THE AUTHOR.
JOHN BUNYAN.

"Wouldst see
A man I' the clouds, and hear him speak to thee?"

Who has not read Pilgrim's Progress? Who has not, in childhood, followed the wandering Christian on his way to the Celestial City? Who has not laid at night his young head on the pillow, to paint on the walls of darkness pictures of the Wicket Gate and the Archers, the Hill of Difficulty, the Lions and Giants, Doubting Castle and Vanity Fair, the sunny Delectable Mountains and the Shepherds, the Black River and the wonderful glory beyond it; and at last fallen asleep, to dream over the strange story, to hear the sweet welcomings of the sisters at the House Beautiful, and the song of birds from the window of that "upper chamber which opened towards the sunrising?" And who, looking back to the green spots in his childish experiences, does not bless the good Tinker of Elstow?

And who, that has reperused the story of the Pilgrim at a maturer age, and felt the plummet of its truth sounding in the deep places of the soul, has not reason to bless the author for some timely warning or grateful encouragement? Where is the scholar, the poet, the man of taste and feeling, who does not, with Cowper,

"Even in transitory life's late day,
Revere the man whose Pilgrim marks the road,
And guides the Progress of the soul to God!"

We have just been reading, with no slight degree of interest, that simple but wonderful piece of autobiography, entitled Grace abounding to the Chief of Sinners, from the pen of the author of Pilgrim's Progress. It is the record of a journey more terrible than that of the ideal Pilgrim; "truth stranger than fiction;" the painful upward struggling of a spirit from the blackness of despair and blasphemy, into the high, pure air of Hope and Faith. More earnest words were never written. It is the entire unveiling of a human heart; the tearing off of the fig-leaf covering of its sin. The voice which speaks to us from these old pages seems not so much that of a denizen of the world in which we live, as of a soul at the last solemn confessional. Shorn of all ornament, simple and direct as the contrition and prayer of childhood, when for the first time the Spectre of Sin stands by its bedside, the style is that of a man dead to self-gratification, careless of the world's opinion, and only desirous to convey to others, in all truthfulness and sincerity, the lesson of his inward trials, temptations, sins, weaknesses, and dangers; and to give glory to Him who had mercifully led him through all, and enabled him, like his own Pilgrim, to leave behind the Valley of the Shadow of Death, the snares of the Enchanted Ground, and the terrors of Doubting Castle, and to reach the land of Beulah, where the air was sweet and pleasant, and the birds sang and the flowers sprang up around him, and the Shining Ones walked in the brightness of the not distant Heaven. In the introductory pages he says "he could have dipped into a style higher than this in which I have discoursed, and could have adorned all things more than here I have seemed to do; but I dared not. God did not play in tempting me; neither did I play when I sunk, as it were, into a bottomless pit, when the pangs of hell took hold on me; wherefore, I may not play in relating of them, but be plain and simple, and lay down the thing as it was."

This book, as well as Pilgrim's Progress, was written in Bedford prison, and was designed especially for the comfort and edification of his "children, whom God had counted him worthy to beget in faith by his ministry." In his introduction he tells them, that, although taken from them, and tied up, "sticking, as it were, between the teeth of the lions of the wilderness," he once again, as before, from the top of Shemer and Hermon, so now, from the lion's den and the mountain of leopards, would look after then with fatherly care and desires for their everlasting welfare. "If," said he, "you have sinned against light; if you are tempted to blaspheme; if you are drowned in despair; if you think God fights against you; or if Heaven is hidden from your eyes, remember it was so with your father. But out of all the Lord delivered me."

He gives no dates; he affords scarcely a clue to his localities; of the man, as he worked, and ate, and drank, and lodged, of his neighbors and contemporaries, of all he saw and heard of the world about him, we have only an occasional glimpse, here and there, in his narrative. It is the story of his inward life only that he relates. What had time and place to do with one who trembled always with the awful consciousness of an immortal nature, and about whom fell alternately the shadows of hell and the splendors of heaven? We gather, indeed, from his record, that he was not an idle on-looker in the time of England's great struggle for freedom, but a soldier of the Parliament, in his young years, among the praying sworders and psalm-singing pikemen, the Greathearts and Holdfasts whom he has immortalized in his allegory; but the only allusion which he makes to this portion of his experience is by way of illustration of the goodness of God in preserving him on occasions of peril.

He was born at Elstow, in Bedfordshire, in 1628; and, to use his own words, his "father's house was of that rank which is the meanest and most despised of all the families of the land." His father was a tinker, and the son followed the same calling, which necessarily brought him into association with the lowest and most depraved classes of English society. The estimation in which the tinker and his occupation were held, in the seventeenth century, may be learned from the quaint and humorous description of Sir Thomas Overbury. "The tinker," saith he, "is a movable, for he hath no abiding in one place; he seems to be devout, for his life is a continual pilgrimage, and sometimes, in humility, goes barefoot, therein making necessity a virtue; he is a gallant, for he carries all his wealth upon his back; or a philosopher, for he bears all his substance with him. He is always furnished with a song, to which his hammer, keeping tune, proves that he was the first founder of the kettle- drum; where the best ale is, there stands his music most upon crotchets. The companion of his travel is some foul, sun-burnt quean, that, since the terrible statute, has recanted gypsyism, and is turned pedlaress. So marches he all over England, with his bag and baggage; his conversation is irreprovable, for he is always mending. He observes truly the statutes, and therefore had rather steal than beg. He is so strong an enemy of idleness, that in mending one hole he would rather make three than want work; and when he hath done, he throws the wallet of his faults behind him. His tongue is very voluble, which, with canting, proves him a linguist. He is entertained in every place, yet enters no farther than the door, to avoid suspicion. To conclude, if he escape Tyburn and Banbury, he dies a beggar."

Truly, but a poor beginning for a pious life was the youth of John Bunyan. As might have been expected, he was a wild, reckless, swearing boy, as his father doubtless was before him. "It was my delight," says he, "to be taken captive by the Devil. I had few equals, both for cursing and swearing, lying and blaspheming." Yet, in his ignorance and darkness, his powerful imagination early lent terror to the reproaches of conscience.

He was scared, even in childhood, with dreams of hell and apparitions of devils. Troubled with fears of eternal fire, and the malignant demons who fed it in the regions of despair, he says that he often wished either that there was no hell, or that he had been born a devil himself, that he might be a tormentor rather than one of the tormented.

At an early age he appears to have married. His wife was as poor as himself, for he tells us that they had not so much as a dish or spoon between them; but she brought with her two books on religious subjects, the reading of which seems to have had no slight degree of influence on his mind. He went to church regularly, adored the priest and all things pertaining to his office, being, as he says, "overrun with superstition." On one occasion, a sermon was preached against the breach of the Sabbath by sports or labor, which struck him at the moment as especially designed for himself; but by the time he had finished his dinner he was prepared to "shake it out of his mind, and return to his sports and gaming."

"But the same day," he continues, "as I was in the midst of a game of cat, and having struck it one blow from the hole, just as I was about to strike it a second time, a voice did suddenly dart from Heaven into my soul, which said, 'Wilt thou leave thy sins and go to heaven, or have thy sins and go to hell?' At this, I was put to an exceeding maze; wherefore, leaving my cat upon the ground, I looked up to Heaven, and it was as if I had, with the eyes of my understanding, seen the Lord Jesus look down upon me, as being very hotly displeased with me, and as if He did severely threaten me with some grievous punishment for those and other ungodly practices.

"I had no sooner thus conceived in my mind, but suddenly this conclusion fastened on my spirit, (for the former hint did set my sins again before my face,) that I had been a great and grievous sinner, and that it was now too late for me to look after Heaven; for Christ would not forgive me nor pardon my transgressions. Then, while I was thinking of it, and fearing lest it should be so, I felt my heart sink in despair, concluding it was too late; and therefore I resolved in my mind to go on in sin; for, thought I, if the case be thus, my state is surely miserable; miserable if I leave my sins, and but miserable if I follow them; I can but be damned; and if I must be so, I had as good be damned for many sins as be damned for few."

The reader of Pilgrim's Progress cannot fail here to call to mind the wicked suggestions of the Giant to Christian, in the dungeon of Doubting Castle.

"I returned," he says, "desperately to my sport again; and I well remember, that presently this kind of despair did so possess my soul, that I was persuaded I could never attain to other comfort than what I should get in sin; for Heaven was gone already, so that on that I must not think; wherefore, I found within me great desire to take my fill of sin, that I might taste the sweetness of it; and I made as much haste as I could to fill my belly with its delicates, lest I should die before I had my desires; for that I feared greatly. In these things, I protest before God, I lie not, neither do I frame this sort of speech; these were really, strongly, and with all my heart, my desires; the good Lord, whose mercy is unsearchable, forgive my transgressions."

One day, while standing in the street, cursing and blaspheming, he met with a reproof which startled him. The woman of the house in front of which the wicked young tinker was standing, herself, as he remarks, "a very loose, ungodly wretch," protested that his horrible profanity made her tremble; that he was the ungodliest fellow for swearing she had ever heard, and able to spoil all the youth of the town who came in his company. Struck by this wholly unexpected rebuke, he at once abandoned the practice of swearing; although previously he tells us that "he had never known how to speak, unless he put an oath before and another behind."

The good name which he gained by this change was now a temptation to him. "My neighbors," he says, "were amazed at my great conversion from prodigious profaneness to something like a moral life and sober man. Now, therefore, they began to praise, to commend, and to speak well of me, both to my face and behind my back. Now I was, as they said, become godly; now I was become a right honest man. But oh! when I understood those were their words and opinions of me, it pleased me mighty well; for though as yet I was nothing but a poor painted hypocrite, yet I loved to be talked of as one that was truly godly. I was proud of my godliness, and, indeed, I did all I did either to be seen of or well spoken of by men; and thus I continued for about a twelvemonth or more."

The tyranny of his imagination at this period is seen in the following relation of his abandonment of one of his favorite sports.

"Now, you must know, that before this I had taken much delight in ringing, but my conscience beginning to be tender, I thought such practice was but vain, and therefore forced myself to leave it; yet my mind hankered; wherefore, I would go to the steeple-house and look on, though I durst not ring; but I thought this did not become religion neither; yet I forced myself, and would look on still. But quickly after, I began to think, 'How if one of the bells should fall?' Then I chose to stand under a main beam, that lay overthwart the steeple, from side to side, thinking here I might stand sure; but then I thought again, should the bell fall with a swing, it might first hit the wall, and then, rebounding upon me, might kill me for all this beam. This made me stand in the steeple door; and now, thought I, I am safe enough; for if a bell should then fall, I can slip out behind these thick walls, and so be preserved notwithstanding.

"So after this I would yet go to see them ring, but would not go any farther than the steeple-door. But then it came in my head, 'How if the steeple itself should fall?' And this thought (it may, for aught I know, when I stood and looked on) did continually so shake my mind, that I durst not stand at the steeple-door any longer, but was forced to flee, for fear the steeple should fall upon my head."

About this time, while wandering through Bedford in pursuit of employment, he chanced to see three or four poor old women sitting at a door, in the evening sun, and, drawing near them, heard them converse upon the things of God; of His work in their hearts; of their natural depravity; of the temptations of the Adversary; and of the joy of believing, and of the peace of reconciliation. The words of the aged women found a response in the soul of the listener. "He felt his heart shake," to use his own words; he saw that he lacked the true tokens of a Christian. He now forsook the company of the profane and licentious, and sought that of a poor man who had the reputation of piety, but, to his grief, he found him "a devilish ranter, given up to all manner of uncleanness; he would laugh at all exhortations to sobriety, and deny that there was a God, an angel, or a spirit."

"Neither," he continues, "was this man only a temptation to me, but, my calling lying in the country, I happened to come into several people's company, who, though strict in religion formerly, yet were also drawn away by these ranters. These would also talk with me of their ways, and condemn me as illegal and dark; pretending that they only had attained to perfection, that they could do what they would, and not sin. Oh! these temptations were suitable to my flesh, I being but a young man, and my nature in its prime; but God, who had, as I hope, designed me for better things, kept me in the fear of His name, and did not suffer me to accept such cursed principles."

At this time he was sadly troubled to ascertain whether or not he had that faith which the Scriptures spake of. Travelling one day from Elstow to Bedford, after a recent rain, which had left pools of water in the path, he felt a strong desire to settle the question, by commanding the pools to become dry, and the dry places to become pools. Going under the hedge, to pray for ability to work the miracle, he was struck with the thought that if he failed he should know, indeed, that he was a castaway, and give himself up to despair. He dared not attempt the experiment, and went on his way, to use his own forcible language, "tossed up and down between the Devil and his own ignorance."

Soon after, he had one of those visions which foreshadowed the wonderful dream of his Pilgrim's Progress. He saw some holy people of Bedford on the sunny side of an high mountain, refreshing themselves in the pleasant air and sunlight, while he was shivering in cold and darkness, amidst snows and never-melting ices, like the victims of the Scandinavian hell. A wall compassed the mountain, separating him from the blessed, with one small gap or doorway, through which, with great pain and effort, he was at last enabled to work his way into the sunshine, and sit down with the saints, in the light and warmth thereof.

But now a new trouble assailed him. Like Milton's metaphysical spirits, who sat apart,

"And reasoned of foreknowledge, will, and fate," he grappled with one of those great questions which have always perplexed and baffled human inquiry, and upon which much has been written to little purpose. He was tortured with anxiety to know whether, according to the Westminster formula, he was elected to salvation or damnation. His old adversary vexed his soul with evil suggestions, and even quoted Scripture to enforce them. "It may be you are not elected," said the Tempter; and the poor tinker thought the supposition altogether too probable. "Why, then," said Satan, "you had as good leave off, and strive no farther; for if, indeed, you should not be elected and chosen of God, there is no hope of your being saved; for it is neither in him that willeth nor in him that runneth, but in God who showeth mercy." At length, when, as he says, he was about giving up the ghost of all his hopes, this passage fell with weight upon his spirit: "Look at the generations of old, and see; did ever any trust in God, and were confounded?" Comforted by these words, he opened his Bible took note them, but the most diligent search and inquiry of his neighbors failed to discover them. At length his eye fell upon them in the Apocryphal book of Ecclesiasticus. This, he says, somewhat doubted him at first, as the book was not canonical; but in the end he took courage and comfort from the passage. "I bless God," he says, "for that word; it was good for me. That word doth still oftentimes shine before my face."

A long and weary struggle was now before him. "I cannot," he says, "express with what longings and breathings of my soul I cried unto Christ to call me. Gold! could it have been gotten by gold, what would I have given for it. Had I a whole world, it had all gone ten thousand times over for this, that my soul might have been in a converted state. How lovely now was every one in my eyes, that I thought to be converted men and women. They shone, they walked like a people who carried the broad seal of Heaven with them."

With what force and intensity of language does he portray in the following passage the reality and earnestness of his agonizing experience: —

"While I was thus afflicted with the fears of my own damnation, there were two things would make me wonder: the one was, when I saw old people hunting after the things of this life, as if they should live here always;

the other was, when I found professors much distressed and cast down, when they met with outward losses; as of husband, wife, or child. Lord, thought I, what seeking after carnal things by some, and what grief in others for the loss of them! If they so much labor after and shed so many tears for the things of this present life, how am I to be bemoaned, pitied, and prayed for! My soul is dying, my soul is damning. Were my soul but in a good condition, and were I but sure of it, ah I how rich should I esteem myself, though blessed but with bread and water! I should count these but small afflictions, and should bear them as little burdens. 'A wounded spirit who can bear!'"

He looked with envy, as he wandered through the country, upon the birds in the trees, the hares in the preserves, and the fishes in the streams. They were happy in their brief existence, and their death was but a sleep. He felt himself alienated from God, a discord in the harmonies of the universe. The very rooks which fluttered around the old church spire seemed more worthy of the Creator's love and care than himself. A vision of the infernal fire, like that glimpse of hell which was afforded to Christian by the Shepherds, was continually before him, with its "rumbling noise, and the cry of some tormented, and the scent of brimstone." Whithersoever he went, the glare of it scorched him, and its dreadful sound was in his ears. His vivid but disturbed imagination lent new terrors to the awful figures by which the sacred writers conveyed the idea of future retribution to the Oriental mind. Bunyan's World of Woe, if it lacked the colossal architecture and solemn vastness of Milton's Pandemonium, was more clearly defined; its agonies were within the pale of human comprehension; its victims were men and women, with the same keen sense of corporeal suffering which they possessed in life; and who, to use his own terrible description, had "all the loathed variety of hell to grapple with; fire unquenchable, a lake of choking brimstone, eternal chains, darkness more black than night, the everlasting gnawing of the worm, the sight of devils, and the yells and outcries of the damned."

His mind at this period was evidently shaken in some degree from its balance. He was troubled with strange, wicked thoughts, confused by doubts and blasphemous suggestions, for which he could only account by supposing himself possessed of the Devil. He wanted to curse and swear, and had to clap his hands on his mouth to prevent it. In prayer, he felt, as he supposed, Satan behind him, pulling his clothes, and telling him to have done, and break off; suggesting that he had better pray to him, and calling up before his mind's eye the figures of a bull, a tree, or some other object, instead of the awful idea of God.

He notes here, as cause of thankfulness, that, even in this dark and clouded state, he was enabled to see the "vile and abominable things fomented by the Quakers," to be errors. Gradually, the shadow wherein he had so long

> "Walked beneath the day's broad glare,
>
> A darkened man,"

passed from him, and for a season he was afforded an "evidence of his salvation from Heaven, with many golden seals thereon hanging in his sight." But, ere long, other temptations assailed him. A strange suggestion haunted him, to sell or part with his Saviour. His own account of this hallucination is too painfully vivid to awaken any other feeling than that of sympathy and sadness.

"I could neither eat my food, stoop for a pin, chop a stick, or cast mine eye to look on this or that, but still the temptation would come, Sell Christ for this, or sell Christ for that; sell him, sell him.

"Sometimes it would run in my thoughts, not so little as a hundred times together, Sell him, sell him; against which, I may say, for whole hours together, I have been forced to stand as continually leaning and forcing my spirit against it, lest haply, before I were aware, some wicked thought might arise in my heart, that might consent thereto; and sometimes the tempter would make me believe I had consented to it; but then I should be as tortured upon a rack, for whole days together.

"This temptation did put me to such scares, lest I should at sometimes, I say, consent thereto, and be overcome therewith, that, by the very force of my mind, my very body would be put into action or motion, by way of pushing or thrusting with my hands or elbows; still answering, as fast as the destroyer said, Sell him, I will not, I will not, I will not; no, not for thousands, thousands, thousands of worlds; thus reckoning, lest I should set too low a value on him, even until I scarce well knew where I was, or how to be composed again.

"But to be brief: one morning, as I did lie in my bed, I was, as at other times, most fiercely assaulted with this temptation, to sell and part with Christ; the wicked suggestion still running in my mind, Sell him, sell him, sell him, sell him, sell him, as fast as a man could speak; against which, also, in my mind, as at other times, I answered, No, no, not for thousands, thousands, thousands, at least twenty times together; but at last, after much striving, I felt this thought pass through my heart, Let him go if he will; and I thought also, that I felt my heart freely consent thereto. Oh, the diligence of Satan! Oh, the desperateness of man's heart!

"Now was the battle won, and down fell I, as a bird that is shot from the top of a tree, into great guilt, and fearful despair. Thus getting out of my bed, I went moping into the field; but God knows with as heavy a heart as mortal man, I think, could bear; where, for the space of two hours, I was like a man bereft of life; and, as now, past all recovery, and bound over to eternal punishment.

"And withal, that Scripture did seize upon my soul: 'Or profane person, as Esau, who, for one morsel of meat, sold his birthright; for ye know, how that afterward, when he would have inherited the blessing, he was rejected; for he found no place for repentance, though he sought it carefully with tears."

For two years and a half, as he informs us, that awful scripture sounded in his ears like the knell of a lost soul. He believed that he had committed they unpardonable sin. His mental anguish 'was united with bodily illness and suffering. His nervous system became fearfully deranged; his limbs trembled; and he supposed this visible tremulousness and agitation to be the mark of Cain. 'Troubled with pain and distressing sensations in his chest, he began to fear that his breast- bone would split open, and that he should perish like Judas Iscariot. He feared that the tiles of the houses would fall upon him as he walked in the streets. He was like his own Man in the Cage at the House of the Interpreter, shut out from the promises, and looking forward to certain judgment. "Methought," he says, "the very sun that shineth in heaven did grudge to give me light." And still the dreadful words, "He found no place for repentance, though he sought it carefully with tears," sounded in the depths of his soul. They were, he says, like fetters of brass to his legs, and their continual clanking followed him for months. Regarding himself elected and predestined for damnation, he thought that all things worked for his damage and eternal overthrow, while all things wrought for the best and to do good to the elect and called of God unto salvation. God and all His universe had, he thought, conspired against him; the green earth, the bright waters, the sky itself, were written over with His irrevocable curse.

Well was it said by Bunyan's contemporary, the excellent Cudworth, in his eloquent sermon before the Long Parliament, that "We are nowhere commanded to pry into the secrets of God, but the wholesome advice given us is this: 'To make our calling and election sure.' We have no warrant from Scripture to peep into the hidden rolls of eternity, to spell out our names among the stars." "Must we say that God sometimes, to exercise His uncontrollable dominion, delights rather in plunging wretched souls down into infernal night and everlasting darkness? What, then, shall we make the God of the whole world? Nothing but a cruel and dreadful *Erinnys*, with curled fiery snakes about His head, and firebrands in His hand; thus governing the world! Surely, this will make us either secretly think there is no God in the world, if He must needs be such, or else to wish heartily there were none." It was thus at times with Bunyan. He was tempted, in this season of despair, to believe that there was no resurrection and no judgment.

One day, he tells us, a sudden rushing sound, as of wind or the wings of angels, came to him through the window, wonderfully sweet and pleasant; and it was as if a voice spoke to him from heaven words of encouragement and hope, which, to use his language, commanded, for the time, "a silence in his heart to all those tumultuous thoughts that did use, like masterless hell-hounds, to roar and bellow and make a hideous noise within him." About this time, also, some comforting passages of Scripture were called to mind; but he remarks, that whenever he strove to apply them to his case, Satan would thrust the curse of Esau in his face, and wrest the good word from him. The blessed promise "Him that cometh to me, I will in no wise cast out" was the chief instrumentality in restoring his lost peace. He says of it: "If ever Satan and I did strive for any word of God in all my life, it was for this good word of Christ; he at one end, and I at the other. Oh, what work we made! It was for this in John, I say, that we did so tug and strive; he pulled, and I pulled, but, God be praised! I overcame him; I got sweetness from it. Oh, many a pull hath my heart had with Satan for this blessed sixth chapter of John!" Who does not here call to mind the struggle between Christian and Apollyon in the valley!

That was no fancy sketch; it was the narrative of the author's own grapple with the Spirit of Evil. Like his ideal Christian, he "conquered through Him that loved him." Love wrought the victory the Scripture of Forgiveness overcame that of Hatred.

He never afterwards relapsed into that state of religious melancholy from which he so hardly escaped. He speaks of his deliverance as the waking out of a troublesome dream. His painful experience was not lost upon him; for it gave him, ever after, a tender sympathy for the weak, the sinful, the ignorant, and desponding. In some measure, he had been "touched with the feeling of their infirmities." He could feel for those in the bonds of sin and despair, as bound with them. Hence his power as a preacher; hence the wonderful adaptation of his great allegory to all the variety of spiritual conditions. Like Fearing, he had lain a month in the Slough of Despond, and had played, like him, the long melancholy bass of spiritual heaviness. With Feeble-mind, he had fallen into the hands of Slay-good, of the nature of Man-eaters: and had limped along his difficult way upon the crutches of Ready-to-halt. Who better than himself could describe the condition of Despondency, and his daughter Much-afraid, in the dungeon of Doubting Castle? Had he not also fallen among thieves, like Little-faith?

His account of his entering upon the solemn duties of a preacher of the Gospel is at once curious and instructive. He deals honestly with himself, exposing all his various moods, weaknesses, doubts, and temptations. "I preached," he says, "what I felt; for the terrors of the law and the guilt of transgression lay heavy on my conscience. I have been as one sent to them from the dead. I went, myself in chains, to preach to them in chains; and carried that fire in my conscience which I persuaded them to beware of." At times, when he stood up to preach, blasphemies and evil doubts rushed into his mind, and he felt a strong desire to utter them aloud to his congregation; and at other seasons, when he was about to apply to the sinner some searching and fearful text of Scripture, he was tempted to withhold it, on the ground that it condemned himself also; but, withstanding the suggestion of the Tempter, to use his own simile, he bowed himself like Samson to condemn sin wherever he found it, though he brought guilt and condemnation upon himself thereby, choosing rather to die with the Philistines than to deny the truth.

Foreseeing the consequences of exposing himself to the operation of the penal laws by holding conventicles and preaching, he was deeply afflicted at the thought of the suffering and destitution to which his wife and children might be exposed by his death or imprisonment. Nothing can be more touching than his simple and earnest words on this point. They show how warm and deep were him human affections, and what a tender and loving heart he laid as a sacrifice on the altar of duty.

"I found myself a man compassed with infirmities; the parting with my wife and poor children hath often been to me in this place as the pulling the flesh from the bones; and also it brought to my mind the many hardships, miseries, and wants, that my poor family was like to meet with, should I be taken from them, especially my poor blind child, who lay nearer my heart than all beside. Oh, the thoughts of the hardships I thought my poor blind one might go under would break my heart to pieces.

"Poor child! thought I, what sorrow art thou like to have for thy portion in this world! thou must be beaten, must beg, suffer hunger, cold, nakedness, and a thousand calamities, though I cannot now endure the wind should blow upon thee. But yet, thought I, I must venture you all with God, though it goeth to the quick to leave you: oh! I saw I was as a man who was pulling down his house upon the heads of his wife and children; yet I thought on those 'two milch kine that were to carry the ark of God into another country, and to leave their calves behind them.'

"But that which helped me in this temptation was divers considerations: the first was, the consideration of those two Scriptures, 'Leave thy fatherless children, I will preserve them alive; and let thy widows trust in me;' and again, 'The Lord said, verily it shall go well with thy remnant; verily I will cause the enemy to entreat them well in the time of evil.'"

He was arrested in 1660, charged with "devilishly and perniciously abstaining from church," and of being "a common upholder of conventicles." At the Quarter Sessions, where his trial seems to have been conducted somewhat like that of Faithful at Vanity Fair, he was sentenced to perpetual banishment. This sentence, however, was never executed, but he was remanded to Bedford jail, where he lay a prisoner for twelve years.

Here, shut out from the world, with no other books than the Bible and Fox's Martyrs, he penned that great work which has attained a wider and more stable popularity than any other book in the English tongue. It is alike the favorite of the nursery and the study. Many experienced Christians hold it only second to the Bible; the infidel himself would not willingly let it die. Men of all sects read it with delight, as in the main a truthful representation of the 'Christian pilgrimage, without indeed assenting to all the doctrines which the author puts in the month of his fighting sermonizer, Great-heart, or which may be deduced from some other portions of his allegory. A recollection of his fearful sufferings, from misapprehension of a single text in the Scriptures, relative to the question of election, we may suppose gave a milder tone to the theology of his Pilgrim than was altogether consistent with the Calvinism of the seventeenth century. "Religion," says Macaulay, "has scarcely ever worn a form so calm and soothing as in Bunyan's allegory." In composing it, he seems never to have altogether lost sight of the fact, that, in his life-and-death struggle with Satan for the blessed promise recorded by the Apostle of Love, the adversary was generally found on the Genevan side of the argument. Little did the short-sighted persecutors of Bunyan dream, when they closed upon him the door of Bedford jail, that God would overrule their poor spite and envy to His own glory and the worldwide renown of their victim. In the solitude of his prison, the ideal forms of beauty and sublimity, which had long flitted before him vaguely, like the vision of the Temanite, took shape and coloring; and he was endowed with power to reduce them to order, and arrange them in harmonious groupings. His powerful imagination, no longer self-tormenting, but under the direction of reason and grace, expanded his narrow cell into a vast theatre, lighted up for the display of its wonders. To this creative faculty of his mind might have been aptly applied the language which George Wither, a contemporary prisoner, addressed to his Muse:—

> "The dull loneness, the black shade
> Which these hanging vaults have made,
> The rude portals that give light
> More to terror than delight;
> This my chamber of neglect,
> Walled about with disrespect,—
> From all these, and this dull air,
> A fit object for despair,
> She hath taught me by her might,
> To draw comfort and delight."

That stony cell of his was to him like the rock of Padan-aram to the wandering Patriarch. He saw angels ascending and descending. The House Beautiful rose up before him, and its holy sisterhood welcomed him. He looked, with his Pilgrim, from the Chamber of Peace. The Valley of Humiliation lay stretched out beneath his eye, and he heard "the curious, melodious note of the country birds, who sing all the day long in the spring time, when the flowers appear, and the sun shines warm, and make the woods and groves and solitary places glad." Side by side with the good Christiana and the loving Mercy, he walked through the green and lowly valley, "fruitful as any the crow flies over," through "meadows beautiful with lilies;" the song of the poor but fresh-faced shepherd- boy, who lived a merry life, and wore the herb heartsease in his bosom, sounded through his cell:—

"He that is down need fear no fall;
He that is low no pride."

The broad and pleasant "river of the Water of Life" glided peacefully before him, fringed "on either side with green trees, with all manner of fruit," and leaves of healing, with "meadows beautified with lilies, and green all the year long;" he saw the Delectable Mountains, glorious with sunshine, overhung with gardens and orchards and vineyards; and beyond all, the Land of Beulah, with its eternal sunshine, its song of birds, its music of fountains, its purple clustered vines, and groves through which walked the Shining Ones, silver-winged and beautiful.

What were bars and bolts and prison-walls to him, whose eyes were anointed to see, and whose ears opened to hear, the glory and the rejoicing of the City of God, when the pilgrims were conducted to its golden gates, from the black and bitter river, with the sounding trumpeters, the transfigured harpers with their crowns of gold, the sweet voices of angels, the welcoming peal of bells in the holy city, and the songs of the redeemed ones? In reading the concluding pages of the first part of Pilgrim's Progress, we feel as if the mysterious glory of the Beatific Vision was unveiled before us. We are dazzled with the excess of light. We are entranced with the mighty melody; overwhelmed by the great anthem of rejoicing spirits. It can only be adequately described in the language of Milton in respect to the Apocalypse, as "a seven-fold chorus of hallelujahs and harping symphonies."

Few who read Bunyan nowadays think of him as one of the brave old English confessors, whose steady and firm endurance of persecution baffled and in the end overcame the tyranny of the Established Church in the reign of Charles II. What Milton and Penn and Locke wrote in defence of Liberty, Bunyan lived out and acted. He made no concessions to worldly rank. Dissolute lords and proud bishops he counted less than the humblest and poorest of his disciples at Bedford. When first arrested and thrown into prison, he supposed he should be called to suffer death for his faithful testimony to the truth; and his great fear was, that he should not meet his fate with the requisite firmness, and so dishonor the cause of his Master. And when dark clouds came over him, and he sought in vain for a sufficient evidence that in the event of his death it would be well with him, he girded up his soul with the reflection, that, as he suffered for the word and way of God, he was engaged not to shrink one hair's breadth from it. "I will leap," he says, "off the ladder blindfold into eternity, sink or swim, come heaven, come hell. Lord Jesus, if thou wilt catch me, do; if not, I will venture in thy name!"

The English revolution of the seventeenth century, while it humbled the false and oppressive aristocracy of rank and title, was prodigal in the development of the real nobility of the mind and heart. Its history is bright with the footprints of men whose very names still stir the hearts of freemen, the world over, like a trumpet peal. Say what we may of its fanaticism, laugh as we may at its extravagant enjoyment of newly acquired religious and civil liberty, who shall now venture to deny that it was the golden age of England? Who that regards freedom above slavery, will now sympathize with the outcry and lamentation of those interested in the continuance of the old order of things, against the prevalence of sects and schism, but who, at the same time, as Milton shrewdly intimates, dreaded more the rending of their pontifical sleeves than the rending of the Church? Who shall now sneer at Puritanism, with the Defence of Unlicensed Printing before him? Who scoff at Quakerism over the Journal of George Fox? Who shall join with debauched lordlings and fat-witted prelates in ridicule of Anabaptist levellers and dippers, after rising from the perusal of Pilgrim's Progress? "There were giants in those days." And foremost amidst that band of liberty-loving and God- fearing men,

> "The slandered Calvinists of Charles's time,
>
> Who fought, and won it, Freedom's holy fight,"

stands the subject of our sketch, the Tinker of Elstow. Of his high merit as an author there is no longer any question. The Edinburgh Review expressed the common sentiment of the literary world, when it declared that the two great creative minds of the seventeenth century were those which produced Paradise Lost and the Pilgrim's Progress.

THOMAS ELLWOOD

Commend us to autobiographies! Give us the veritable notchings of Robinson Crusoe on his stick, the indubitable records of a life long since swallowed up in the blackness of darkness, traced by a hand the very dust of which has become undistinguishable. The foolishest egotist who ever chronicled his daily experiences, his hopes and fears, poor plans and vain reachings after happiness, speaking to us out of the Past, and thereby giving us to understand that it was quite as real as our Present, is in no mean sort our benefactor, and commands our attention, in spite of his folly. We are thankful for the very vanity which prompted him to bottle up his poor records, and cast them into the great sea of Time, for future voyagers to pick up. We note, with the deepest interest, that in him too was enacted that miracle of a conscious existence, the reproduction of which in ourselves awes and perplexes us. He, too, had a mother; he hated and loved; the light from old-quenched hearths shone over him; he walked in the sunshine over the dust of those who had gone before him, just as we are now walking over his. These records of him remain, the footmarks of a long-extinct life, not of mere animal organism, but of a being like ourselves, enabling us, by studying their hieroglyphic significance, to decipher and see clearly into the mystery of existence centuries ago. The dead generations live again in these old self-biographies. Incidentally, unintentionally, yet in the simplest and most natural manner, they make us familiar with all the phenomena of life in the bygone ages. We are brought in contact with actual flesh-and-blood men and women, not the ghostly outline figures which pass for such, in what is called History. The horn lantern of the biographer, by the aid of which, with painful minuteness, he chronicled, from day to day, his own outgoings and incomings, making visible to us his pitiful wants, labors, trials, and tribulations of the stomach and of the conscience, sheds, at times, a strong clear light upon contemporaneous activities; what seemed before half fabulous, rises up in distinct and full proportions; we look at statesmen, philosophers, and poets, with the eyes of those who lived perchance their next-door neighbors, and sold them beer, and mutton, and household stuffs, had access to their kitchens, and took note of the fashion of their wigs and the color of their breeches. Without some such light, all history would be just about as unintelligible and unreal as a dimly remembered dream.

The journals of the early Friends or Quakers are in this respect invaluable. Little, it is true, can be said, as a general thing, of their literary merits. Their authors were plain, earnest men and women, chiefly intent upon the substance of things, and having withal a strong testimony to bear against carnal wit and outside show and ornament. Yet, even the scholar may well admire the power of certain portions of George Fox's Journal, where a strong spirit clothes its utterance in simple, downright Saxon words; the quiet and beautiful enthusiasm of Pennington; the torrent energy of Edward Burrough; the serene wisdom of Penn; the logical acuteness of Barclay; the honest truthfulness of Sewell; the wit and humor of John Roberts, (for even Quakerism had its apostolic jokers and drab-coated Robert Halls;) and last, not least, the simple beauty of Woolman's Journal, the modest record of a life of good works and love.

Let us look at the Life of Thomas Ellwood. The book before us is a hardly used Philadelphia reprint, bearing date of 1775. The original was published some sixty years before. It is not a book to be found in fashionable libraries, or noticed in fashionable reviews, but is none the less deserving of attention.

Ellwood was born in 1639, in the little town of Crowell, in Oxfordshire. Old Walter, his father, was of "gentlemanly lineage," and held a commission of the peace under Charles I. One of his most intimate friends was Isaac Pennington, a gentleman of estate and good reputation, whose wife, the widow of Sir John Springette, was a lady of superior endowments. Her only daughter, Gulielma, was the playmate and companion of Thomas. On making this family a visit, in 1658, in company with his father, he was surprised to find that they had united with the Quakers, a sect then little known, and everywhere spoken against. Passing through the vista of nearly two centuries, let us cross the threshold, and look with the eyes of young Ellwood upon this Quaker family. It will doubtless give us a good idea of the earnest and solemn spirit of that age of religious awakening.

"So great a change from a free, debonair, and courtly sort of behavior, which we had formerly found there, into so strict a gravity as they now received us with, did not a little amuse us, and disappointed our expectations of such a pleasant visit as we had promised ourselves.

"For my part, I sought, and at length found, means to cast myself into the company of the daughter, whom I found gathering flowers in the garden, attended by her maid, also a Quaker. But when I addressed her after my accustomed manner, with intention to engage her in discourse on the foot of our former acquaintance, though she treated me with a courteous mien, yet, as young as she was, the gravity of her looks and behavior struck such an awe upon me, that I found myself not so much master of myself as to pursue any further converse with her.

"We staid dinner, which was very handsome, and lacked nothing to recommend it to me but the want of mirth and pleasant discourse, which we could neither have with them, nor, by reason of them, with one another; the weightiness which was upon their spirits and countenances keeping down the lightness that would have been up in ours."

Not long after, they made a second visit to their sober friends, spending several days, during which they attended a meeting, in a neighboring farmhouse, where we are introduced by Ellwood to two remarkable personages, Edward Burrough, the friend and fearless reprover of Cromwell, and by far the most eloquent preacher of his sect and James Nayler, whose melancholy after-history of fanaticism, cruel sufferings, and beautiful repentance, is so well known to the readers of English history under the Protectorate. Under the preaching of these men, and the influence of the Pennington family, young Ellwood was brought into fellowship with the Quakers. Of the old Justice's sorrow and indignation at this sudden blasting of his hopes and wishes in respect to his son, and of the trials and difficulties of the latter in his new vocation, it is now scarcely worth while to speak. Let us step forward a few years, to 1662, considering meantime how matters, political and spiritual, are changed in that brief period. Cromwell, the Maccabeus of Puritanism, is no longer among men; Charles the Second sits in his place; profane and licentious cavaliers have thrust aside the sleek-haired, painful-faced Independents, who used to groan approval to the Scriptural illustrations of Harrison and Fleetwood; men easy of virtue, without sincerity, either in religion or politics, occupying the places made honorable by the Miltons, Whitlocks, and Vanes of the Commonwealth. Having this change in view, the light which the farthing candle of Ellwood sheds upon one of these illustrious names will not be unwelcome. In his intercourse with Penn, and other learned Quakers, he had reason to lament his own deficiencies in scholarship, and his friend Pennington undertook to put him in a way of remedying the defect.

"He had," says Ellwood, "an intimate acquaintance with Dr. Paget, a physician of note in London, and he with John Milton, a gentleman of great note for learning throughout the learned world, for the accurate pieces he had written on various subjects and occasions.

"This person, having filled a public station in the former times, lived a private and retired life in London, and, having lost his sight, kept always a man to read for him, which usually was the son of some gentleman of his acquaintance, whom, in kindness, he took to improve in his learning.

"Thus, by the mediation of my friend Isaac Pennington with Dr. Paget, and through him with John Milton, was I admitted to come to him, not as a servant to him, nor to be in the house with him, but only to have the liberty of coming to his house at certain hours when I would, and read to him what books he should appoint, which was all the favor I desired.

"He received me courteously, as well for the sake of Dr. Paget, who introduced me, as of Isaac Pennington, who recommended me, to both of whom he bore a good respect. And, having inquired divers things of me, with respect to my former progression in learning, he dismissed me, to provide myself with such accommodations as might be most suitable to my studies.

"I went, therefore, and took lodgings as near to his house (which was then in Jewen Street) as I conveniently could, and from thenceforward went every day in the afternoon, except on the first day of the week, and, sitting by him in his dining-room, read to him such books in the Latin tongue as he pleased to have me read.

"He perceiving with what earnest desire I had pursued learning, gave me not only all the encouragement, but all the help he could. For, having a curious ear, he understood by my tone when I understood what I read and when I did not, and accordingly would stop me, examine me, and open the most difficult passages to me."

Thanks, worthy Thomas, for this glimpse into John Milton's dining-room!

He had been with "Master Milton," as he calls him, only a few weeks, when, being one "first day morning," at the Bull and Mouth meeting, Aldersgate, the train-bands of the city, "with great noise and clamor," headed by Major Rosewell, fell upon him and his friends. The immediate cause of this onslaught upon quiet worshippers was the famous plot of the Fifth Monarchy men, grim old fanatics, who (like the Millerites of the present day) had been waiting long for the personal reign of Christ and the saints upon earth, and in their zeal to hasten such a consummation had sallied into London streets with drawn swords and loaded matchlocks. The government took strong measures for suppressing dissenters' meetings or "conventicles;" and the poor Quakers, although not at all implicated in the disturbance, suffered more severely than any others. Let us look at the "freedom of conscience and worship" in England under that irreverent Defender of the Faith, Charles II. Ellwood says: "He that commanded the party gave us first a general charge to come out of the room. But we, who came thither at God's requiring to worship Him, (like that good man of old, who said, we ought to obey God rather than man,) stirred not, but kept our places. Whereupon, he sent some of his soldiers among us, with command to drag or drive us out, which they did roughly enough." Think of it: grave men and women, and modest maidens, sitting there with calm, impassive countenances, motionless as death, the pikes of the soldiery closing about them in a circle of bristling steel! Brave and true ones! Not in vain did ye thus oppose God's silence to the Devil's uproar; Christian endurance and calm persistence in the exercise of your rights as Englishmen and men to the hot fury of impatient tyranny! From your day down to this, the world has been the better for your faithfulness.

Ellwood and some thirty of his friends were marched off to prison in Old Bridewell, which, as well as nearly all the other prisons, was already crowded with Quaker prisoners. One of the rooms of the prison was used as a torture chamber. "I was almost affrighted," says Ellwood, "by the dismalness of the place; for, besides that the walls were all laid over with black, from top to bottom, there stood in the middle a great whipping-post.

"The manner of whipping there is, to strip the party to the skin, from the waist upward, and, having fastened him to the whipping-post, (so that he can neither resist nor shun the strokes,) to lash his naked body with long, slender twigs of holly, which will bend almost like thongs around the body; and these, having little knots upon them, tear the skin and flesh, and give extreme pain."

To this terrible punishment aged men and delicately nurtured young females were often subjected, during this season of hot persecution.

From the Bridewell, Ellwood was at length removed to Newgate, and thrust in, with other "Friends," amidst the common felons. He speaks of this prison, with its thieves, murderers, and prostitutes, its over-crowded apartments and loathsome cells, as "a hell upon earth." In a closet, adjoining the room where he was lodged, lay for several days the quartered bodies of Phillips, Tongue, and Gibbs, the leaders of the Fifth Monarchy rising, frightful and loathsome, as they came from the bloody hands of the executioners! These ghastly remains were at length obtained by the friends of the dead, and buried. The heads were ordered to be prepared for setting up in different parts of the city. Read this grim passage of description:—

"I saw the heads when they were brought to be boiled. The hangman fetched them in a dirty basket, out of some by-place, and, setting them down among the felons, he and they made sport of them. They took them by the hair, flouting, jeering, and laughing at them; and then giving them some ill names, boxed them on their ears and cheeks; which done, the hangman put them into his kettle, and parboiled them with bay-salt and cummin-seed: that to keep them from putrefaction, and this to keep off the fowls from seizing upon them. The whole sight, as well that of the bloody quarters first as this of the heads afterwards, was both frightful and loathsome, and begat an abhorrence in my nature."

At the next session of the municipal court at the Old Bailey, Ellwood obtained his discharge. After paying a visit to "my Master Milton," he made his way to Chalfont, the home of his friends the Penningtons, where he was soon after engaged as a Latin teacher. Here he seems to have had his trials and temptations. Gulielma Springette, the daughter of Pennington's wife, his old playmate, had now grown to be "a fair woman of marriageable age," and, as he informs us, "very desirable, whether regard was had to her outward person, which wanted nothing to make her completely comely, or to the endowments of her mind, which were every way extraordinary, or to her outward fortune, which was fair." From all which, we are not surprised to learn that "she was secretly and openly sought for by many of almost every rank and condition." "To whom," continues Thomas, "in their respective turns, (till he at length came for whom she was reserved,) she carried herself with so much evenness of temper, such courteous freedom, guarded by the strictest modesty, that as it gave encouragement or ground of hope to none, so neither did it administer any matter of offence or just cause of complaint to any."

Beautiful and noble maiden! How the imagination fills up this outline limning by her friend, and, if truth must be told, admirer! Serene, courteous, healthful; a ray of tenderest and blandest light, shining steadily in the sober gloom of that old household! Confirmed Quaker as she is, shrinking from none of the responsibilities and dangers of her profession, and therefore liable at any time to the penalties of prison and whipping-post, under that plain garb and in spite of that "certain gravity of look and behavior," — which, as we have seen, on one occasion awed young Ellwood into silence, — youth, beauty, and refinement assert their prerogatives; love knows no creed; the gay, and titled, and wealthy crowd around her, suing in vain for her favor.

> *"Followed, like the tided moon,*
>
> *She moves as calmly on,"*

"until he at length comes for whom she was reserved," and her name is united with that of one worthy even of her, the world-renowned William Penn.

Meantime, one cannot but feel a good degree of sympathy with young Ellwood, her old schoolmate and playmate, placed, as he was, in the same family with her, enjoying her familiar conversation and unreserved confidence, and, as he says, the "advantageous opportunities of riding and walking abroad with her, by night as well as by day, without any other company than her maid; for so great, indeed, was the confidence that her mother had in me, that she thought her daughter safe, if I was with her, even from the plots and designs of others upon her." So near, and yet, alas! in truth, so distant! The serene and gentle light which shone upon him, in the sweet solitudes of Chalfont, was that of a star, itself unapproachable.

As he himself meekly intimates, she was reserved for another. He seems to have fully understood his own position in respect to her; although, to use his own words, "others, measuring him by the propensity of their own inclinations, concluded he would steal her, run away with her, and marry her." Little did these jealous surmisers know of the true and really heroic spirit of the young Latin master. His own apology and defence of his conduct, under circumstances of temptation which St. Anthony himself could have scarcely better resisted, will not be amiss.

"I was not ignorant of the various fears which filled the jealous heads of some concerning me, neither was I so stupid nor so divested of all humanity as not to be sensible of the real and innate worth and virtue which adorned that excellent dame, and attracted the eyes and hearts of so many, with the greatest importunity, to seek and solicit her; nor was I so devoid of natural heat as not to feel some sparklings of desire, as well as others; but the force of truth and sense of honor suppressed whatever would have risen beyond the bounds of fair and virtuous friendship. For I easily foresaw that, if I should have attempted any thing in a dishonorable way, by fraud or force, upon her, I should have thereby brought a wound upon mine own soul, a foul scandal upon my religious profession, and an infamous stain upon mine honor, which was far more dear unto me than my life. Wherefore, having observed how some others had befooled themselves, by misconstruing her common kindness (expressed in an innocent, open, free, and familiar conversation, springing from the abundant affability, courtesy, and sweetness of her natural temper) to be the effect of a singular regard and peculiar affection to them, I resolved to shun the rock whereon they split; and, remembering the saying of the poet

'Felix quem faciunt aliena Pericula cantum,'

I governed myself in a free yet respectful carriage towards her, thereby preserving a fair reputation with my friends, and enjoying as much of her favor and kindness, in a virtuous and firm friendship, as was fit for her to show or for me to seek."

Well and worthily said, poor Thomas! Whatever might be said of others, thou, at least, wast no coxcomb. Thy distant and involuntary admiration of "the fair Guli" needs, however, no excuse. Poor human nature, guard it as one may, with strictest discipline and painfully cramping environment, will sometimes act out itself; and, in thy case, not even George Fox himself, knowing thy beautiful young friend, (and doubtless admiring her too, for he was one of the first to appreciate and honor the worth and dignity or woman,) could have found it in his heart to censure thee!

At this period, as was indeed most natural, our young teacher solaced himself with occasional appeals to what he calls "the Muses." There is reason to believe, however, that the Pagan sisterhood whom he ventured to invoke seldom graced his study with their personal attendance. In these rhyming efforts, scattered up and down his Journal, there are occasional sparkles of genuine wit, and passages of keen sarcasm, tersely and fitly expressed. Others breathe a warm, devotional feeling; in the following brief prayer, for instance, the wants of the humble Christian are condensed in a manner worthy of Quarles or Herbert:—

"Oh! that mine eye might closed be
To what concerns me not to see;
That deafness might possess mine ear
To what concerns me not to hear;
That Truth my tongue might always tie
From ever speaking foolishly;
That no vain thought might ever rest
Or be conceived in my breast;
That by each word and deed and thought
Glory may to my God be brought!
But what are wishes? Lord, mine eye
On Thee is fixed, to Thee I cry
Wash, Lord, and purify my heart,
And make it clean in every part;
And when 't is clean, Lord, keep it too,
For that is more than I can do."

The thought in the following extracts from a poem written on the death of his friend Pennington's son is trite, but not inaptly or inelegantly expressed: —

"What ground, alas, has any man
To set his heart on things below,
Which, when they seem most like to stand,
Fly like the arrow from the bow!
Who's now atop erelong shall feel
The circling motion of the wheel!

"The world cannot afford a thing
Which to a well-composed mind
Can any lasting pleasure bring,
But in itself its grave will find.
All things unto their centre tend
What had beginning must have end!

"No disappointment can befall
Us, having Him who's all in all!
What can of pleasure him prevent
Who lath the Fountain of Content?"

In the year 1663 a severe law was enacted against the "sect called Quakers," prohibiting their meetings, with the penalty of banishment for the third offence! The burden of the prosecution which followed fell upon the Quakers of the metropolis, large numbers of whom were heavily fined, imprisoned, and sentenced to be banished from their native land. Yet, in time, our worthy friend Ellwood came in for his own share of trouble, in consequence of attending the funeral of one of his friends. An evil-disposed justice of the county obtained information of the Quaker gathering; and, while the body of the dead was "borne on Friends' shoulders through the street, in order to be carried to the burying- ground, which was at the town's end," says Ellwood, "he rushed out upon us with the constables and a rabble of rude fellows whom he had gathered together, and, having his drawn sword in his hand, struck one of the foremost of the bearers with it, commanding them to set down the coffin. But the Friend who was so stricken, being more concerned for the safety of the dead body than for his own, lest it should fall, and any indecency thereupon follow, held the coffin fast; which the justice observing, and being enraged that his word was not forthwith obeyed, set his hand to the coffin, and with a forcible thrust threw it off from the bearers' shoulders, so, that it fell to the ground in the middle of the street, and there we were forced to leave it; for the constables and rabble fell upon us, and drew some and drove others into the inn. Of those thus taken," continues Ellwood, "I was one. They picked out ten of us, and sent us to Aylesbury jail.

"They caused the body to lie in the open street and cartway, so that all travellers that passed, whether horsemen, coaches, carts, or wagons, were fain to break out of the way to go by it, until it was almost night. And then, having caused a grave to be made in the unconsecrated part of what is called the Churchyard, they forcibly took the body from the widow, and buried it there."

He remained a prisoner only about two months, during which period he comforted himself by such verse-making as follows, reminding us of similar enigmas in Bunyan's *Pilgrim's Progress*:

"Lo! a Riddle for the wise,
In the which a Mystery lies.

RIDDLE.

"Some men are free whilst they in prison lie;
Others who ne'er saw prison captives die.

CAUTION.

"He that can receive it may,
He that cannot, let him stay,

Not be hasty, but suspend
Judgment till he sees the end.

Beneath this stone, depressed,

SOLUTION.
"He's only free, indeed, who's free from sin,
And he is fastest bound that's bound therein."

In the mean time, where is our "Master Milton"? We, left him deprived of his young companion and reader, sitting lonely in his small dining-room, in Jewen Street. It is now the year 1665; is not the pestilence in London? A sinful and godless city, with its bloated bishops fawning around the Nell Gwyns of a licentious and profane Defender of the Faith; its swaggering and drunken cavaliers; its ribald jesters; its obscene ballad-singers; its loathsome prisons, crowded with Godfearing men and women: is not the measure of its iniquity already filled up? Three years only have passed since the terrible prayer of Vane went upward from the scaffold on Tower Hill: "When my blood is shed upon the block, let it, O God, have a voice afterward!" Audible to thy ear, O bosom friend of the martyr! has that blood cried from earth; and now, how fearfully is it answered! Like the ashes which the Seer of the Hebrews cast towards Heaven, it has returned in boils and blains upon the proud and oppressive city. John Milton, sitting blind in Jewen Street, has heard the toll of the death-bells, and the nightlong rumble of the burial-carts, and the terrible summons, "Bring out your dead!" The Angel of the Plague, in yellow mantle, purple-spotted, walks the streets. Why should he tarry in a doomed city, forsaken of God! Is not the command, even to him, "Arise and flee, for thy life"? In some green nook of the quiet country, he may finish the great work which his hands have found to do. He bethinks him of his old friends, the Penningtons, and his young Quaker companion, the patient and gentle Ellwood. "Wherefore," says the latter, "some little time before I went to Aylesbury jail, I was desired by my quondam Master Milton to take an house for him in the neighborhood where I dwelt, that he might go out of the city for the safety of himself and his family, the pestilence then growing hot in London. I took a pretty box for him in Giles Chalfont, a mile from me, of which I gave him notice, and intended to have waited on him and seen him well settled, but was prevented by that imprisonment. But now being released and returned home, I soon made a visit to him, to welcome him into the country. After some common discourse had passed between us, he called for a manuscript of his, which, having brought, he delivered to me, bidding me take it home with me and read it at my leisure, and when I had so done return it to him, with my judgment thereupon."

Now, what does the reader think young Ellwood carried in his gray coat pocket across the dikes and hedges and through the green lanes of Giles Chalfont that autumn day? Let us look farther "When I came home, and had set myself to read it, I found it was that excellent poem which he entitled *Paradise Lost*. After I had, with the best attention, read it through, I made him another visit; and, returning his book with due acknowledgment of the favor he had done me in communicating it to me, he asked me how I liked it and what I thought of it, which I modestly but freely told him; and, after some farther discourse about it, I pleasantly said to him, 'Thou hast said much here of Paradise Lost; what hast thou to say of Paradise Found?' He made me no answer, but sat some time in a muse; then brake off that discourse, and fell upon another subject."

"I modestly but freely told him what I thought" of Paradise Lost! What he told him remains a mystery. One would like to know more precisely what the first critical reader of that song "of Man's first disobedience" thought of it. Fancy the young Quaker and blind Milton sitting, some pleasant afternoon of the autumn of that old year, in "the pretty box" at Chalfont, the soft wind through the open window lifting the thin hair of the glorious old Poet! Back-slidden England, plague-smitten, and accursed with her faithless Church and libertine King, knows little of poor "Master Milton," and takes small note of his Puritanic verse-making. Alone, with his humble friend, he sits there, conning over that poem which, he fondly hoped, the world, which had grown all dark and strange to the author, "would not willingly let die." The suggestion in respect to Paradise Found, to which, as we have seen, "he made no answer, but sat some time in a muse," seems not to have been lost; for, "after the sickness was over," continues Ellwood, "and the city well cleansed, and become safely habitable again, he returned thither; and when afterwards I waited on him there, which I seldom failed of doing whenever my occasions drew me to London, he showed me his second poem, called Paradise Gained; and, in a pleasant tone, said to me, 'This is owing to you, for you put it into my head by the question you put to me at Chalfont, which before I had not thought of.'"

Golden days were these for the young Latin reader, even if it be true, as we suspect, that he was himself very far from appreciating the glorious privilege which he enjoyed, of the familiar friendship and confidence of Milton. But they could not last. His amiable host, Isaac Pennington, a blameless and quiet country gentleman, was dragged from his house by a military force, and lodged in Aylesbury jail; his wife and family forcibly ejected from their pleasant home, which was seized upon by the government as security for the fines imposed upon its owner. The plague was in the village of Aylesbury, and in the very prison itself; but the noble-hearted Mary Pennington followed her husband, sharing with him the dark peril. Poor Ellwood, while attending a monthly meeting at Hedgerly, with six others, (among them one Morgan Watkins, a poor old Welshman, who, painfully endeavoring to utter his testimony in his own dialect, was suspected by the Dogberry of a justice of being a Jesuit trolling over his Latin,) was arrested, and committed to Wiccomb House of Correction.

This was a time of severe trial for the sect with which Ellwood had connected himself. In the very midst of the pestilence, when thousands perished weekly in London, fifty-four Quakers were marched through the almost deserted streets, and placed on board a ship, for the purpose of being conveyed, according to their sentence of banishment, to the West Indies. The ship lay for a long time, with many others similarly situated, a helpless prey to the pestilence. Through that terrible autumn, the prisoners sat waiting for the summons of the ghastly Destroyer; and, from their floating dungeon.

> "Heard the groan
> Of agonizing ships from shore to shore;
> Heard nightly plunged beneath the sullen wave
> The frequent corse."

When the vessel at length set sail, of the fifty-four who went on board, twenty-seven only were living. A Dutch privateer captured her, when two days out, and carried the prisoners to North Holland, where they were set at liberty. The condition of the jails in the city, where were large numbers of Quakers, was dreadful in the extreme. Ill ventilated, crowded, and loathsome with the accumulated filth of centuries, they invited the disease which daily decimated their cells. "Go on!" says Pennington, writing to the King and bishops from his plague-infected cell in the Aylesbury prison: "try it out with the Spirit of the Lord! Come forth with your laws, and prisons, and spoiling of goods, and banishment, and death, if the Lord please, and see if ye can carry it! Whom the Lord loveth He can save at His pleasure. Hath He begun to break our bonds and deliver us, and shall we now distrust Him? Are we in a worse condition than Israel was when the sea was before them, the mountains on either side, and the Egyptians behind, pursuing them?"

Brave men and faithful! It is not necessary that the present generation, how quietly reaping the fruit of your heroic endurance, should see eye to eye with you in respect to all your testimonies and beliefs, in order to recognize your claim to gratitude and admiration. For, in an age of hypocritical hollowness and mean self-seeking, when, with noble exceptions, the very Puritans of Cromwell's Reign of the Saints were taking profane lessons from their old enemies, and putting on an outside show of conformity, for the sake of place or pardon, ye maintained the austere dignity of virtue, and, with King and Church and Parliament arrayed against you, vindicated the Rights of Conscience, at the cost of home, fortune, and life. English liberty owes more to your unyielding firmness than to the blows stricken for her at Worcester and Naseby.

In 1667, we find the Latin teacher in attendance at a great meeting of Friends, in London, convened at the suggestion of George Fox, for the purpose of settling a little difficulty which had arisen among the Friends, even under the pressure of the severest persecution, relative to the very important matter of "wearing the hat." George Fox, in his love of truth and sincerity in word and action, had discountenanced the fashionable doffing of the hat, and other flattering obeisances towards men holding stations in Church or State, as savoring of man-worship, giving to the creature the reverence only due to the Creator, as undignified and wanting in due self-respect, and tending to support unnatural and oppressive distinctions among those equal in the sight of God. But some of his disciples evidently made much more of this "hat testimony" than their teacher. One John Perrott, who had just returned from an unsuccessful attempt to convert the Pope, at Rome, (where that dignitary, after listening to his exhortations, and finding him in no condition to be benefited by the spiritual physicians of the Inquisition, had quietly turned him over to the temporal ones of the Insane Hospital,) had broached the doctrine that, in public or private worship, the hat was not to be taken off, without an immediate revelation or call to do so! Ellwood himself seems to have been on the point of yielding to this notion, which appears to have been the occasion of a good deal of dissension and scandal. Under these circumstances, to save truth from reproach, and an important testimony to the essential equality of mankind from running into sheer fanaticism, Fox summoned his tried and faithful friends together, from all parts of the United Kingdom, and, as it appears, with the happiest result. Hat-revelations were discountenanced, good order and harmony reestablished, and John Perrott's beaver and the crazy head under it were from thenceforth powerless for evil. Let those who are disposed to laugh at this notable "Ecumenical Council of the Hat" consider that ecclesiastical history has brought down to us the records of many larger and more imposing convocations, wherein grave bishops and learned fathers took each other by the beard upon matters of far less practical importance.

In 1669, we find Ellwood engaged in escorting his fair friend, Gulielma, to her uncle's residence in Sussex. Passing through London, and taking the Tunbridge road, they stopped at Seven Oak to dine. The Duke of York was on the road, with his guards and hangers-on, and the inn was filled with a rude company. "Hastening," says Ellwood, "from a place where we found nothing but rudeness, the roysterers who swarmed there, besides the damning oaths they belched out against each other, looked very sourly upon us, as if they grudged us the horses which we rode and the clothes we wore." They had proceeded but a little distance, when they were overtaken by some half dozen drunken rough-riding cavaliers, of the Wildrake stamp, in full pursuit after the beautiful Quakeress. One of them impudently attempted to pull her upon his horse before him, but was held at bay by Ellwood, who seems, on this occasion, to have relied somewhat upon his "stick," in defending his fair charge. Calling up Gulielma's servant, he bade him ride on one side of his mistress, while he guarded her on the other. "But he," says Ellwood, "not thinking it perhaps decent to ride so near his mistress, left room enough for another to ride between." In dashed the drunken retainer, and Gulielma was once more in peril. It was clearly no time for exhortations and expostulations; "so," says Ellwood, "I chopped in upon him, by a nimble turn, and kept him at bay. I told him I had hitherto spared him, but wished him not to provoke me further. This I spoke in such a tone as bespoke an high resentment of the abuse put upon us, and withal pressed him so hard with my horse that I suffered him not to come up again to Guli." By this time, it became evident to the companions of the ruffianly assailant that the young Quaker was in earnest, and they hastened to interfere. "For they," says Ellwood, "seeing the contest rise so high, and probably fearing it would rise higher, not knowing where it might stop, came in to part us; which they did by taking him away."

Escaping from these sons of Belial, Ellwood and his fair companion rode on through Tunbridge Wells, "the street thronged with men, who looked very earnestly at them, but offered them no affront," and arrived, late at night, in a driving rain, at the mansion-house of Herbert Springette. The fiery old gentleman was so indignant at the insult offered to his niece, that he was with difficulty dissuaded from demanding satisfaction at the hands of the Duke of York.

This seems to have been his last ride with Gulielma. She was soon after married to William Penn, and took up her abode at Worminghurst, in Sussex. How blessed and beautiful was that union may be understood from the following paragraph of a letter, written by her husband, on the eve of his departure for America to lay the foundations of a Christian colony:—

"My dear wife! remember thou wast the love of my youth, and much the joy of my life, the most beloved as well as the most worthy of all my earthly comforts; and the reason of that love was more thy inward than thy outward excellences, which yet were many. God knows, and thou knowest it, I can say it was a match of Providence's making; and God's image in us both was the first thing and the most amiable and engaging ornament in our eyes."

About this time our friend Thomas, seeing that his old playmate at Chalfont was destined for another, turned his attention towards a "young Friend, named Mary Ellis." He had been for several years acquainted with her, but now he "found his heart secretly drawn and inclining towards her." "At length," he tells us, "as I was sitting all alone, waiting upon the Lord for counsel and guidance in this, in itself and to me, important affair, I felt a word sweetly arise in me, as if I had heard a Voice which said, Go, and prevail! and faith springing in my heart at the word, I immediately rose and went, nothing doubting." On arriving at her residence, he states that he "solemnly opened his mind to her, which was a great surprisal to her, for she had taken in an apprehension, as others had also done," that his eye had been fixed elsewhere and nearer home. "I used not many words to her," he continues, "but I felt a Divine Power went along with the words, and fixed the matter expressed by them so fast in her breast, that, as she afterwards acknowledged to me, she could not shut it out."

"I continued," he says, "my visits to my best-beloved Friend until we married, which was on the 28th day of the eighth month, 1669. We took each other in a select meeting of the ancient and grave Friends of that country. A very solemn meeting it was, and in a weighty frame of spirit we were." His wife seems to have had some estate; and Ellwood, with that nice sense of justice which marked all his actions, immediately made his will, securing to her, in case of his decease, all her own goods and moneys, as well as all that he had himself acquired before marriage. "Which," he tells, "was indeed but little, yet, by all that little, more than I had ever given her ground to expect with me." His father, who was yet unreconciled to the son's religious views, found fault with his marriage, on the ground that it was unlawful and unsanctioned by priest or liturgy, and consequently refused to render him any pecuniary assistance. Yet, in spite of this and other trials, he seems to have preserved his serenity of spirit. After an unpleasant interview with his father, on one occasion, he wrote, at his lodgings in an inn, in London, what he calls *A Song of Praise*. An extract from it will serve to show the spirit of the good man in affliction: —

"Unto the Glory of Thy Holy Name,
Eternal God! whom I both love and fear,
I hereby do declare, I never came
Before Thy throne, and found Thee loath to hear,
But always ready with an open ear;
And, though sometimes Thou seem'st Thy face to hide,
As one that had withdrawn his love from me,
'T is that my faith may to the full, be tried,
And that I thereby may the better see
How weak I am when not upheld by Thee!"

The next year, 1670, an act of Parliament, in relation to "Conventicles," provided that any person who should be present at any meeting, under color or pretence of any exercise of religion, in other manner than according to the liturgy and practice of the Church of England, "should be liable to fines of from five to ten shillings; and any person preaching at or giving his house for the meeting, to a fine of twenty pounds: one third of the fines being received by the informer or informers." As a natural consequence of such a law, the vilest scoundrels in the land set up the trade of informers and heresy-hunters. Wherever a dissenting meeting or burial took place, there was sure to be a mercenary spy, ready to bring a complaint against all in attendance. The Independents and Baptists ceased, in a great measure, to hold public meetings, yet even they did not escape prosecution. Bunyan, for instance, in these days, was dreaming, like another Jacob, of angels ascending and descending, in Bedford prison. But upon the poor Quakers fell, as usual, the great force of the unjust enactment. Some of these spies or informers, men of sharp wit, close countenances, pliant tempers, and skill in dissimulation, took the guise of Quakers, Independents, or Baptists, as occasion required, thrusting themselves into the meetings of the proscribed sects, ascertaining the number who attended, their rank and condition, and then informing against them. Ellwood, in his Journal for 1670, describes several of these emissaries of evil. One of them came to a Friend's house, in Bucks, professing to be a brother in the faith, but, overdoing his counterfeit Quakerism, was detected and dismissed by his host. Betaking himself to the inn, he appeared in his true character, drank and swore roundly, and confessed over his cups that he had been sent forth on his mission by the Rev. Dr. Mew, Vice- Chancellor of Oxford. Finding little success in counterfeiting Quakerism, he turned to the Baptists, where, for a time, he met with better success. Ellwood, at this time, rendered good service to his friends, by exposing the true character of these wretches, and bringing them to justice for theft, perjury, and other misdemeanors.

While this storm of persecution lasted, (a period of two or three years,) the different dissenting sects felt, in some measure, a common sympathy, and, while guarding themselves against their common foe, had little leisure for controversy with each other; but, as was natural, the abatement of their mutual suffering and danger was the signal for renewing their suspended quarrels. The Baptists fell upon the Quakers, with pamphlet and sermon; the latter replied in the same way. One of the most conspicuous of the Baptist disputants was the famous Jeremy Ives, with whom our friend Ellwood seems to have had a good deal of trouble. "His name," says Ellwood, "was up for a topping Disputant. He was well, read in the fallacies of logic, and was ready in framing syllogisms. His chief art lay in tickling the humor of rude, unlearned, and injudicious hearers."

The following piece of Ellwood's, entitled "An Epitaph for Jeremy Ives," will serve to show that wit and drollery were sometimes found even among the proverbially sober Quakers of the seventeenth century:—

"Beneath this stone, depressed, doth lie
The Mirror of Hypocrisy—
Ives, whose mercenary tongue
Like a Weathercock was hung,
And did this or that way play,
As Advantage led the way.
If well hired, he would dispute,
Otherwise he would be mute.
But he'd bawl for half a day,
If he knew and liked his pay.

"For his person, let it pass;
Only note his face was brass.
His heart was like a pumice-stone,
And for Conscience he had none.
Of Earth and Air he was composed,
With Water round about enclosed.
Earth in him had greatest share,
Questionless, his life lay there;
Thence his cankered Envy sprung,
Poisoning both his heart and tongue.

"Air made him frothy, light, and vain,
And puffed him with a proud disdain.
Into the Water oft he went,
And through the Water many sent
That was, ye know, his element!
The greatest odds that did appear
Was this, for aught that I can hear,
That he in cold did others dip,
But did himself hot water sip.

"And his cause he'd never doubt,
If well soak'd o'er night in Stout;
But, meanwhile, he must not lack
Brandy and a draught of Sack.

One dispute would shrink a bottle
Of three pints, if not a pottle.
One would think he fetched from thence
All his dreamy eloquence.

"Let us now bring back the Sot
To his Aqua Vita pot,
And observe, with some content,
How he framed his argument.
That his whistle he might wet,
The bottle to his mouth he set,
And, being Master of that Art,
Thence he drew the Major part,
But left the Minor still behind;
Good reason why, he wanted wind;
If his breath would have held out,
He had Conclusion drawn, no doubt."

The residue of Ellwood's life seems to have glided on in serenity and peace. He wrote, at intervals, many pamphlets in defence of his Society, and in favor of Liberty of Conscience. At his hospitable residence, the leading spirits of the sect were warmly welcomed. George Fox and William Penn seem to have been frequent guests. We find that, in 1683, he was arrested for seditious publications, when on the eve of hastening to his early friend, Gulielma, who, in the absence of her husband, Governor Penn, had fallen dangerously ill. On coming before the judge, "I told him," says Ellwood, "that I had that morning received an express out of Sussex, that William Penn's wife (with whom I had an intimate acquaintance and strict friendship, *ab ipsis fere incunabilis*, at least, *a teneris unguiculis*) lay now ill, not without great danger, and that she had expressed her desire that I would come to her as soon as I could." The judge said "he was very sorry for Madam Penn's illness," of whose virtues he spoke very highly, but not more than was her due. Then he told me, "that, for her sake, he would do what he could to further my visit to her." Escaping from the hands of the law, he visited his friend, who was by this time in a way of recovery, and, on his return, learned that the prosecution had been abandoned.

At about this date his narrative ceases. We learn, from other sources, that he continued to write and print in defence of his religious views up to the year of his death, which took place in 1713. One of his productions, a poetical version of the Life of David, may be still met with, in the old

Quaker libraries. On the score of poetical merit, it is about on a level with Michael Drayton's verses on the same subject. As the history of one of the firm confessors of the old struggle for religious freedom, of a genial-hearted and pleasant scholar, the friend of Penn and Milton, and the suggester of Paradise Regained, we trust our hurried sketch has not been altogether without interest; and that, whatever may be the religious views of our readers, they have not failed to recognize a good and true man in Thomas Ellwood.

JAMES NAYLER

"You will here read the true story of that much injured, ridiculed man, James Nayler; what dreadful sufferings, with what patience he endured, even to the boring of the tongue with hot irons, without a murmur; and with what strength of mind, when the delusion he had fallen into, which they stigmatized as blasphemy, had given place to clearer thoughts, he could renounce his error in a strain of the beautifullest humility." — Essays of Elia.

"Would that Carlyle could now try his hand at the English Revolution!" was our exclamation, on laying down the last volume of his remarkable History of the French Revolution with its brilliant and startling word-pictures still flashing before us. To some extent this wish has been realized in the Letters and Speeches of Oliver Cromwell. Yet we confess that the perusal of these volumes has disappointed us. Instead of giving himself free scope, as in his French Revolution, and transferring to his canvas all the wild and ludicrous, the terrible and beautiful phases of that moral phenomenon, he has here concentrated all his artistic skill upon a single figure, whom he seems to have regarded as the embodiment and hero of the great event. All else on his canvas is subordinated to the grim image of the colossal Puritan. Intent upon presenting him as the fitting object of that "hero-worship," which, in its blind admiration and adoration of mere abstract Power, seems to us at times nothing less than devil-worship, he dwarfs, casts into the shadow, nay, in some instances caricatures and distorts, the figures which surround him. To excuse Cromwell in his usurpation, Henry Vane, one of those exalted and noble characters, upon whose features the lights held by historical friends or foes detect no blemish, is dismissed with a sneer and an utterly unfounded imputation of dishonesty. To reconcile, in some degree, the discrepancy between the declarations of Cromwell, in behalf of freedom of conscience, and that mean and cruel persecution which the Quakers suffered under the Protectorate, the generally harmless fanaticism of a few individuals bearing that name is gravely urged. Nay, the fact that some weak-brained enthusiasts undertook to bring about the millennium, by associating together, cultivating the earth, and "dibbling beans" for the New Jerusalem market, is regarded by our author as the "germ of Quakerism;" and furnishes an occasion for sneering at "my poor friend Dryasdust, lamentably tearing his hair over the intolerance of that old time to Quakerism and such like."

The readers of this (with all its faults) powerfully written Biography cannot fail to have been impressed with the intensely graphic description (Part I., vol. ii., pp. 184, 185) of the entry of the poor fanatic, James Nayler, and his forlorn and draggled companions into Bristol. Sadly ludicrous is it; affecting us like the actual sight of tragic insanity enacting its involuntary comedy, and making us smile through our tears.

In another portion of the work, a brief account is given of the trial and sentence of Nayler, also in the serio-comic view; and the poor man is dismissed with the simple intimation, that after his punishment he "repented, and confessed himself mad." It was no part of the author's business, we are well aware, to waste time and words upon the history of such a man as Nayler; he was of no importance to him, otherwise than as one of the disturbing influences in the government of the Lord Protector. But in our mind the story of James Nayler has always been one of interest; and in the belief that it will prove so to others, who, like Charles Lamb, can appreciate the beautiful humility of a forgiven spirit, we have taken some pains to collect and embody the facts of it.

James Nayler was born in the parish of Ardesley, in Yorkshire, 1616. His father was a substantial farmer, of good repute and competent estate and be, in consequence, received a good education: At the age of twenty-two, he married and removed to Wakefield parish, which has since been made classic ground by the pen of Goldsmith. Here, an honest, God-fearing farmer, he tilled his soil, and alternated between cattle-markets and Independent conventicles. In 1641, he obeyed the summons of "my Lord Fairfax" and the Parliament, and joined a troop of horse composed of sturdy Independents, doing such signal service against "the man of Belial, Charles Stuart," that he was promoted to the rank of quartermaster, in which capacity he served under General Lambert, in his Scottish campaign. Disabled at length by sickness, he was honorably dismissed from the service, and returned to his family in 1649.

For three or four years, he continued to attend the meetings of the Independents, as a zealous and devout member. But it so fell out, that in the winter of 1651, George Fox, who had just been released from a cruel imprisonment in Derby jail, felt a call to set his face towards Yorkshire. "So travelling," says Fox, in his Journal, "through the countries, to several places, preaching Repentance and the Word of Life, I came into the parts about Wakefield, where James Nayler lived." The worn and weary soldier, covered with the scars of outward battle, received, as he believed, in the cause of God and his people, against Antichrist and oppression, welcomed with thankfulness the veteran of another warfare; who, in conflict with a principalities and powers, and spiritual wickedness in high places, had made his name a familiar one in every English hamlet. "He and Thomas Goodyear," says Fox, "came to me, and were both convinced, and received the truth." He soon after joined the Society of Friends. In the spring of the next year he was in his field following his plough, and meditating, as he was wont, on the great questions of life and duty, when he seemed to hear a voice bidding him go out from his kindred and his father's house, with an assurance that the Lord would be with him, while laboring in his service. Deeply impressed, he left his employment, and, returning to his house, made immediate preparations for a journey. But hesitation and doubt followed; he became sick from anxiety of mind, and his recovery, for a time, was exceedingly doubtful. On his restoration to bodily health, he obeyed what he regarded as a clear intimation of duty, and went forth a preacher of the doctrines he had embraced. The Independent minister of the society to which he had formerly belonged sent after him the story that he was the victim of sorcery; that George Fox carried with him a bottle, out of which he made people drink; and that the draught had the power to change a Presbyterian or Independent into a Quaker at once; that, in short, the Arch-Quaker, Fox, was a wizard, and could be seen at the same moment of time riding on the same black horse, in two places widely separated. He had scarcely commenced his exhortations, before the mob, excited by such stories, assailed him. In the early summer of the year we hear of him in Appleby jail. On his release, he fell in company with George Fox. At Walney Island, he was furiously assaulted, and beaten with clubs and stones; the poor priest-led fishermen being fully persuaded that they were dealing with a wizard. The spirit of the man, under these circumstances, may be seen in the following extract from a letter to his friends, dated at "Killet, in Lancashire, the 30th of 8th Month, 1652:" —

"Dear friends! Dwell in patience, and wait upon the Lord, who will do his own work. Look not at man who is in the work, nor at any man opposing it; but rest in the will of the Lord, that so ye may be furnished with patience, both to do and to suffer what ye shall be called unto, that your end in all things may be His praise. Meet often together; take heed of what exalteth itself above its brother; but keep low, and serve one another in love."

Laboring thus, interrupted only by persecution, stripes, and imprisonment, he finally came to London, and spoke with great power and eloquence in the meetings of Friends in that city. Here he for the first time found himself surrounded by admiring and sympathizing friends. He saw and rejoiced in the fruits of his ministry. Profane and drunken cavaliers, intolerant Presbyters, and blind Papists, owned the truths which he uttered, and counted themselves his disciples. Women, too, in their deep trustfulness and admiring reverence, sat at the feet of the eloquent stranger. Devout believers in the doctrine of the inward light and manifestation of God in the heart of man, these latter, at length, thought they saw such unmistakable evidences of the true life in James Nayler, that they felt constrained to declare that Christ was, in an especial manner, within him, and to call upon all to recognize in reverent adoration this new incarnation of the divine and heavenly. The wild enthusiasm of his disciples had its effect on the teacher. Weak in body, worn with sickness, fasting, stripes, and prison-penance, and naturally credulous and imaginative, is it strange that in some measure he yielded to this miserable delusion? Let those who would harshly judge him, or ascribe his fall to the peculiar doctrines of his sect, think of Luther, engaged in personal combat with the Devil, or conversing with him on points of theology in his bed-chamber; or of Bunyan at actual fisticuffs with the adversary; or of Fleetwood and Vane and Harrison millennium-mad, and making preparations for an earthly reign of King Jesus. It was an age of intense religious excitement. Fanaticism had become epidemic. Cromwell swayed his Parliaments by "revelations" and Scripture phrases in the painted chamber; stout generals and sea-captains exterminated the Irish, and swept Dutch navies from the ocean, with old Jewish war-cries, and hymns of Deborah and Miriam; country justices charged juries in Hebraisms, and cited the laws of Palestine oftener than those of England. Poor Nayler found himself in the very midst of this seething and confused moral maelstrom. He struggled against it for a time, but human nature was weak; he became, to use his own words, "bewildered and darkened," and the floods went over him.

Leaving London with some of his more zealous followers, not without solemn admonition and rebuke from Francis Howgill and Edward Burrough, who at that period were regarded as the most eminent and gifted of the Society's ministers, he bent his steps towards Exeter. Here, in consequence of the extravagance of his language and that of his disciples, he was arrested and thrown into prison. Several infatuated women surrounded the jail, declaring that "Christ was in prison," and on being admitted to see him, knelt down and kissed his feet, exclaiming, "Thy name shall be no more called James Nayler, but Jesus!" Let us pity him and them. They, full of grateful and extravagant affection for the man whose voice had called them away from worldly vanities to what they regarded as eternal realities, whose hand they imagined had for them swung back the pearl gates of the celestial city, and flooded their atmosphere with light from heaven; he, receiving their homage (not as offered to a poor, weak, sinful Yorkshire trooper, but rather to the hidden man of the heart, the "Christ within" him) with that self-deceiving humility which is but another name for spiritual pride. Mournful, yet natural; such as is still in greater or less degree manifested between the Catholic enthusiast and her confessor; such as the careful observer may at times take note of in our Protestant revivals and camp meetings.

How Nayler was released from Exeter jail does not appear, but the next we hear of him is at Bristol, in the fall of the year. His entrance into that city shows the progress which he and his followers had made in the interval. Let us look at Carlyle's description of it: "A procession of eight persons one, a man on horseback riding single, the others, men and women partly riding double, partly on foot, in the muddiest highway in the wettest weather; singing, all but the single rider, at whose bridle walk and splash two women, 'Hosannah! Holy, holy! Lord God of Sabaoth,' and other things, 'in a buzzing tone,' which the impartial hearer could not make out. The single rider is a raw-boned male figure, 'with lank hair reaching below his cheeks,' hat drawn close over his brows, 'nose rising slightly in the middle,' of abstruse 'down look,' and large dangerous jaws strictly closed: he sings not, sits there covered, and is sung to by the others bare. Amid pouring deluges and mud knee-deep, 'so that the rain ran in at their necks and vented it at their hose and breeches: 'a spectacle to the West of England and posterity! Singing as above; answering no question except in song. From Bedminster to Ratcliffgate, along the streets to the High Cross of Bristol: at the High Cross they are laid hold of by the authorities: turn out to be James Nayler and Company."

Truly, a more pitiful example of "hero-worship" is not well to be conceived of. Instead of taking the rational view of it, however, and mercifully shutting up the actors in a mad-house, the authorities of that day, conceiving it to be a stupendous blasphemy, and themselves God's avengers in the matter, sent Nayler under strong guard up to London, to be examined before the Parliament. After long and tedious examinations and cross-questionings, and still more tedious debates, some portion of which, not uninstructive to the reader, may still be found in Burton's Diary, the following horrible resolution was agreed upon:—

"That James Nayler be set in the pillory, with his head in the pillory in the Palace Yard, Westminster, during the space of two hours on Thursday next; and be whipped by the hangman through the streets from Westminster to the Old Exchange, and there, likewise, be set in the pillory, with his head in the pillory for the space of two hours, between eleven and one, on Saturday next, in each place wearing a paper containing a description of his crimes; and that at the Old Exchange his tongue be bored through with a hot iron, and that he be there stigmatized on the forehead with the letter 'B;' and that he be afterwards sent to Bristol, to be conveyed into and through the said city on horseback with his face backward, and there, also, publicly whipped the next market-day after he comes thither; that from thence he be committed to prison in Bridewell, London, and there restrained from the society of people, and there to labor hard until he shall be released by Parliament; and during that time be debarred the use of pen, ink, and paper, and have no relief except what he earns by his daily labor."

Such, neither more nor less, was, in the opinion of Parliament, required on their part to appease the divine vengeance. The sentence was pronounced on the 17th of the twelfth month; the entire time of the Parliament for the two months previous having been occupied with the case. The Presbyterians in that body were ready enough to make the most of an offence committed by one who had been an Independent; the Independents, to escape the stigma of extenuating the crimes of one of their quondam brethren, vied with their antagonists in shrieking over the atrocity of Nayler's blasphemy, and in urging its severe punishment. Here and there among both classes were men disposed to leniency, and more than one earnest plea was made for merciful dealing with a man whose reason was evidently unsettled, and who was, therefore, a fitting object of compassion; whose crime, if it could indeed be called one, was evidently the result of a clouded intellect, and not of wilful intention of evil. On the other hand, many were in favor of putting him to death as a sort of peace-offering to the clergy, who, as a matter of course, were greatly scandalized by Nayler's blasphemy, and still more by the refusal of his sect to pay tithes, or recognize their divine commission.

Nayler was called into the Parliament-house to receive his sentence. "I do not know mine offence," he said mildly. "You shall know it," said Sir Thomas Widrington, "by your sentence." When the sentence was read, he attempted to speak, but was silenced. "I pray God," said Nayler, "that he may not lay this to your charge."

The next day, the 18th of the twelfth month, he stood in the pillory two hours, in the chill winter air, and was then stripped and scourged by the hangman at the tail of a cart through the streets. Three hundred and ten stripes were inflicted; his back and arms were horribly cut and mangled, and his feet crushed and bruised by the feet of horses treading on him in the crowd. He bore all with uncomplaining patience; but was so far exhausted by his sufferings, that it was found necessary to postpone the execution of the residue of the sentence for one week. The terrible severity of his sentence, and his meek endurance of it, had in the mean time powerfully affected many of the humane and generous of all classes in the city; and a petition for the remission of the remaining part of the penalty was numerously signed and presented to Parliament. A debate ensued upon it, but its prayer was rejected. Application was then made to Cromwell, who addressed a letter to the Speaker of the House, inquiring into the affair, protesting an "abhorrence and detestation of giving or occasioning the least countenance to such opinions and practices" as were imputed to Nayler; "yet we, being intrusted in the present government on behalf of the people of these nations, and not knowing how far such proceeding entered into wholly without us may extend in the consequence of it, do hereby desire the House may let us know the grounds and reasons whereon they have proceeded." From this, it is not unlikely that the Protector might have been disposed to clemency, and to look with a degree of charity upon the weakness and errors of one of his old and tried soldiers who had striven like a brave man, as he was, for the rights and liberties of Englishmen; but the clergy here interposed, and vehemently, in the name of God and His Church, demanded that the executioner should finish his work. Five of the most eminent of them, names well known in the Protectorate, Caryl, Manton, Nye, Griffith, and Reynolds, were deputed by Parliament to visit the mangled prisoner. A reasonable request was made, that some impartial person might be present, that justice might be done Nayler in the report of his answers. This was refused. It was, however, agreed that the conversation should be written down and a copy of it left with the jailer. He was asked if he was sorry for his blasphemies. He said he did not know to what blasphemies they alluded; that he did believe in Jesus Christ; that He had taken up His dwelling in his own heart, and for the testimony of Him he now suffered. "I believe," said one of the ministers, "in a Christ who was never in any man's heart." "I know no such Christ," rejoined the prisoner; "the Christ I witness to fills Heaven and Earth, and dwells in the hearts of all true believers." On being asked why he allowed the women to adore and worship him, he said he "denied bowing to the creature; but if they beheld the power of Christ, wherever it was, and bowed to it, he could not resist it, or say aught against it."

After some further parley, the reverend visitors grew angry, threw the written record of the conversation in the fire, and left the prison, to report the prisoner incorrigible.

On the 27th of the month, he was again led out of his cell and placed upon the pillory. Thousands of citizens were gathered around, many of them earnestly protesting against the extreme cruelty of his punishment. Robert Rich, an influential and honorable merchant, followed him up to the pillory with expressions of great sympathy, and held him by the hand while the red-hot iron was pressed through his tongue and the brand was placed on his forehead. He was next sent to Bristol, and publicly whipped through the principal streets of that city; and again brought back to the Bridewell prison, where he remained about two years, shut out from all intercourse with his fellow-beings. At the expiration of this period, he was released by order of Parliament. In the solitude of his cell, the angel of patience had been with him.

Through the cloud which had so long rested over him, the clear light of truth shone in upon his spirit; the weltering chaos of a disordered intellect settled into the calm peace of a reconciliation with God and man. His first act on leaving prison was to visit Bristol, the scene of his melancholy fall.

There he publicly confessed his errors, in the eloquent earnestness of a contrite spirit, humbled in view of the past, yet full of thanksgiving and praise for the great boon of forgiveness. A writer who was present says, the "assembly was tendered, and broken into tears; there were few dry eyes, and many were bowed in their minds."

In a paper which he published soon after, he acknowledges his lamentable delusion. "Condemned forever," he says, "be all those false worships with which any have idolized my person in that Night of my Temptation, when the Power of Darkness was above rue; all that did in any way tend to dishonor the Lord, or draw the minds of any from the measure of Christ Jesus in themselves, to look at flesh, which is as grass, or to ascribe that to the visible which belongs to Him. Darkness came over me through want of watchfulness and obedience to the pure Eye of God. I was taken captive from the true light; I was walking in the Night, as a wandering bird fit for a prey. And if the Lord of all my mercies had not rescued me, I had perished; for I was as one appointed to death and destruction, and there was none to deliver me."

"It is in my heart to confess to God, and before men, my folly and offence in that day; yet there were many things formed against me in that day, to take away my life and bring scandal upon the truth, of which I was not guilty at all." "The provocation of that Time of Temptation was exceeding great against the Lord, yet He left me not; for when Darkness was above, and the Adversary so prevailed that all things were turned and perverted against my right seeing, hearing, or understanding, only a secret hope and faith I had in my God, whom I had served, that He would bring me through it and to the end of it, and that I should again see the day of my redemption from under it all,—this quieted my soul in its greatest tribulation." He concludes his confession with these words: "He who hath saved my soul from death, who hath lifted my feet up out of the pit, even to Him be glory forever; and let every troubled soul trust in Him, for his mercy endureth forever!" ¬

Among his papers, written soon after his release, is a remarkable prayer, or rather thanksgiving. The limit I have prescribed to myself will only allow me to copy an extract:—

"It is in my heart to praise Thee, O my God! Let me never forget Thee, what Thou hast been to me in the night, by Thy presence in my hour of trial, when I was beset in darkness, when I was cast out as a wandering bird; when I was assaulted with strong temptations, then Thy presence, in secret, did preserve me, and in a low state I felt Thee near me; when my way was through the sea, when I passed under the mountains, there wast Thou present with me; when the weight of the hills was upon me, Thou upheldest me. Thou didst fight, on my part, when I wrestled with death; when darkness would have shut me up, Thy light shone about me; when my work was in the furnace, and I passed through the fire, by Thee I was not consumed; when I beheld the dreadful visions, and was among the fiery spirits, Thy faith staid me, else through fear I had fallen. I saw Thee, and believed, so that the enemy could not prevail." After speaking of his humiliation and sufferings, which Divine Mercy had overruled for his spiritual good, he thus concludes: "Thou didst lift me out from the pit, and set me forth in the sight of my enemies; Thou proclaimedst liberty to the captive; Thou calledst my acquaintances near me; they to whom I had been a wonder looked upon me; and in Thy love I obtained favor with those who had deserted me. Then did gladness swallow up sorrow, and I forsook my troubles; and I said, How good is it that man be proved in the night, that he may know his folly, that every mouth may become silent, until Thou makest man known unto himself, and has slain the boaster, and shown him the vanity which vexeth Thy spirit."

All honor to the Quakers of that day, that, at the risk of misrepresentation and calumny, they received back to their communion their greatly erring, but deeply repentant, brother. His life, ever after, was one of self-denial and jealous watchfulness over himself, — blameless and beautiful in its humility and lowly charity.

Thomas Ellwood, in his autobiography for the year 1659, mentions Nayler, whom he met in company with Edward Burrough at the house of Milton's friend, Pennington. Ellwood's father held a discourse with the two Quakers on their doctrine of free and universal grace. "James Nailer," says Ellwood, "handled the subject with so much perspicuity and clear demonstration, that his reasoning seemed to be irresistible. As for Edward Burrough, he was a brisk young Man, of a ready Tongue, and might have been for aught I then knew, a Scholar, which made me less admire his Way of Reasoning. But what dropt from James Nailer had the greater Force upon me, because he lookt like a simple Countryman, having the appearance of an Husbandman or Shepherd."

In the latter part of the eighth month, 1660, he left London on foot, to visit his wife and children in Wakefield. As he journeyed on, the sense of a solemn change about to take place seemed with him; the shadow of the eternal world fell over him. As he passed through Huntingdon, a friend who saw him describes him as "in an awful and weighty frame of mind, as if he had been redeemed from earth, and a stranger on it, seeking a better home and inheritance." A few miles beyond the town, he was found, in the dusk of the evening, very ill, and was taken to the house of a friend, who lived not far distant. He died shortly after, expressing his gratitude for the kindness of his attendants, and invoking blessings upon them. About two hours before his death, he spoke to the friend at his bedside these remarkable words, solemn as eternity, and beautiful as the love which fills it: —

"There is a spirit which I feel which delights to do no evil, nor to avenge any wrong; but delights to endure all things, in hope to enjoy its own in the end; its hope is to outlive all wrath and contention, and to weary out all exultation and cruelty, or whatever is of a nature contrary to itself. It sees to the end of all temptations; as it bears no evil in itself, so it conceives none in thought to any other: if it be betrayed, it bears it, for its ground and spring is the mercy and forgiveness of God. Its crown is meekness; its life is everlasting love unfeigned; it takes its kingdom with entreaty, and not with contention, and keeps it by lowliness of mind. In God alone it can rejoice, though none else regard it, or can own its life. It is conceived in sorrow, and brought forth with none to pity it; nor doth it murmur at grief and oppression. It never rejoiceth but through sufferings, for with the world's joy it is murdered. I found it alone, being forsaken. I have fellowship therein with them who lived in dens and desolate places of the earth, who through death obtained resurrection and eternal Holy Life."

So died James Nayler. He was buried in "Thomas Parnell's burying-ground, at King's Rippon," in a green nook of rural England. Wrong and violence, and temptation and sorrow, and evil-speaking, could reach him no more. And in taking leave of him, let us say, with old Joseph Wyeth, where he touches upon this case in his *Anguis Flagellatus*: "Let none insult, but take heed lest they also, in the hour of their temptation, do fall away."

ANDREW MARVELL

"They who with a good conscience and an upright heart do their civil duties in the sight of God, and in their several places, to resist tyranny and the violence of superstition banded both against them, will never seek to be forgiven that which may justly be attributed to their immortal praise." — *Answer to Eikon Basilike.*

Among, the great names which adorned the Protectorate, — that period of intense mental activity, when political and religious rights and duties were thoroughly discussed by strong and earnest statesmen and theologians, — that of Andrew Marvell, the friend of Milton, and Latin Secretary of Cromwell, deserves honorable mention. The magnificent prose of Milton, long neglected, is now perhaps as frequently read as his great epic; but the writings of his friend and fellow secretary, devoted like his own to the cause of freedom and the rights of the people, are scarcely known to the present generation. It is true that Marvell's political pamphlets were less elaborate and profound than those of the author of the glorious *Defence of Unlicensed Printing*. He was light, playful, witty, and sarcastic; he lacked the stern dignity, the terrible invective, the bitter scorn, the crushing, annihilating retort, the grand and solemn eloquence, and the devout appeals, which render immortal the controversial works of Milton. But he, too, has left his foot-prints on his age; he, too, has written for posterity that which they "will not willingly let die." As one of the inflexible defenders of English liberty, sowers of the seed, the fruits of which we are now reaping, he has a higher claim on the kind regards of this generation than his merits as a poet, by no means inconsiderable, would warrant.

Andrew Marvell was born in Kingston-upon-Hull, in 1620. At the age of eighteen he entered Trinity College, whence he was enticed by the Jesuits, then actively seeking proselytes. After remaining with them a short time, his father found him, and brought him back to his studies. On leaving college, he travelled on the Continent. At Rome he wrote his first satire, a humorous critique upon Richard Flecknoe, an English Jesuit and verse writer, whose lines on Silence Charles Lamb quotes in one of his Essays. It is supposed that he made his first acquaintance with Milton in Italy.

At Paris he made the Abbot de Manihan the subject of another satire. The Abbot pretended to skill in the arts of magic, and used to prognosticate the fortunes of people from the character of their handwriting. At what period he returned from his travels we are not aware. It is stated, by some of his biographers, that he was sent as secretary of a Turkish mission. In 1653, he was appointed the tutor of Cromwell's nephew; and, four years after, doubtless through the instrumentality of his friend Milton, he received the honorable appointment of Latin Secretary of the Commonwealth. In 1658, he was selected by his townsmen of Hull to represent them in Parliament. In this service he continued until 1663, when, notwithstanding his sturdy republican principles, he was appointed secretary to the Russian embassy. On his return, in 1665, he was again elected to Parliament, and continued in the public service until the prorogation of the Parliament of 1675.

The boldness, the uncompromising integrity and irreproachable consistency of Marvell, as a statesman, have secured for him the honorable appellation of "the British Aristides." Unlike too many of his old associates under the Protectorate, he did not change with the times. He was a republican in Cromwell's day, and neither threats of assassination, nor flatteries, nor proffered bribes, could make him anything else in that of Charles II. He advocated the rights of the people at a time when patriotism was regarded as ridiculous folly; when a general corruption, spreading downwards from a lewd and abominable Court, had made legislation a mere scramble for place and emolument. English history presents no period so disgraceful as the Restoration. To use the words of Macaulay, it was "a day of servitude without loyalty and sensuality without love, of dwarfish talents and gigantic vices, the paradise of cold hearts and narrow minds, the golden age of the coward, the bigot, and the slave. The principles of liberty were the scoff of every grinning courtier, and the Anathema Maranatha of every fawning dean." It is the peculiar merit of Milton and Marvell, that in such an age they held fast their integrity, standing up in glorious contrast with clerical apostates and traitors to the cause of England's liberty.

In the discharge of his duties as a statesman Marvell was as punctual and conscientious as our own venerable Apostle of Freedom, John Quincy Adams. He corresponded every post with his constituents, keeping them fully apprised of all that transpired at Court or in Parliament. He spoke but seldom, but his great personal influence was exerted privately upon the members of the Commons as well as upon the Peers. His wit, accomplished manners, and literary eminence made him a favorite at the Court itself. The voluptuous and careless monarch laughed over the biting satire of the republican poet, and heartily enjoyed his lively conversation. It is said that numerous advances were made to him by the courtiers of Charles II., but he was found to be incorruptible. The personal compliments of the King, the encomiums of Rochester, the smiles and flatteries of the frail but fair and high-born ladies of the Court; nay, even the golden offers of the King's treasurer, who, climbing with difficulty to his obscure retreat on an upper floor of a court in the Strand, laid a tempting bribe of L1,000 before him, on the very day when he had been compelled to borrow a guinea, were all lost upon the inflexible patriot. He stood up manfully, in an age of persecution, for religious liberty, opposed the oppressive excise, and demanded frequent Parliaments and a fair representation of the people.

In 1672, Marvell engaged in a controversy with the famous High-Churchman, Dr. Parker, who had taken the lead in urging the persecution of Non- conformists. In one of the works of this arrogant divine, he says that "it is absolutely necessary to the peace and government of the world that the supreme magistrate should be vested with power to govern and conduct the consciences of subjects in affairs of religion. Princes may with less hazard give liberty to men's vices and debaucheries than to their consciences." And, speaking of the various sects of Non-conformists, he counsels princes and legislators that "tenderness and indulgence to such men is to nourish vipers in their own bowels, and the most sottish neglect of our quiet and security." Marvell replied to him in a severely satirical pamphlet, which provoked a reply from the Doctor. Marvell rejoined, with a rare combination of wit and argument. The effect of his sarcasm on the Doctor and his supporters may be inferred from an anonymous note sent him, in which the writer threatens by the eternal God to cut his throat, if he uttered any more libels upon Dr. Parker. Bishop Burnet remarks that "Marvell writ in a burlesque strain, but with so peculiar and so entertaining a conduct 'that from the King down to the tradesman his books were read with great pleasure, and not only humbled Parker, but his whole party, for Marvell had all the wits on his side.'" The Bishop further remarks that Marvell's satire "gave occasion to the only piece of modesty with which Dr. Parker was ever charged, namely, of withdrawing from town, and not importuning the press for some years, since even a face of brass must grow red when it is burnt as his has been."

Dean Swift, in commenting upon the usual fate of controversial pamphlets, which seldom live beyond their generation, says: "There is indeed an exception, when a great genius undertakes to expose a foolish piece; so we still read Marvell's answer to Parker with pleasure, though the book it answers be sunk long ago."

Perhaps, in the entire compass of our language, there is not to be found a finer piece of satirical writing than Marvell's famous parody of the speeches of Charles II., in which the private vices and public inconsistencies of the King, and his gross violations of his pledges on coming to the throne, are exposed with the keenest wit and the most laugh-provoking irony. Charles himself, although doubtless annoyed by it, could not refrain from joining in the mirth which it excited at his expense.

The friendship between Marvell and Milton remained firm and unbroken to the last. The former exerted himself to save his illustrious friend from persecution, and omitted no opportunity to defend him as a politician and to eulogize him as a poet. In 1654 he presented to Cromwell Milton's noble tract in *Defence of the People of England*, and, in writing to the author, says of the work, "When I consider how equally it teems and rises with so many figures, it seems to me a Trajan's column, in whose winding ascent we see embossed the several monuments of your learned victories." He was one of the first to appreciate *Paradise Lost*, and to commend it in some admirable lines. One couplet is exceedingly beautiful, in its reference to the author's blindness: —

> "Just Heaven, thee like Tiresias to requite,
> Rewards with prophecy thy loss of sight."

His poems, written in the "snatched leisure" of an active political life, bear marks of haste, and are very unequal. In the midst of passages of pastoral description worthy of Milton himself, feeble lines and hackneyed phrases occur. His *Nymph lamenting the Death of her Fawn* is a finished and elaborate piece, full of grace and tenderness. *Thoughts in a Garden* will be remembered by the quotations of that exquisite critic, Charles Lamb. How pleasant is this picture!

> "What wondrous life is this I lead!
> Ripe apples drop about my head;
> The luscious clusters of the vine
> Upon my mouth do crush their wine;
> The nectarine and curious peach
> Into my hands themselves do reach;
> Stumbling on melons as I pass,
> Ensnared with flowers, I fall on grass.

> "Here at this fountain's sliding foot,
> Or at the fruit-tree's mossy root,
> Casting the body's vest aside,
> My soul into the boughs does glide.
> There like a bird it sits and sings,
> And whets and claps its silver wings;
> And, till prepared for longer flight,
> Waves in its plumes the various light.

> *"How well the skilful gard'ner drew*
> *Of flowers and herbs this dial true!*
> *Where, from above, the milder sun*
> *Does through a fragrant zodiac run;*
> *And, as it works, the industrious bee*
> *Computes his time as well as we.*
> *How could such sweet and wholesome hours*
> *Be reckoned but with herbs and flowers!"*

One of his longer poems, *Appleton House*, contains passages of admirable description, and many not unpleasing conceits. Witness the following: —

> *"Thus I, an easy philosopher,*
> *Among the birds and trees confer,*
> *And little now to make me wants,*
> *Or of the fowl or of the plants.*
> *Give me but wings, as they, and I*
> *Straight floating on the air shall fly;*
> *Or turn me but, and you shall see*
> *I am but an inverted tree.*
> *Already I begin to call*
> *In their most learned original;*
> *And, where I language want, my signs*
> *The bird upon the bough divines.*
> *No leaf does tremble in the wind,*
> *Which I returning cannot find.*
> *Out of these scattered Sibyl's leaves,*
> *Strange prophecies my fancy weaves:*
> *What Rome, Greece, Palestine, e'er said,*
> *I in this light Mosaic read.*
> *Under this antic cope I move,*
> *Like some great prelate of the grove;*
> *Then, languishing at ease, I toss*
> *On pallets thick with velvet moss;*
> *While the wind, cooling through the boughs,*
> *Flatters with air my panting brows.*
> *Thanks for my rest, ye mossy banks!*

And unto you, cool zephyrs, thanks!
Who, as my hair, my thoughts too shed,
And winnow from the chaff my head.
How safe, methinks, and strong behind
These trees have I encamped my mind!"

Here is a picture of a piscatorial idler and his trout stream, worthy of the pencil of Izaak Walton:—

"See in what wanton harmless folds
It everywhere the meadow holds:
Where all things gaze themselves, and doubt
If they be in it or without;
And for this shade, which therein shines
Narcissus-like, the sun too pines.
Oh! what a pleasure 't is to hedge
My temples here in heavy sedge;
Abandoning my lazy side,
Stretched as a bank unto the tide;
Or, to suspend my sliding foot
On the osier's undermining root,
And in its branches tough to hang,
While at my lines the fishes twang."

A little poem of Marvell's, which he calls Eyes and Tears, has the following passages:—

"How wisely Nature did agree
With the same eyes to weep and see!
That having viewed the object vain,
They might be ready to complain.
And, since the self-deluding sight
In a false angle takes each height,
These tears, which better measure all,
Like watery lines and plummets fall."

"Happy are they whom grief doth bless,
That weep the more, and see the less;
And, to preserve their sight more true,
Bathe still their eyes in their own dew;

So Magdalen, in tears more wise,
Dissolved those captivating eyes,
Whose liquid chains could, flowing, meet
To fetter her Redeemer's feet.
The sparkling glance, that shoots desire,
Drenched in those tears, does lose its fire;
Yea, oft the Thunderer pity takes,
And there his hissing lightning slakes.
The incense is to Heaven dear,
Not as a perfume, but a tear;
And stars shine lovely in the night,
But as they seem the tears of light.
Ope, then, mine eyes, your double sluice,
And practise so your noblest use;
For others, too, can see or sleep,
But only human eyes can weep."

The Bermuda Emigrants has some happy lines, as the following:—

"He hangs in shade the orange bright,
Like golden lamps in a green night."

Or this, which doubtless suggested a couplet in Moore's *Canadian Boat Song*:—

"And all the way, to guide the chime,
With falling oars they kept the time."

His facetious and burlesque poetry was much admired in his day; but a great portion of it referred to persons and events no longer of general interest. The satire on Holland is an exception. There is nothing in its way superior to it in our language. Many of his best pieces were originally written in Latin, and afterwards translated by himself. There is a splendid Ode to Cromwell—a worthy companion of Milton's glorious sonnet—which is not generally known, and which we transfer entire to our pages. Its simple dignity and the melodious flow of its versification commend themselves more to our feelings than its eulogy of war. It is energetic and impassioned, and probably affords a better idea of the author, as an actor in the stirring drama of his time, than the "soft Lydian airs" of the poems that we have quoted.

AN HORATIAN ODE UPON CROMWELL'S RETURN
FROM IRELAND.

The forward youth that would appear
Must now forsake his Muses dear;
Nor in the shadows sing
His numbers languishing.

'T is time to leave the books in dust,
And oil the unused armor's rust;
Removing from the wall
The corslet of the hall.

So restless Cromwell could not cease
In the inglorious arts of peace,
But through adventurous war
Urged his active star.

And, like the three-forked lightning, first
Breaking the clouds wherein it nurst,
Did thorough his own side
His fiery way divide.

For 't is all one to courage high,
The emulous, or enemy;
And with such to enclose
Is more than to oppose.

Then burning through the air he went,
And palaces and temples rent;
And Caesar's head at last
Did through his laurels blast.

'T is madness to resist or blame
The face of angry Heaven's flame;
And, if we would speak true,
Much to the man is due,

Who, from his private gardens, where
He lived reserved and austere,
(As if his highest plot
To plant the bergamot,)

Could by industrious valor climb
To ruin the great work of time,

And cast the kingdoms old
Into another mould!

Though justice against fate complain,
And plead the ancient rights in vain, —
But those do hold or break,
As men are strong or weak.

Nature, that hateth emptiness,
Allows of penetration less,
And therefore must make room
Where greater spirits come.

What field of all the civil war,
Where his were not the deepest scar?
And Hampton shows what part
He had of wiser art;
Where, twining subtle fears with hope,
He wove a net of such a scope,
That Charles himself might chase
To Carisbrook's narrow case;

That hence the royal actor borne,
The tragic scaffold might adorn,
While round the armed bands
Did clap their bloody hands.

HE nothing common did or mean
Upon that memorable scene,
But with his keener eye
The axe's edge did try

Nor called the gods, with vulgar spite,
To vindicate his helpless right!
But bowed his comely head,
Down, as upon a bed.

This was that memorable hour,
Which first assured the forced power;
So when they did design
The Capitol's first line,

A bleeding head, where they begun,
Did fright the architects to run;
And yet in that the state
Foresaw its happy fate.

And now the Irish are ashamed
To see themselves in one year tamed;
So much one man can do,
That does best act and know.

They can affirm his praises best,
And have, though overcome, confest
How good he is, how just,
And fit for highest trust.

Nor yet grown stiffer by command,
But still in the Republic's hand,
How fit he is to sway
That can so well obey.

He to the Commons' feet presents
A kingdom for his first year's rents,
And, what he may, forbears
His fame to make it theirs.

And has his sword and spoils ungirt,
To lay them at the public's skirt;
So when the falcon high
Falls heavy from the sky,

She, having killed, no more does search,
But on the next green bough to perch,
Where, when he first does lure,
The falconer has her sure.

What may not, then, our isle presume,
While Victory his crest does plume?
What may not others fear,
If thus he crowns each year?

As Caesar, he, erelong, to Gaul;
To Italy as Hannibal,

And to all states not free
Shall climacteric be.

The Pict no shelter now shall find
Within his parti-contoured mind;
But from his valor sad
Shrink underneath the plaid,
Happy if in the tufted brake
The English hunter him mistake,
Nor lay his hands a near
The Caledonian deer.

But thou, the war's and fortune's son,
March indefatigably on;
And, for the last effect,
Still keep the sword erect.

Besides the force, it has to fright
The spirits of the shady night
The same arts that did gain
A power, must it maintain.

Marvell was never married. The modern critic, who affirms that bachelors have done the most to exalt women into a divinity, might have quoted his extravagant panegyric of Maria Fairfax as an apt illustration:—

"'T is she that to these gardens gave
The wondrous beauty which they have;
She straitness on the woods bestows,
To her the meadow sweetness owes;
Nothing could make the river be
So crystal pure but only she,—
She, yet more pure, sweet, strait, and fair,
Than gardens, woods, meals, rivers are
Therefore, what first she on them spent
They gratefully again present:
The meadow carpets where to tread,
The garden flowers to crown her head,
And for a glass the limpid brook
Where she may all her beauties look;
But, since she would not have them seen,

The wood about her draws a screen;
For she, to higher beauty raised,
Disdains to be for lesser praised;
She counts her beauty to converse
In all the languages as hers,
Nor yet in those herself employs,
But for the wisdom, not the noise,
Nor yet that wisdom could affect,
But as 't is Heaven's dialect."

It has been the fashion of a class of shallow Church and State defenders to ridicule the great men of the Commonwealth, the sturdy republicans of England, as sour-featured, hard-hearted ascetics, enemies of the fine arts and polite literature. The works of Milton and Marvell, the prose- poem of Harrington, and the admirable discourses of Algernon Sydney are a sufficient answer to this accusation. To none has it less application than to the subject of our sketch. He was a genial, warmhearted man, an elegant scholar, a finished gentleman at home, and the life of every circle which he entered, whether that of the gay court of Charles II., amidst such men as Rochester and L'Estrange, or that of the republican philosophers who assembled at Miles's Coffee House, where he discussed plans of a free representative government with the author of Oceana, and Cyriack Skinner, that friend of Milton, whom the bard has immortalized in the sonnet which so pathetically, yet heroically, alludes to his own blindness. Men of all parties enjoyed his wit and graceful conversation. His personal appearance was altogether in his favor. A clear, dark, Spanish complexion, long hair of jetty blackness falling in graceful wreaths to his shoulders, dark eyes, full of expression and fire, a finely chiselled chin, and a mouth whose soft voluptuousness scarcely gave token of the steady purpose and firm will of the inflexible statesman: these, added to the prestige of his genius, and the respect which a lofty, self-sacrificing patriotism extorts even from those who would fain corrupt and bribe it, gave him a ready passport to the fashionable society of the metropolis. He was one of the few who mingled in that society, and escaped its contamination, and who,

"Amidst the wavering days of sin,
Kept himself icy chaste and pure."

The tone and temper of his mind may be most fitly expressed in his own paraphrase of Horace:—

"Climb at Court for me that will,
Tottering Favor's pinnacle;
All I seek is to lie still!

Settled in some secret nest,
In calm leisure let me rest;
And, far off the public stage,
Pass away my silent age.
Thus, when, without noise, unknown,
I have lived out all my span,
I shall die without a groan,
An old, honest countryman.
Who, exposed to other's eyes,
Into his own heart ne'er pries,
Death's to him a strange surprise."

He died suddenly in 1678, while in attendance at a popular meeting of his old constituents at Hull. His health had previously been remarkably good; and it was supposed by many that he was poisoned by some of his political or clerical enemies. His monument, erected by his grateful constituency, bears the following inscription:—

"Near this place lyeth the body of Andrew Marvell, Esq., a man so
endowed by Nature, so improved by Education, Study, and Travel,
so

consummated by Experience, that, joining the peculiar graces of
Wit

and Learning, with a singular penetration and strength of
judgment;

and exercising all these in the whole course of his life, with an
unutterable steadiness in the ways of Virtue, he became the
ornament

and example of his age, beloved by good men, feared by bad, admired
by all, though imitated by few; and scarce paralleled by any. But a
Tombstone can neither contain his character, nor is Marble
necessary

to transmit it to posterity; it is engraved in the minds of this
generation, and will be always legible in his inimitable writings,
nevertheless. He having served twenty years successfully in
Parliament, and that with such Wisdom, Dexterity, and Courage,
as

becomes a true Patriot, the town of Kingston-upon-Hull, from
whence

he was deputed to that Assembly, lamenting in his death the public
loss, have erected this Monument of their Grief and their Gratitude,
1688."

Thus lived and died Andrew Marvell. His memory is the inheritance of Americans as well as Englishmen. His example commends itself in an especial manner to the legislators of our Republic. Integrity and fidelity to principle are as greatly needed at this time in our halls of Congress as in the Parliaments of the Restoration; men are required who can feel, with Milton, that "it is high honor done them from God, and a special mark of His favor, to have been selected to stand upright and steadfast in His cause, dignified with the defence of Truth and public liberty."

JOHN ROBERTS

Thomas Carlyle, in his history of the stout and sagacious Monk of St. Edmunds, has given us a fine picture of the actual life of Englishmen in the middle centuries. The dim cell-lamp of the somewhat apocryphal Jocelin of Brakelond becomes in his hands a huge Drummond-light, shining over the Dark Ages like the naphtha-fed cressets over Pandemonium, proving, as he says in his own quaint way, that "England in the year 1200 was no dreamland, but a green, solid place, which grew corn and several other things; the sun shone on it; the vicissitudes of seasons and human fortunes were there; cloth was woven, ditches dug, fallow fields ploughed, and houses built." And if, as the writer just quoted insists, it is a matter of no small importance to make it credible to the present generation that the Past is not a confused dream of thrones and battle- fields, creeds and constitutions, but a reality, substantial as hearth and home, harvest-field and smith-shop, merry-making and death, could make it, we shall not wholly waste our time and that of our readers in inviting them to look with us at the rural life of England two centuries ago, through the eyes of John Roberts and his worthy son, Daniel, yeomen, of Siddington, near Cirencester.

The Memoirs of John Roberts, alias Haywood, by his son, Daniel Roberts, (the second edition, printed verbatim from the original one, with its picturesque array of italics and capital letters,) is to be found only in a few of our old Quaker libraries. It opens with some account of the family. The father of the elder Roberts "lived reputably, on a little estate of his own," and it is mentioned as noteworthy that he married a sister of a gentleman in the Commission of the Peace. Coming of age about the beginning of the civil wars, John and one of his young neighbors enlisted in the service of Parliament. Hearing that Cirencester had been taken by the King's forces, they obtained leave of absence to visit their friends, for whose safety they naturally felt solicitous. The following account of the reception they met with from the drunken and ferocious troopers of Charles I., the "bravos of Alsatia and the pages of Whitehall," throws a ghastly light upon the horrors of civil war:—

"As they were passing by Cirencester, they were discovered, and pursued by two soldiers of the King's party, then in possession of the town. Seeing themselves pursued, they quitted their horses, and took to their heels; but, by reason of their accoutrements, could make little speed. They came up with my father first; and, though he begged for quarter, none they would give him, but laid on him with their swords, cutting and slashing his hands and arms, which he held up to save his head; as the marks upon them did long after testify. At length it pleased the Almighty to put it into his mind to fall down on his face; which he did. Hereupon the soldiers, being on horseback, cried to each other, *Alight, and cut his throat*! but neither of them did; yet continued to strike and prick him about the jaws, till they thought him dead. Then they left him, and pursued his neighbor, whom they presently overtook and killed. Soon after they had left my father, it was said in his heart, *Rise, and flee for thy life*! which call he obeyed; and, starting upon his feet, his enemies espied him in motion, and pursued him again. He ran down a steep hill, and through a river which ran at the bottom of it; though with exceeding difficulty, his boots filling with water, and his wounds bleeding very much. They followed him to the top of the hill; but, seeing he had got over, pursued him no farther."

The surgeon who attended him was a Royalist, and bluntly told his bleeding patient that if he had met him in the street he would have killed him himself, but now he was willing to cure him. On his recovery, young Roberts again entered the army, and continued in it until the overthrow, of the Monarchy. On his return, he married "Lydia Tindall, of the denomination of Puritans." A majestic figure rises before us, on reading the statement that Sir Matthew Hale, afterwards Lord Chief Justice of England, the irreproachable jurist and judicial saint, was "his wife's kinsman, and drew her marriage settlement."

No stronger testimony to the high-toned morality and austere virtue of the Puritan yeomanry of England can be adduced than the fact that, of the fifty thousand soldiers who were discharged on the accession of Charles II., and left to shift for themselves, comparatively few, if any, became chargeable to their parishes, although at that very time one out of six of the English population were unable to support themselves. They carried into their farm-fields and workshops the strict habits of Cromwell's discipline; and, in toiling to repair their wasted fortunes, they manifested the same heroic fortitude and self-denial which in war had made them such formidable and efficient "Soldiers of the Lord." With few exceptions, they remained steadfast in their uncompromising non- conformity, abhorring Prelacy and Popery, and entertaining no very orthodox notions with respect to the divine right of Kings. From them the Quakers drew their most zealous champions; men who, in renouncing the "carnal weapons" of their old service, found employment for habitual combativeness in hot and wordy sectarian warfare. To this day the vocabulary of Quakerism abounds in the military phrases and figures which were in use in the Commonwealth's time. Their old force and significance are now in a great measure lost; but one can well imagine that, in the assemblies of the primitive Quakers, such stirring battle-cries and warlike tropes, even when employed in enforcing or illustrating the doctrines of peace, must have made many a stout heart' to beat quicker, tinder its drab coloring, with recollections of Naseby and Preston; transporting many a listener from the benches of his place of worship to the ranks of Ireton and Lambert, and causing him to hear, in the place of the solemn and nasal tones of the preacher, the blast of Rupert's bugles, and the answering shout of Cromwell's pikemen: "Let God arise, and let his enemies be scattered!"

Of this class was John Roberts. He threw off his knapsack, and went back to his small homestead, contented with the privilege of supporting himself and family by daily toil, and grumbling in concert with his old campaign brothers at the new order of things in Church and State. To his apprehension, the Golden Days of England ended with the parade on Blackheath to receive the restored King. He manifested no reverence for Bishops and Lords, for he felt none. For the Presbyterians he had no good will; they had brought in the King, and they denied the liberty of prophesying. John Milton has expressed the feeling of the Independents and Anabaptists towards this latter class, in that famous line in which he defines Presbyter as "old priest writ large." Roberts was by no means a gloomy fanatic; he had a great deal of shrewdness and humor, loved a quiet joke; and every gambling priest and swearing magistrate in the neighborhood stood in fear of his sharp wit. It was quite in course for such a man to fall in with the Quakers, and he appears to have done so at the first opportunity.

In the year 1665, "it pleased the Lord to send two women Friends out of the North to Cirencester," who, inquiring after such as feared God, were directed to the house of John Roberts. He received them kindly, and, inviting in some of his neighbors, sat down with them, whereupon "the Friends spake a few words, which had a good effect." After the meeting was over, he was induced to visit a "Friend" then confined in Banbury jail, whom he found preaching through the grates of his cell to the people in the street. On seeing Roberts he called to mind the story of Zaccheus, and declared that the word was now to all who were seeking Christ by climbing the tree of knowledge, "Come down, come down; for that which is to be known of God is manifested within." Returning home, he went soon after to the parish meeting-house, and, entering with his hat on, the priest noticed him, and, stopping short in his discourse, declared that he could not go on while one of the congregation wore his hat. He was thereupon led out of the house, and a rude fellow, stealing up behind, struck him on the back with a heavy stone. "Take that for God's sake," said the ruffian. "So I do," answered Roberts, without looking back to see his assailant, who the next day came and asked his forgiveness for the injury, as he could not sleep in consequence of it.

We next find him attending the Quarter Sessions, where three "Friends" were arraigned for entering Cirencester Church with their hats on. Venturing to utter a word of remonstrance against the summary proceedings of the Court, Justice Stephens demanded his name, and, on being told, exclaimed, in the very tone and temper of Jeffreys:

"I 've heard of you. I'm glad I have you here. You deserve a stone doublet. There's many an honester man than you hanged."

"It may be so," said Roberts, "but what becomes of such as hang honest men?"

The Justice snatched a ball of wax and hurled it at the quiet questioner. "I 'll send you to prison," said he; "and if any insurrection or tumult occurs, I 'll come and cut your throat with my own sword." A warrant was made out, and he was forthwith sent to the jail. In the evening, Justice Sollis, his uncle, released him, on condition of his promise to appear at the next Sessions. He returned to his home, but in the night following he was impressed with a belief that it was his duty to visit Justice Stephens. Early in the morning, with a heavy heart, without eating or drinking, he mounted his horse and rode towards the residence of his enemy. When he came in sight of the house, he felt strong misgivings that his uncle, Justice Sollis, who had so kindly released him, and his neighbors generally, would condemn him for voluntarily running into danger, and drawing down trouble upon himself and family. He alighted from his horse, and sat on the ground in great doubt and sorrow, when a voice seemed to speak within him, "Go, and I will go with thee." The Justice met him at the door. "I am come," said Roberts, "in the fear and dread of Heaven, to warn thee to repent of thy wickedness with speed, lest the Lord send thee to the pit that is bottomless!" This terrible summons awed the Justice; he made Roberts sit down on his couch beside him, declaring that he received the message from God, and asked forgiveness for the wrong he had done him.

The parish vicar of Siddington at this time was George Bull, afterwards Bishop of St. David's, whom Macaulay speaks of as the only rural parish priest who, during the latter part of the seventeenth century, was noted as a theologian, or Who possessed a respectable library. Roberts refused to pay the vicar his tithes, and the vicar sent him to prison. It was the priest's "Short Method with Dissenters." While the sturdy Non- conformist lay in prison, he was visited by the great woman of the neighborhood, Lady Dunch, of Down Amney. "What do you lie in jail for?" inquired the lady.

Roberts replied that it was because he could not put bread into the mouth of a hireling priest. The lady suggested that he might let somebody else satisfy the demands of the priest; and that she had a mind to do this herself, as she wished to talk with him on religious subjects. To this Roberts objected; there were poor people who needed her charities, which would be wasted on such devourers as the priests, who, like Pharaoh's lean kine, were eating up the fat and the goodly, without looking a whit the better. But the lady, who seems to have been pleased and amused by the obstinate prisoner, paid the tithe and the jail fees, and set him at liberty, making him fix a day when he would visit her. At the time appointed he went to Down Amney, and was overtaken on the way by the priest of Cirencester, who had been sent for to meet the Quaker. They found the lady ill in bed; but she had them brought to her chamber, being determined not to lose the amusement of hearing a theological discussion, to which she at once urged them, declaring that it would divert her and do her good. The parson began by accusing the Quakers of holding Popish doctrines. The Quaker retorted by telling him that if he would prove the Quakers like the Papists in one thing, by the help of God, he would prove him like them in ten. After a brief and sharp dispute, the priest, finding his adversary's wit too keen for his comfort, hastily took his leave.

The next we hear of Roberts he is in Gloucester Castle, subjected to the brutal usage of a jailer, who took a malicious satisfaction in thrusting decent and respectable Dissenters, imprisoned for matters of conscience, among felons and thieves. A poor vagabond tinker was hired to play at night on his hautboy, and prevent their sleeping; but Roberts spoke to him in such a manner that the instrument fell from his hand; and he told the jailer that he would play no more, though he should hang him up at the door for it.

How he was released from jail does not appear; but the narrative tells us that some time after an apparitor came to cite him to the Bishop's Court at Gloucester. When he was brought before the Court, Bishop Nicholson, a kind-hearted and easy-natured prelate, asked him the number of his children, and how many of them had been *bishoped*?

"None, that I know of," said Roberts.

"What reason," asked the Bishop, "do you give for this?"

"A very good one," said the Quaker: "most of my children were born in Oliver's days, when Bishops were out of fashion."

The Bishop and the Court laughed at this sally, and proceeded to question him touching his views of baptism. Roberts admitted that John had a Divine commission to baptize with water, but that he never heard of anybody else that had. The Bishop reminded him that Christ's disciples baptized. "What 's that to me?" responded Roberts. "Paul says he was not sent to baptize, but to preach the Gospel. And if he was not sent, who required it at his hands? Perhaps he had as little thanks for his labor as thou hast for thine; and I would willingly know who sent thee to baptize?"

The Bishop evaded this home question, and told him he was there to answer for not coming to church. Roberts denied the charge; sometimes he went to church, and sometimes it came to him. "I don't call that a church which you do, which is made of wood and stone."

"What do you call it?" asked the Bishop.

"It might be properly called a mass-house," was the reply; "for it was built for that purpose." The Bishop here told him he might go for the present; he would take another opportunity to convince him of his errors.

The next person called was a Baptist minister, who, seeing that Roberts refused to put off his hat, kept on his also. The Bishop sternly reminded him that he stood before the King's Court, and the representative of the majesty of England; and that, while some regard might be had to the scruples of men who made a conscience of putting off the hat, such contempt could not be tolerated on the part of one who could put it off to every mechanic be met. The Baptist pulled off his hat, and apologized, on the ground of illness.

We find Roberts next following George Fox on a visit to Bristol. On his return, reaching his house late in the evening, he saw a man standing in the moonlight at his door, and knew him to be a bailiff.

"Hast thou anything against me?" asked Roberts.

"No," said the bailiff, "I've wronged you enough, God forgive me! Those who lie in wait for you are my Lord Bishop's bailiffs; they are merciless rogues. Ever, my master, while you live, please a knave, for an honest man won't hurt you."

The next morning, having, as he thought, been warned by a dream to do so, he went to the Bishop's house at Cleave, near Gloucester. Confronting the Bishop in his own hall, he told him that he had come to know why he was hunting after him with his bailiffs, and why he was his adversary. "The King is your adversary," said the Bishop; "you have broken the King's law." Roberts ventured to deny the justice of the law. "What!" cried the Bishop, "do such men as you find fault with the laws?" "Yes," replied the other, stoutly; "and I tell thee plainly to thy face, it is high time wiser men were chosen, to make better laws."

The discourse turning upon the Book of Common Prayer, Roberts asked the Bishop if the sin of idolatry did not consist in worshipping the work of men's hands. The Bishop admitted it, as in the case of Nebuchadnezzar's image.

"Then," said Roberts, "whose hands made your Prayer Book? It could not make itself."

"Do you compare our Prayer Book to Nebuchadnezzar's image?" cried the Bishop.

"Yes," returned Roberts, "that was his image; this is thine. I no more dare bow to thy Common-Prayer Book than the Three Children to Nebuchadnezzar's image."

"Yours is a strange upstart religion," said the Bishop.

Roberts told him it was older than his by several hundred years. At this claim of antiquity the prelate was greatly amused, and told Roberts that if he would make out his case, he should speed the better for it.

"Let me ask thee," said Roberts, "where thy religion was in Oliver's days, when thy Common-Prayer Book was as little regarded as an old almanac, and your priests, with a few honest exceptions, turned with the tide, and if Oliver had put mass in their mouths would have conformed to it for the sake of their bellies."

"What would you have us do?" asked the Bishop. "Would you have had Oliver cut our throats?"

"No," said Roberts; "but what sort of religion was that which you were afraid to venture your throats for?"

The Bishop interrupted him to say, that in Oliver's days he had never owned any other religion than his own, although he did not dare to openly maintain it as he then did.

"Well," continued Roberts, "if thou didst not think thy religion worth venturing thy throat for then, I desire thee to consider that it is not worth the cutting of other men's throats now for not conforming to it."

"You are right," responded the frank Bishop. "I hope we shall have a care how we cut men's throats."

The following colloquy throws some light on the condition and character of the rural clergy at this period, and goes far to confirm the statements of Macaulay, which many have supposed exaggerated. Baxter's early religious teachers were more exceptionable than even the maudlin mummer whom Roberts speaks of, one of them being "the excellentest stage- player in all the country, and a good gamester and goodfellow, who, having received Holy Orders, forged the like for a neighbor's son, who on the strength of that title officiated at the desk and altar; and after him came an attorney's clerk, who had tippled himself into so great poverty that he had no other way to live than to preach."

J. ROBERTS. I was bred up under a Common-Prayer Priest; and a poor drunken old Man he was. Sometimes he was so drunk he could not say his Prayers, and at best he could but say them; though I think he was by far a better Man than he that is Priest there now.

BISHOP. Who is your Minister now?

J. ROBERTS. My Minister is Christ Jesus, the Minister of the everlasting Covenant; but the present Priest of the Parish is George Bull.

BISHOP. Do you say that drunken old Man was better than Mr. Bull? I tell you, I account Mr. Bull as sound, able, and orthodox a Divine as any we have among us.

J. ROBERT. I am sorry for that; for if he be one of the best of you, I believe the Lord will not suffer you long; for he is a proud, ambitious, ungodly Man: he hath often sued me at Law, and brought his Servants to swear against me wrongfully. His Servants themselves have confessed to my Servants, that I might have their Ears; for their Master made them drunk, and then told them they were set down in the List as Witnesses against me, and they must swear to it: And so they did, and brought treble Damages. They likewise owned they took Tithes from my Servants, threshed them out, and sold them for their Master. They have also several Times took my Cattle out of my Grounds, drove them to Fairs and Markets, and sold them, without giving me any Account.

BISHOP. I do assure you I will inform Mr. Bull of what you say.

J. ROBERTS. Very well. And if thou pleasest to send for me to face him, I shall make much more appear to his Face than I'll say behind his Back.

After much more discourse, Roberts told the Bishop that if it would do him any good to have him in jail, he would voluntarily go and deliver himself up to the keeper of Gloucester Castle. The good-natured prelate relented at this, and said he should not be molested or injured, and further manifested his good will by ordering refreshments. One of the Bishop's friends who was present was highly offended by the freedom of Roberts with his Lordship, and undertook to rebuke him, but was so readily answered that he flew into a rage. "If all the Quakers in England," said he, "are not hanged in a month's time, I 'll be hanged for them." "Prithee, friend," quoth Roberts, "remember and be as good as thy word!"

Good old Bishop Nicholson, it would seem, really liked his incorrigible Quaker neighbor, and could enjoy heartily his wit and humor, even when exercised at the expense of his own ecclesiastical dignity. He admired his blunt honesty and courage. Surrounded by flatterers and self- seekers, he found satisfaction in the company and conversation of one who, setting aside all conventionalisms, saw only in my Lord Bishop a poor fellow-probationer, and addressed him on terms of conscious equality. The indulgence which he extended to him naturally enough provoked many of the inferior clergy, who had been sorely annoyed by the sturdy Dissenter's irreverent witticisms and unsparing ridicule. Vicar Bull, of Siddington, and

Priest Careless, of Cirencester, in particular, urged the Bishop to deal sharply with him. The former accused him of dealing in the Black Art, and filled the Bishop's ear with certain marvellous stories of his preternatural sagacity and discernment in discovering cattle which were lost. The Bishop took occasion to inquire into these stories; and was told by Roberts that, except in a single instance, the discoveries were the result of his acquaintance with the habits of animals and his knowledge of the localities where they were lost. The circumstance alluded to, as an exception, will be best related in his own words.

"I had a poor Neighbor, who had a Wife and six Children, and whom the chief men about us permitted to keep six or seven Cows upon the Waste, which were the principal Support of the Family, and preserved them from becoming chargeable to the Parish. One very stormy night the Cattle were left in the Yard as usual, but could not be found in the morning. The Man and his Sons had sought them to no purpose; and, after they had been lost four days, his Wife came to me, and, in a great deal of grief, cried, 'O Lord! Master Hayward, we are undone! My Husband and I must go a begging in our old age! We have lost all our Cows. My Husband and the Boys have been round the country, and can hear nothing of them. I'll down on my bare knees, if you'll stand our Friend!' I desired she would not be in such an agony, and told her she should not down on her knees to me; but I would gladly help them in what I could. 'I know,' said she, 'you are a good Man, and God will hear your Prayers.' I desire thee, said I, to be still and quiet in thy mind; perhaps thy Husband or Sons may hear of them to-day; if not, let thy Husband get a horse, and come to me to-morrow morning as soon as he will; and I think, if it please God, to go with him to seek then. The Woman seemed transported with joy, crying, 'Then we shall have our Cows again.' Her Faith being so strong, brought the greater Exercise on me, with strong cries to the Lord, that he would be pleased to make me instrumental in his Hand, for the help of the poor Family. In the Morning early comes the old Man. In the Name of God, says he, which way shall we go to seek them? I, being deeply concerned in my Mind, did not answer him till he had thrice repeated it; and then I answered, In the Name of God, I would go to seek them; and said (before I was well aware) we will go to Malmsbury, and at the Horse- Fair we shall find them. When I had spoken the Words, I was much troubled lest they should not prove true. It was very early, and the first Man we saw, I asked him if he had seen any stray Milch Cows thereabouts. What manner of Cattle are they? said he. And the old Man describing their Mark and Number, he told us there were some stood chewing their Cuds in the Horse-Fair; but thinking they belonged to some in the Neighborhood, he did not take particular Notice of them. When we came to the Place, the old Man found them to be his; but suffered his Transports of Joy to rise so high, that I was ashamed of his behavior; for he fell a hallooing, and threw up his Montier Cap in the Air several times, till he raised the Neighbors out of their Beds to see what was the Matter. 'O!' said he, 'I had lost my Cows four or five days ago, and thought I should never see them again; and this honest Neighbor of mine told me this Morning, by his own Fire's Side, nine Miles off, that here I should find them, and here I have them!' Then up goes his Cap again. I begged of the poor Man to be quiet, and take his Cows home, and be thankful; as indeed I was, being reverently bowed in my Spirit before the Lord, in that he was pleased to put the words of Truth into my mouth. And the Man drove his Cattle home, to the great Joy of his Family."

Not long after the interview with the Bishop at his own palace, which has been related, that dignitary, with the Lord Chancellor, in their coaches, and about twenty clergymen on horseback, made a call at the humble dwelling of Roberts, on their way to Tedbury, where the Bishop was to hold a Visitation. "I could not go out of the country without seeing you," said the prelate, as the farmer came to his coach door and pressed him to alight.

"John," asked Priest Evans, the Bishop's kinsman, "is your house free to entertain such men as we are?"

"Yes, George," said Roberts; "I entertain honest men, and sometimes others."

"My Lord," said Evans, turning to the Bishop, "John's friends are the honest men, and we are the others."

The Bishop told Roberts that they could not then alight, but would gladly drink with him; whereupon the good wife brought out her best beer. "I commend you, John," quoth the Bishop, as he paused from his hearty draught; "you keep a cup of good beer in your house. I have not drank any that has pleased me better since I left home." The cup passed next to the Chancellor, and finally came to Priest Bull, who thrust it aside, declaring that it was full of hops and heresy. As to hops, Roberts replied, he could not say, but as for heresy, he bade the priest take note that the Lord Bishop had drank of it, and had found no heresy in the cup.

The Bishop leaned over his coach door and whispered: "John, I advise you to take care you don't offend against the higher Powers. I have heard great complaints against you, that you are the Ringleader of the Quakers in this Country; and that, if you are not suppressed, all will signify nothing. Therefore, pray, John, take care, for the future, you don't offend any more."

"I like thy Counsel very well," answered Roberts, "and intend to take it. But thou knowest God is the higher Power; and you mortal Men, however advanced in this World, are but the lower Power; and it is only because I endeavor to be obedient to the will of the higher Powers, that the lower Powers are angry with me. But I hope, with the assistance of God, to take thy Counsel, and be subject to the higher Powers, let the lower Powers do with me as it may please God to suffer them."

The Bishop then said he would like to talk with him further, and requested him to meet him at Tedbury the next day. At the time appointed, Roberts went to the inn where the Bishop lodged, and was invited to dine with him. After dinner was over, the prelate told him that he must go to church, and leave off holding conventicles at his house, of which great complaint was made. This he flatly refused to do; and the Bishop, losing patience, ordered the constable to be sent for. Roberts told him that if, after coming to his house under the guise of friendship, he should betray him and send him to prison, he, who had hitherto commended him for his moderation, would put his name in print, and cause it to stink before all sober people. It was the priests, he told him, who set him on; but, instead of hearkening to them, he should commend them to some honest vocation, and not suffer them to rob their honest neighbors, and feed on the fruits of other men's toil, like caterpillars.

"Whom do you call caterpillars?" cried Priest Rich, of North Surrey.

"We farmers," said Roberts, "call those so who live on other men's fields, and by the sweat of other men's brows; and if thou dost so, thou mayst be one of them."

This reply so enraged the Bishop's attendants that they could only be appeased by an order for the constable to take him to jail. In fact, there was some ground for complaint of a lack of courtesy on the part of the blunt farmer; and the Christian virtue of forbearance, even in Bishops, has its limits.

The constable, obeying the summons, came to the inn, at the door of which the landlady met him. "What do you here!" cried the good woman, "when honest John is going to be sent to prison? Here, come along with me." The constable, nothing loath, followed her into a private room, where she concealed him. Word was sent to the Bishop, that the constable was not to be found; and the prelate, telling Roberts he could send him to jail in the afternoon, dismissed him until evening. At the hour appointed, the latter waited upon the Bishop, and found with him only one priest and a lay gentleman. The priest begged the Bishop to be allowed to discourse with the prisoner; and, leave being granted, he began by telling Roberts that the knowledge of the Scriptures had made him mad, and that it was a great pity he had ever seen them.

"Thou art an unworthy man," said the Quaker, "and I'll not dispute with thee. If the knowledge of the Scriptures has made me mad, the knowledge of the sack-pot hath almost made thee mad; and if we two madmen should dispute about religion, we should make mad work of it."

"An 't please you, my Lord," said the scandalized priest, "he says I 'm drunk."

The Bishop asked Roberts to repeat his words; and, instead of reprimanding him, as the priest expected, was so much amused that he held up his hands and laughed; whereupon the offended inferior took a hasty leave. The Bishop, who was evidently glad to be rid of him, now turned to Roberts, and complained that he had dealt hardly with him, in telling him, before so many gentlemen, that he had sought to betray him by professions of friendship, in order to send him to prison; and that, if he had not done as he did, people would have reported him as an encourager of the Quakers. "But now, John," said the good prelate, "I'll burn the warrant against you before your face." "You know, Mr. Burnet," he continued, addressing his attendant, "that a Ring of Bells may be made of excellent metal, but they may be out of tune; so we may say of John: he is a man of as good metal as I ever met with, but quite out of tune."

"Thou mayst well say so," quoth Roberts, "for I can't tune after thy pipe."

The inferior clergy were by no means so lenient as the Bishop. They regarded Roberts as the ringleader of Dissent, an impracticable, obstinate, contumacious heretic, not only refusing to pay them tithes himself, but encouraging others to the same course. Hence, they thought it necessary to visit upon him the full rigor of the law. His crops were taken from his field, and his cattle from his yard. He was often committed to the jail, where, on one occasion, he was kept, with many others, for a long time, through the malice of the jailer, who refused to put the names of his prisoners in the Calendar, that they might have a hearing. But the spirit of the old Commonwealth's man remained steadfast. When Justice George, at the Ram in Cirencester, told him he must conform, and go to church, or suffer the penalty of the law, he replied that he had heard indeed that some were formerly whipped out of the Temple, but he had never heard of any being whipped in. The Justice, pointing, through the open window of the inn, at the church tower, asked him what that was. "Thou mayst call it a daw-house," answered the incorrigible Quaker. "Dost thou not see how the jackdaws flock about it?"

Sometimes it happened that the clergyman was also a magistrate, and united in his own person the authority of the State and the zeal of the Church. Justice Parsons, of Gloucester, was a functionary of this sort. He wielded the sword of the Spirit on the Sabbath against Dissenters, and on week days belabored them with the arm of flesh and the constable's staff. At one time he had between forty and fifty of them locked up in Gloucester Castle, among them Roberts and his sons, on the charge of attending conventicles. But the troublesome prisoners baffled his vigilance, and turned their prison into a meeting-house, and held their conventicles in defiance of him. The Reverend Justice pounced upon them on one occasion, with his attendants. An old, gray-haired man, formerly a strolling fencing-master, was preaching when he came in. The Justice laid hold of him by his white locks, and strove to pull him down, but the tall fencing-raster stood firm and spoke on; he then tried to gag him, but failed in that also. He demanded the names of the prisoners, but no one answered him. A voice (we fancy it was that of our old friend Roberts) called out: "The Devil must be hard put to it to have his drudgery done, when the Priests must leave their pulpits to turn informers against poor prisoners." The Justice obtained a list of the names of the prisoners, made out on their commitment, and, taking it for granted that all were still present, issued warrants for the collection of fines by levies upon their estates. Among the names was that of a poor widow, who had been discharged, and was living, at the time the clerical magistrate swore she was at the meeting, twenty miles distant from the prison.

Soon after this event, our old friend fell sick. He had been discharged from prison, but his sons were still confined. The eldest had leave, however, to attend him in his illness, and he bears his testimony that the Lord was pleased to favor his father with His living presence in his last moments. In keeping with the sturdy Non-conformist's life, he was interred at the foot of his own orchard, in Siddington, a spot he had selected for a burial-ground long before, where neither the foot of a priest nor the shadow of a steeple-house could rest upon his grave.

In closing our notice of this pleasant old narrative, we may remark that the light it sheds upon the antagonistic religious parties of the time is calculated to dissipate prejudices and correct misapprehensions, common alike to Churchmen and Dissenters. The genial humor, sound sense, and sterling virtues of the Quaker farmer should teach the one class that poor James Nayler, in his craziness and folly, was not a fair representative of his sect; while the kind nature, the hearty appreciation of goodness, and the generosity and candor of Bishop Nicholson should convince the other class that a prelate is not necessarily, and by virtue of his mitre, a Laud or a Bonner. The Dissenters of the seventeenth century may well be forgiven for the asperity of their language; men whose ears had been cropped because they would not recognize Charles I. as a blessed martyr, and his scandalous son as the head of the Church, could scarcely be expected to make discriminations, or suggest palliating circumstances, favorable to any class of their adversaries. To use the homely but apt simile of McFingal,

> "The will's confirmed by treatment horrid,
>
> As hides grow harder when they're curried."

They were wronged, and they told the world of it. Unlike Shakespeare's cardinal, they did not die without a sign. They branded, by their fierce epithets, the foreheads of their persecutors more deeply than the sheriff's hot iron did their own. If they lost their ears, they enjoyed the satisfaction of making those of their oppressors tingle. Knowing their persecutors to be in the wrong, they did not always inquire whether they themselves had been entirely right, and had done no unrequired works of supererogation by the way of "testimony" against their neighbors' mode cf worship. And so from pillory and whipping-post, from prison and scaffold, they sent forth their wail and execration, their miserere and anathema, and the sound thereof has reached down to our day. May it never wholly die away until, the world over, the forcing of conscience is regarded as a crime against humanity and a usurpation of God's prerogative. But abhorring, as we must, persecution under whatever pretext it is employed, we are not, therefore, to conclude that all persecutors were bad and unfeeling men. Many of their severities, upon which we now look back with horror, were, beyond a question, the result of an intense anxiety for the well-being of immortal souls, endangered by the poison which, in their view, heresy was casting into the waters of life. Coleridge, in one of the moods of a mind which traversed in imagination the vast circle of human experience, reaches this point in his Table-Talk. "It would require," says he, "stronger arguments than any I have seen to convince me that men in authority have not a right, involved in an imperative duty, to deter those under their control from teaching or countenancing doctrines which they believe to be damnable, and even to punish with death those who violate such prohibition." It would not be very difficult for us to imagine a tender-hearted Inquisitor of this stamp, stifling his weak compassion for the shrieking wretch under bodily torment by his strong pity for souls in danger of perdition from the sufferer's heresy. We all know with what satisfaction the gentle-spirited Melanethon heard of the burning of Servetus, and with what zeal he defended it. The truth is, the notion that an intellectual recognition of certain dogmas is the essential condition of salvation lies at the bottom of all intolerance in matters of religion. Under this impression, men are too apt to forget that the great end of Christianity is love, and that charity is its crowning virtue; they overlook the beautiful significance of the parable of the heretic Samaritan and the orthodox Pharisee: and thus, by suffering their speculative opinions of the next world to make them uncharitable and cruel in this, they are really the worse for them, even admitting them to be true.

SAMUEL HOPKINS

Three quarters of a century ago, the name of Samuel Hopkins was as familiar as a household word throughout New England. It was a spell wherewith to raise at once a storm of theological controversy. The venerable minister who bore it had his thousands of ardent young disciples, as well as defenders and followers of mature age and acknowledged talent; a hundred pulpits propagated the dogmas which he had engrafted on the stock of Calvinism. Nor did he lack numerous and powerful antagonists. The sledge ecclesiastic, with more or less effect, was unceasingly plied upon the strong-linked chain of argument which he slowly and painfully elaborated in the seclusion of his parish. The press groaned under large volumes of theological, metaphysical, and psychological disquisition, the very thought of which is now "a weariness to the flesh;" in rapid succession pamphlet encountered pamphlet, horned, beaked, and sharp of talon, grappling with each other in mid-air, like Milton's angels. That loud controversy, the sound whereof went over Christendom, awakening responses from beyond the Atlantic, has now died away; its watchwords no longer stir the blood of belligerent sermonizers; its very terms and definitions have well-nigh become obsolete and unintelligible. The hands which wrote and the tongues which spoke in that day are now all cold and silent; even Emmons, the brave old intellectual athlete of Franklin, now sleeps with his fathers, — the last of the giants. Their fame is still in all the churches; effeminate clerical dandyism still affects to do homage to their memories; the earnest young theologian, exploring with awe the mountainous debris of their controversial lore, ponders over the colossal thoughts entombed therein, as he would over the gigantic fossils of an early creation, and endeavors in vain to recall to the skeleton abstractions before him the warm and vigorous life wherewith they were once clothed; but Hopkinsianism, as a distinct and living school of philosophy, theology, and metaphysics, no longer exists. It has no living oracles left; and its memory survives only in the doctrinal treatises of the elder and younger Edwards, Hopkins, Bellamy, and Emmons.

It is no part of our present purpose to discuss the merits of the system in question. Indeed, looking at the great controversy which divided New England Calvinism in the eighteenth century, from a point of view which secures our impartiality and freedom from prejudice, we find it exceedingly difficult to get a precise idea of what was actually at issue. To our poor comprehension, much of the dispute hinges upon names rather than things; on the manner of reaching conclusions quite as much as upon the conclusions themselves. Its origin may be traced to the great religious awakening of the middle of the past century, when the dogmas of the Calvinistic faith were subjected to the inquiry of acute and earnest minds, roused up from the incurious ease and passive indifference of nominal orthodoxy. Without intending it, it broke down some of the barriers which separated Arminianism and Calvinism; its product, Hopkinsianism, while it pushed the doctrine of the Genevan reformer on the subject of the Divine decrees and agency to that extreme point where it well-nigh loses itself in Pantheism, held at the same time that guilt could not be hereditary; that man, being responsible for his sinful acts, and not for his sinful nature, can only be justified by a personal holiness, consisting not so much in legal obedience as in that disinterested benevolence which prefers the glory of God and the welfare of universal being above the happiness of self. It had the merit, whatever it may be, of reducing the doctrines of the Reformation to an ingenious and scholastic form of theology; of bringing them boldly to the test of reason and philosophy. Its leading advocates were not mere heartless reasoners and closet speculators. They taught that sin was selfishness, and holiness self-denying benevolence, and they endeavored to practise accordingly. Their lives recommended their doctrines. They were bold and faithful in the discharge of what they regarded as duty. In the midst of slave-holders, and in an age of comparative darkness on the subject of human rights, Hopkins and the younger Edwards lifted up their voices for the slave. And twelve years ago, when Abolitionism was everywhere spoken against, and the whole land was convulsed with mobs to suppress it, the venerable Emmons, burdened with the weight of ninety years, made a journey to New York, to attend a meeting of the Anti- Slavery Society. Let those who condemn the creed of these men see to it that they do not fall behind them in practical righteousness and faithfulness to the convictions of duty.

Samuel Hopkins, who gave his name to the religious system in question, was born in Waterbury, Connecticut, in 1721. In his fifteenth year he was placed under the care of a neighboring clergyman, preparatory for college, which he entered about a year after. In 1740, the celebrated Whitefield visited New Haven, and awakened there, as elsewhere, serious inquiry on religious subjects. He was followed the succeeding spring by Gilbert Tennent, the New Jersey revivalist, a stirring and powerful preacher. A great change took place in the college. All the phenomena which President Edwards has described in his account of the Northampton awakening were reproduced among the students. The excellent David Brainard, then a member of the college, visited Hopkins in his apartment, and, by a few plain and earnest words, convinced him that he was a stranger to vital Christianity. In his autobiographical sketch, he describes in simple and affecting language the dark and desolate state of his mind at this period, and the particular exercise which finally afforded him some degree of relief, and which he afterwards appears to have regarded as his conversion from spiritual death to life. When he first heard Tennent, regarding him as the greatest as well as the best of men, he made up his mind to study theology with him; but just before the commencement at which he was to take his degree, the elder Edwards preached at New Haven. Struck by the power of the great theologian, he at once resolved to make him his spiritual father. In the winter following, he left his father's house on horseback, on a journey of eighty miles to Northampton. Arriving at the house of President Edwards, he was disappointed by hearing that he was absent on a preaching tour. But he was kindly received by the gifted and accomplished lady of the mansion, and encouraged to remain during the winter. Still doubtful in respect to his own spiritual state, he was, he says, "very gloomy, and retired most of the time in his chamber." The kind heart of his amiable hostess was touched by his evident affliction. After some days she came to his chamber, and, with the gentleness and delicacy of a true woman, inquired into the cause of his unhappiness. The young student disclosed to her, without reserve, the state of his feelings and the extent of his fears. "She told me," says the Doctor, "that she had had peculiar exercises respecting me since I had been in the family; that she trusted I should receive light and comfort, and doubted not that God intended yet to do great things by me."

After pursuing his studies for some months with the Puritan philosopher, young Hopkins commenced preaching, and, in 1743, was ordained at Sheffield, (now Great Barrington') in the western part of Massachusetts. There were at the time only about thirty families in the town. He says it was a matter of great regret to him to be obliged to settle so far from his spiritual guide and tutor but seven years after he was relieved and gratified by the removal of Edwards to Stockbridge, as the Indian missionary at that station, seven miles only from his own residence; and for several years the great metaphysician and his favorite pupil enjoyed the privilege of familiar intercourse with each other. The removal of the former in 1758 to Princeton, New Jersey, and his death, which soon followed, are mentioned in the diary of Hopkins as sore trials and afflictive dispensations.

Obtaining a dismissal from his society in Great Barrington in 1769, he was installed at Newport the next year, as minister of the first Congregational church in that place. Newport, at this period, was, in size, wealth, and commercial importance, the second town in New England. It was the great slave mart of the North. Vessels loaded with stolen men and women and children, consigned to its merchant princes, lay at its wharves; immortal beings were sold daily in its market, like cattle at a fair. The soul of Hopkins was moved by the appalling spectacle. A strong conviction of the great wrong of slavery, and of its utter incompatibility with the Christian profession, seized upon his mind. While at Great Barrington, he had himself owned a slave, whom he had sold on leaving the place, without compunction or suspicion in regard to the rightfulness of the transaction. He now saw the origin of the system in its true light; he heard the seamen engaged in the African trade tell of the horrible scenes of fire and blood which they had witnessed, and in which they had been actors; he saw the half-suffocated wretches brought up from their noisome and narrow prison, their squalid countenances and skeleton forms bearing fearful evidence of the suffering attendant upon the transportation from their native homes. The demoralizing effects of slaveholding everywhere forced themselves upon his attention, for the evil had struck its roots deeply in the community, and there were few families into which it had not penetrated. The right to deal in slaves, and use them as articles of property, was questioned by no one; men of all professions, clergymen and church-members, consulted only their interest and convenience as to their purchase or sale. The magnitude of the evil at first appalled him; he felt it to be his duty to condemn it, but for a time even his strong spirit faltered and turned pale in contemplation of the consequences to be apprehended from an attack upon it. Slavery and slave-trading were at that time the principal source of wealth to the island; his own church and congregation were personally interested in the traffic; all were implicated in its guilt. He stood alone, as it were, in its condemnation; with here and there an exception, all Christendom maintained the rightfulness of slavery. No movement had yet been made in England against the slave-trade; the decision of Granville Sharp's Somerset case had not yet taken place. The Quakers, even, had not at that time redeemed themselves from the opprobrium. Under these circumstances, after a thorough examination of the subject, he resolved, in the strength of the Lord, to take his stand openly and decidedly on the side of humanity. He prepared a sermon for the purpose, and for the first time from a pulpit of New England was heard an emphatic testimony against the sin of slavery. In contrast with the unselfish and disinterested benevolence which formed in his mind the essential element of Christian holiness, he held up the act of reducing human beings to the condition of brutes, to minister to the convenience, the luxury, and lusts of the owner. He had expected bitter complaint and opposition from his hearers, but was agreeably surprised to find that in most cases his sermon only excited astonishment in their minds that they themselves had never before looked at the subject in the light in which he presented it. Steadily and faithfully pursuing the matter, he had the satisfaction to carry with him his church, and obtain from it, in the midst of a slaveholding and slavetrading community, a resolution every way worthy of note in this day of cowardly compromise with the evil on the part of our leading ecclesiastical bodies: —

"Resolved, That the slave-trade and the slavery of the Africans, as it has existed among us, is a gross violation of the righteousness and benevolence which are so much inculcated in the Gospel, and therefore we will not tolerate it in this church."

There are few instances on record of moral heroism superior to that of Samuel Hopkins, in thus rebuking slavery in the time and place of its power. Honor to the true man ever, who takes his life in his hands, and, at all hazards, speaks the word which is given him to utter, whether men will hear or forbear, whether the end thereof is to be praise or censure, gratitude or hatred. It well may be doubted whether on that Sabbath day the angels of God, in their wide survey of His universe, looked upon a nobler spectacle than that of the minister of Newport, rising up before his slaveholding congregation, and demanding, in the name of the Highest, the "deliverance of the captive, and the opening of prison doors to them that were bound."

Dr. Hopkins did not confine his attention solely to slaveholding in his own church and congregation. He entered into correspondence with the early Abolitionists of Europe as well as his own country. He labored with his brethren in the ministry to bring then to his own view of the great wrong of holding men as slaves. In a visit to his early friend, Dr. Bellamy, at Bethlehem, who was the owner of a slave, he pressed the subject kindly but earnestly upon his attention. Dr. Bellamy urged the usual arguments in favor of slavery. Dr. Hopkins refuted them in the most successful manner, and called upon his friend to do an act of simple justice, in giving immediate freedom to his slave. Dr. Bellamy, thus hardly pressed, said that the slave was a most judicious and faithful fellow; that, in the management of his farm, he could trust everything to his discretion; that he treated him well, and he was so happy in his service that he would refuse his freedom if it were offered him.

"Will you," said Hopkins, "consent to his liberation, if he really desires it?"

"Yes, certainly," said Dr. Bellamy.

"Then let us try him," said his guest.

The slave was at work in an adjoining field, and at the call of his master came promptly to receive his commands.

"Have you a good master?" inquired Hopkins.

"O yes; massa, he berry good."

"But are you happy in your present condition?" queried the Doctor.

"O yes, massa; berry happy."

Dr. Bellamy here could scarcely suppress his exultation at what he supposed was a complete triumph over his anti-slavery brother. But the pertinacious guest continued his queries.

"Would you not be more happy if you were free?"

"O yes, massa," exclaimed the negro, his dark face glowing with new life; "berry much more happy!"

To the honor of Dr. Bellamy, he did not hesitate.

"You have your wish," he said to his servant. "From this moment you are free."

Dr. Hopkins was a poor man, but one of his first acts, after becoming convinced of the wrongfulness of slavery, was to appropriate the very sum which, in the days of his ignorance, he had obtained as the price of his slave to the benevolent purpose of educating some pious colored men in the town of Newport, who were desirous of returning to their native country as missionaries. In one instance he borrowed, on his own responsibility, the sum requisite to secure the freedom of a slave in whom he became interested. One of his theological pupils was Newport Gardner, who, twenty years after the death of his kind patron, left Boston as a missionary to Africa. He was a native African, and was held by Captain Gardner, of Newport, who allowed him to labor for his own benefit, whenever by extra diligence he could gain a little time for that purpose. The poor fellow was in the habit of laying up his small earnings on these occasions, in the faint hope of one day obtaining thereby the freedom of himself and his family. But time passed on, and the hoard of purchase-money still looked sadly small. He concluded to try the efficacy of praying. Having gained a day for himself, by severe labor, and communicating his plan only to Dr. Hopkins and two or three other Christian friends, he shut himself up in his humble dwelling, and spent the time in prayer for freedom. Towards the close of the day, his master sent for him. He was told that this was his gained time, and that he was engaged for himself. "No matter," returned the master, "I must see him." Poor Newport reluctantly abandoned his supplications, and came at his master's bidding, when, to his astonishment, instead of a reprimand, he received a paper, signed by his master, declaring him and his family from thenceforth free. He justly attributed this signal blessing to the all-wise Disposer, who turns the hearts of men as the rivers of water are turned; but it cannot be doubted that the labors and arguments of Dr. Hopkins with his master were the human instrumentality in effecting it.

In the year 1773, in connection with Dr. Ezra Stiles, he issued an appeal to the Christian community in behalf of a society which he had been instrumental in forming, for the purpose of educating missionaries for Africa. In the desolate and benighted condition of that unhappy continent he had become painfully interested, by conversing with the slaves brought into Newport. Another appeal was made on the subject in 1776.

The war of the Revolution interrupted, for a time, the philanthropic plans of Dr. Hopkins. The beautiful island on which he lived was at an early period exposed to the exactions and devastations of the enemy. All who could do so left it for the mainland. Its wharves were no longer thronged with merchandise; its principal dwellings stood empty; the very meeting houses were in a great measure abandoned. Dr. Hopkins, who had taken the precaution, at the commencement of hostilities, to remove his family to Great Barrington, remained himself until the year 1776, when the British took possession of the island. During the period of its occupation, he was employed in preaching to destitute congregations. He spent the summer of 1777 at Newburyport, where his memory is still cherished by the few of his hearers who survive. In the spring of 1780, he returned to Newport. Everything had undergone a melancholy change. The garden of New England lay desolate. His once prosperous and wealthy church and congregation were now poor, dispirited, and, worst of all, demoralized. His meeting-house had been used as a barrack for soldiers; pulpit and pews had been destroyed; the very bell had been stolen. Refusing, with his characteristic denial of self, a call to settle in a more advantageous position, he sat himself down once more in the midst of his reduced and impoverished parishioners, and, with no regular salary, dependent entirely on such free-will offerings as from time to time were made him, he remained with them until his death.

In 1776, Dr. Hopkins published his celebrated "Dialogue concerning the Slavery of the Africans; showing it to be the Duty and Interest of the American States to Emancipate all their Slaves." This he dedicated to the Continental Congress, the Signers of the Declaration of Independence. It was republished in 1785, by the New York Abolition Society, and was widely circulated. A few years after, on coming unexpectedly into possession of a few hundred dollars, he devoted immediately one hundred of it to the society for ameliorating the condition of the Africans.

He continued to preach until he had reached his eighty-third year. His last sermon was delivered on the 16th of the tenth month, 1803, and his death took place in the twelfth month following. He died calmly, in the steady faith of one who had long trusted all things in the hand of God. "The language of my heart is," said he, "let God be glorified by all things, and the best interest of His kingdom promoted, whatever becomes of me or my interest." To a young friend, who visited him three days before his death, he said, "I am feeble and cannot say much. I have said all I can say. With my last words, I tell you, religion is the one thing needful." "And now," he continued, affectionately pressing the hand of his friend, "I am going to die, and I am glad of it." Many years before, an agreement had been made between Dr. Hopkins and his old and tried friend, Dr. Hart, of Connecticut, that when either was called home, the survivor should preach the funeral sermon of the deceased. The venerable Dr. Hart accordingly came, true to his promise, preaching at the funeral from the words of Elisha, "My father, my father; the chariots of Israel, and the horsemen thereof." In the burial-ground adjoining his meeting- house lies all that was mortal of Samuel Hopkins.

One of Dr. Hopkins's habitual hearers, and who has borne grateful testimony to the beauty and holiness of his life and conversation, was William Ellery Channing. Widely as he afterwards diverged from the creed of his early teacher, it contained at least one doctrine to the influence of which the philanthropic devotion of his own life to the welfare of man bears witness. He says, himself, that there always seemed to him something very noble in the doctrine of disinterested benevolence, the casting of self aside, and doing good, irrespective of personal consequences, in this world or another, upon which Dr. Hopkins so strongly insisted, as the all-essential condition of holiness.

How widely apart, as mere theologians, stood Hopkins and Channing! Yet how harmonious their lives and practice! Both could forget the poor interests of self, in view of eternal right and universal humanity. Both could appreciate the saving truth, that love to God and His creation is the fulfilling of the divine law. The idea of unselfish benevolence, which they held in common, clothed with sweetness and beauty the stern and repulsive features of the theology of Hopkins, and infused a sublime spirit of self-sacrifice and a glowing humanity into the indecisive and less robust faith of Charming. What is the lesson of this but that Christianity consists rather in the affections than in the intellect; that it is a life rather than a creed; and that they who diverge the widest from each other in speculation upon its doctrines may, after all, be found working side by side on the common ground of its practice.

We have chosen to speak of Dr. Hopkins as a philanthropist rather than as a theologian. Let those who prefer to contemplate the narrow sectarian rather than the universal man dwell upon his controversial works, and extol the ingenuity and logical acumen with which he defended his own dogmas and assailed those of others. We honor him, not as the founder of a new sect, but as the friend of all mankind,—the generous defender of the poor and oppressed. Great as unquestionably were his powers of argument, his learning, and skill in the use of the weapons of theologic warfare, these by no means constitute his highest title to respect and reverence. As the product of an honest and earnest mind, his doctrinal dissertations have at least the merit of sincerity. They were put forth in behalf of what he regarded as truth; and the success which they met with, while it called into exercise his profoundest gratitude, only served to deepen the humility and self-abasement of their author. As the utterance of what a good man believed and felt, as a part of the history of a life remarkable for its consecration to apprehended duty, these writings cannot be without interest even to those who dissent from their arguments and deny their assumptions; but in the time now, we trust, near at hand, when distracted and divided Christendom shall unite in a new Evangelical union, in which orthodoxy in life and practice shall be estimated above orthodoxy in theory, he will be honored as a good man, rather than as a successful creed-maker; as a friend of the oppressed and the fearless rebuker of popular sin rather than as the champion of a protracted sectarian war. Even now his writings, so popular in their day, are little known. The time may come when no pilgrim of sectarianism shall visit his grave. But his memory shall live in the hearts of the good and generous; the emancipated slave shall kneel over his ashes, and bless God for the gift to humanity of a life so devoted to its welfare. To him may be applied the language of one who, on the spot where he labored and lay down to rest, while rejecting the doctrinal views of the theologian, still cherishes the philanthropic spirit of the man:—

> "He is not lost,—he hath not passed away
> Clouds, earths, may pass, but stars shine calmly on;
> And he who doth the will of God, for aye
> Abideth, when the earth and heaven are gone.
>
> "Alas that such a heart is in the grave!'
> Thanks for the life that now shall never end!
> Weep, and rejoice, thou terror-hunted slave,
> That hast both lost and found so great a friend!"

RICHARD BAXTER

The picture drawn by a late English historian of the infamous Jeffreys in his judicial robes, sitting in judgment upon the venerable Richard Baxter, brought before him to answer to an indictment, setting; forth that the said "Richardus Baxter, persona seditiosa et factiosa pravae mentis, impiae, inquietae, turbulent disposition et conversation; falso illicte, injuste nequit factiose seditiose, et irreligiose, fecit, composuit, scripsit quendam falsum, seditiosum, libellosum, factiosum et irreligiosum librum," is so remarkable that the attention of the most careless reader is at once arrested. Who was that old man, wasted with disease and ghastly with the pallor of imprisonment, upon whom the foul- mouthed buffoon in ermine exhausted his vocabulary of abuse and ridicule? Who was Richardus Baxter?

The author of works so elaborate and profound as to frighten by their very titles and ponderous folios the modern ecclesiastical student from their perusal, his hold upon the present generation is limited to a few practical treatises, which, from their very nature, can never become obsolete. The *Call to the Unconverted* and the *Saints' Everlasting Rest* belong to no time or sect. They speak the universal language of the wants and desires of the human soul. They take hold of the awful verities of life and death, righteousness and judgment to come. Through them the suffering and hunted minister of Kidderminster has spoken in warning, entreaty, and rebuke, or in tones of tenderest love and pity, to the hearts of the generations which have succeeded him. His controversial works, his confessions of faith, his learned disputations, and his profound doctrinal treatises are no longer read. Their author himself, towards the close of his life, anticipated, in respect to these favorite productions, the children of his early zeal, labor, and suffering, the judgment of posterity. "I perceive," he says, "that most of the doctrinal controversies among Protestants are far more about equivocal words than matter. Experience since the year 1643 to this year 1675 hath loudly called me to repent of my own prejudices, sidings, and censurings of causes and persons not understood, and of all the miscarriages of my ministry and life which have been thereby caused; and to make it my chief work to call men that are within my bearing to more peaceable thoughts, affections, and practices."

Richard Baxter was born at the village of Eton Constantine, in 1615. He received from officiating curates of the little church such literary instruction as could be given by men who had left the farmer's flail, the tailor's thimble, and the service of strolling stage-players, to perform church drudgery under the parish incumbent, who was old and well-nigh blind. At the age of sixteen, he was sent to a school at Wroxeter, where he spent three years, to little purpose, so far as a scientific education was concerned. His teacher left him to himself mainly, and following the bent of his mind, even at that early period, he abandoned the exact sciences for the perusal of such controversial and metaphysical writings of the schoolmen as his master's library afforded. The smattering of Latin which he acquired only served in after years to deform his treatises with barbarous, ill-adapted, and erroneous citations. "As to myself," said he, in his letter written in old age to Anthony Wood, who had inquired whether he was an Oxonian graduate, "my faults are no disgrace to a university, for I was of none; I have but little but what I had out of books and inconsiderable help of country divines. Weakness and pain helped me to study how to die; that set me a-studying how to live; and that on studying the doctrine from which I must fetch my motives and comforts; beginning with necessities, I proceeded by degrees, and am now going to see that for which I have lived and studied."

Of the first essays of the young theologian as a preacher of the Established Church, his early sufferings from that complication of diseases with which his whole life was tormented, of the still keener afflictions of a mind whose entire outlook upon life and nature was discolored and darkened by its disordered bodily medium, and of the struggles between his Puritan temperament and his reverence for Episcopal formulas, much might be profitably said, did the limits we have assigned ourselves admit. Nor can we do more than briefly allude to the religious doubts and difficulties which darkened and troubled his mind at an early period.

He tells us at length in his Life how he struggled with these spiritual infirmities and temptations. The future life, the immortality of the soul, and the truth of the Scriptures were by turns questioned. "I never," says he in a letter to Dr. More, inserted in the *Sadducisimus Triumphatus,* "had so much ado to overcome a temptation as that to the opinion of Averroes, that, as extinguished candles go all out in an illuminated air, so separated souls go all into one common anima mundi, and lose their individuation." With these and similar "temptations" Baxter struggled long, earnestly, and in the end triumphantly. His faith, when once established, remained unshaken to the last; and although always solemn, reverential, and deeply serious, he was never the subject of religious melancholy, or of that mournful depression of soul which arises from despair of an interest in the mercy and paternal love of our common Father.

The Great Revolution found him settled as a minister in Kidderminster, under the sanction of a drunken vicar, who, yielding to the clamor of his more sober parishioners, and his fear of their appeal to the Long Parliament, then busy in its task of abating church nuisances, had agreed to give him sixty pounds per year, in the place of a poor tippling curate, notorious as a common railer and pothouse encumbrance.

As might have been expected, the sharp contrast which the earnest, devotional spirit and painful strictness of Baxter presented to the irreverent license and careless good humor of his predecessor by no means commended him to the favor of a large class of his parishioners. Sabbath merry-makers missed the rubicund face and maudlin jollity of their old vicar; the ignorant and vicious disliked the new preacher's rigid morality; the better informed revolted at his harsh doctrines, austere life, and grave manner. Intense earnestness characterized all his efforts. Contrasting human nature with the Infinite Purity and Holiness, he was oppressed with the sense of the loathsomeness and deformity of sin, and afflicted by the misery of his fellow-creatures separated from the divine harmony. He tells us that at this period he preached the terrors of the Law and the necessity of repentance, rather than the joys and consolations of the Gospel, upon which he so loved to dwell in his last years. He seems to have felt a necessity laid upon him to startle men from false hope and security, and to call for holiness of life and conformity to the divine will as the only ground of safety. Powerful and impressive as are the appeals and expostulations contained in his written works, they probably convey but a faint idea of the force and earnestness of those which he poured forth from his pulpit. As he advanced in years, these appeals were less frequently addressed to the fears of his auditors, for he had learned to value a calm and consistent life of practical goodness beyond any passionate exhibition of terrors, fervors, and transports. Having witnessed, in an age of remarkable enthusiasm and spiritual awakening, the ill effects of passional excitements and religious melancholy, he endeavored to present cheerful views of Christian life and duty, and made it a special object to repress morbid imaginations and heal diseased consciences. Thus it came to pass that no man of his day was more often applied to for counsel and relief by persons laboring under mental depression than himself. He has left behind him a very curious and not uninstructive discourse, which he entitled The Cure of Melancholy, by Faith and Physick, in which he shows a great degree of skill in his morbid mental anatomy. He had studied medicine to some extent for the benefit of the poor of his parish, and knew something of the intimate relations and sympathy of the body and mind; he therefore did not hesitate to ascribe many of the spiritual complaints of his applicants to disordered bodily functions, nor to prescribe pills and powders in the place of Scripture texts. More than thirty years after the commencement of his labors at Kidderminster he thus writes: "I was troubled this year with multitudes of melancholy persons from several places of the land; some of high quality, some of low, some exquisitely learned, and some unlearned. I know not how it came to pass, but if men fell melancholy I must hear from them or see them, more than any physician I knew." He cautions against ascribing melancholy phantasms and passions to the Holy Spirit, warns the young against licentious imaginations and excitements, and ends by advising all to take heed how they make of religion a matter of "fears, tears, and scruples." "True religion," he remarks, "doth principally consist in obedience, love, and joy."

At this early period of his ministry, however, he had all of Whitefield's intensity and fervor, added to reasoning powers greatly transcending those of the revivalist of the next century. Young in years, he was even then old in bodily infirmity and mental experience. Believing himself the victim of a mortal disease, he lived and preached in the constant prospect of death. His memento mori was in his bed-chamber, and sat by him at his frugal meal. The glory of the world was stained to his vision. He was blind to the beauty of all its "pleasant pictures." No monk of Mount Athos or silent Chartreuse, no anchorite of Indian superstition, ever more completely mortified the flesh, or turned his back more decidedly upon the "good things" of this life. A solemn and funeral atmosphere surrounded him. He walked in the shadows of the cypress, and literally "dwelt among the tombs." Tortured by incessant pain, he wrestled against its attendant languor and debility, as a sinful wasting of inestimable time; goaded himself to constant toil and devotional exercise, and, to use his own words, "stirred up his sluggish soul to speak to sinners with compassion, as a dying man to dying men."

Such entire consecration could not long be without its effect, even upon the "vicious rabble," as Baxter calls them. His extraordinary earnestness, self-forgetting concern for the spiritual welfare of others, his rigid life of denial and sacrifice, if they failed of bringing men to his feet as penitents, could not but awaken a feeling of reverence and awe. In Kidderminster, as in most other parishes of the kingdom, there were at this period pious, sober, prayerful people, diligent readers of the Scriptures, who were derided by their neighbors as Puritans, precisians, and hypocrites. These were naturally drawn towards the new preacher, and he as naturally recognized them as "honest seekers of the word and way of God." Intercourse with such men, and the perusal of the writings of certain eminent Non-conformists, had the effect to abate, in some degree, his strong attachment to the Episcopal formula and polity. He began to doubt the rightfulness of making the sign of the cross in baptism, and to hesitate about administering the sacrament to profane swearers and tipplers.

But while Baxter, in the seclusion of his parish, was painfully weighing the arguments for and against the wearing of surplices, the use of marriage rings, and the prescribed gestures and genuflections of his order, tithing with more or less scruple of conscience the mint and anise and cummin of pulpit ceremonials, the weightier matters of the law, freedom, justice, and truth were claiming the attention of Pym and Hampden, Brook and Vane, in the Parliament House. The controversy between King and Commons had reached the point where it could only be decided by the dread arbitrament of battle. The somewhat equivocal position of the Kidderminster preacher exposed him to the suspicion of the adherents of the King and Bishops. The rabble, at that period sympathizing with the party of license in morals and strictness in ceremonials, insulted and mocked him, and finally drove him from his parish.

On the memorable 23d of tenth month, 1642, he was invited to occupy a friend's pulpit at Alcester.

While preaching, a low, dull, jarring roll, as of continuous thunder, sounded in his ears. It was the cannon-fire of Edgehill, the prelude to the stern battle-piece of revolution. On the morrow, Baxter hurried to the scene of action. "I was desirous," he says, "to see the field. I found the Earl of Essex keeping the ground, and the King's army facing them on a hill about a mile off. There were about a thousand dead bodies in the field between them." Turning from this ghastly survey, the preacher mingled with the Parliamentary army, when, finding the surgeons busy with the wounded, he very naturally sought occasion for the exercise of his own vocation as a spiritual practitioner. He attached himself to the army. So far as we can gather from his own memoirs and the testimony of his contemporaries, he was not influenced to this step by any of the political motives which actuated the Parliamentary leaders. He was no revolutionist. He was as blind and unquestioning in his reverence for the King's person and divine right, and as hearty in his hatred of religious toleration and civil equality, as any of his clerical brethren who officiated in a similar capacity in the ranks of Goring and Prince Rupert. He seems only to have looked upon the soldiers as a new set of parishioners, whom Providence had thrown in his way. The circumstances of his situation left him little choice in the matter. "I had," he says, "neither money nor friends. I knew not who would receive me in a place of safety, nor had I anything to satisfy them for diet and entertainment." He accepted an offer to live in the Governor's house at Coventry, and preach to the soldiers of the garrison. Here his skill in polemics was called into requisition, in an encounter with two New England Antinomians, and a certain Anabaptist tailor who was making more rents in the garrison's orthodoxy than he mended in their doublets and breeches.

Coventry seems at this time to have been the rendezvous of a large body of clergymen, who, as Baxter says, were "for King and Parliament,"—men who, in their desire for a more spiritual worship, most unwillingly found themselves classed with the sentries whom they regarded as troublers and heretics, not to be tolerated; who thought the King had fallen into the hands of the Papists, and that Essex and Cromwell were fighting to restore him; and who followed the Parliamentary forces to see to it that they were kept sound in faith, and free from the heresy of which the Court News-Book accused them. Of doing anything to overturn the order of Church and State, or of promoting any radical change in the social and political condition of the people, they had no intention whatever. They looked at the events of the time, and upon their duties in respect to them, not as politicians or reformers, but simply as ecclesiastics and spiritual teachers, responsible to God for the religious beliefs and practices of the people, rather than for their temporal welfare and happiness. They were not the men who struck down the solemn and imposing prelacy of England, and vindicated the divine right of men to freedom by tossing the head of an anointed tyrant from the scaffold at Whitehall. It was the so-called schismatics, ranters, and levellers, the disputatious corporals and Anabaptist musketeers, the dread and abhorrence alike of prelate and presbyter, who, under the lead of Cromwell,

"*Ruined the great work of time,*
And cast the kingdoms old
Into another mould."

The Commonwealth was the work of the laity, the sturdy yeomanry and God- fearing commoners of England.

The news of the fight of Naseby reaching Coventry, Baxter, who had friends in the Parliamentary forces, wishing, as he says, to be assured of their safety, passed over to the stricken field, and spent a night with them. He was afflicted and confounded by the information which they gave him, that the victorious army was full of hot-headed schemers and levellers, who were against King and Church, prelacy and ritual, and who were for a free Commonwealth and freedom of religious belief and worship. He was appalled to find that the heresies of the Antinomians, Arminians, and Anabaptists had made sadder breaches in the ranks of Cromwell than the pikes of Jacob Astley, or the daggers of the roysterers who followed the mad charge of Rupert. Hastening back to Coventry, he called together his clerical brethren, and told them "the sad news of the corruption of the army." After much painful consideration of the matter, it was deemed best for Baxter to enter Cromwell's army, nominally as its chaplain, but really as the special representative of orthodoxy in politics and religion, against the democratic weavers and prophesying tailors who troubled it. He joined Whalley's regiment, and followed it through many a hot skirmish and siege. Personal fear was by no means one of Baxter's characteristics, and he bore himself through all with the coolness of an old campaigner. Intent upon his single object, he sat unmoved under the hail of cannon-shot from the walls of Bristol, confronted the well-plied culverins of Sherburne, charged side by side with Harrison upon Goring's musketeers at Langford, and heard the exulting thanksgiving of that grim enthusiast, when "with a loud voice he broke forth in praises of God, as one in rapture;" and marched, Bible in hand, with Cromwell himself, to the storming of Basing-House, so desperately defended by the Marquis of Winchester. In truth, these storms of outward conflict were to him of small moment. He was engaged in a sterner battle with spiritual principalities and powers, struggling with Satan himself in the guise of political levellers and Antinomian sowers of heresy. No antagonist was too high and none too low for him. Distrusting Cromwell, he sought to engage him in a discussion of certain points of abstract theology, wherein his soundness seemed questionable; but the wary chief baffled off the young disputant by tedious, unanswerable discourses about free grace, which Baxter admits were not unsavory to others, although the speaker himself had little understanding of the matter. At other times, he repelled his sad-visaged chaplain with unwelcome jests and rough, soldierly merriment; for he had "a vivacity, hilarity, and alacrity as another man hath when he hath taken a cup too much." Baxter says of him, complainingly, "he would not dispute with me at all." But, in the midst of such an army, he could not lack abundant opportunity for the exercise of his peculiar powers of argumentation. At Amersham, he had a sort of pitched battle with the contumacious soldiers. "When the public talking day came," says he, "I took the reading-pew, and Pitchford's cornet and troopers took the gallery. There did the leader of the Chesham men begin, and afterwards Pitchford's soldiers set in; and I alone disputed with them from morning until almost night; for I knew their trick, that if I had gone out first, they would have prated what boasting words they listed, and made the people believe that they had baffled me, or got the best; therefore I stayed it out till they first rose and went away." As usual in such cases, both parties claimed the victory. Baxter got thanks only from the King's adherents; "Pitchford's troops and the leader of the Chesham men" retired from their hard day's work, to enjoy the countenance and favor of Cromwell, as men after his own heart, faithful to the Houses and the Word, against kingcraft and prelacy.

Laughed at and held at arm's length by Cromwell, shunned by Harrison and Berry and other chief officers, opposed on all points by shrewd, earnest men, as ready for polemic controversy as for battle with the

King's malignants, and who set off against his theological and metaphysical distinctions their own personal experiences and spiritual exercises, he had little to encourage him in his arduous labors. Alone in such a multitude, flushed with victory and glowing with religious enthusiasm, he earnestly begged his brother ministers to come to his aid. "If the army," said he, "had only ministers enough, who could have done such little as I did, all their plot might have been broken, and King, Parliament, and Religion might have been preserved." But no one volunteered to assist him, and the "plot" of revolution went on.

After Worcester fight he returned to Coventry, to make his report to the ministers assembled there. He told them of his labors and trials, of the growth of heresy and levelling principles in the army, and of the evident design of its leaders to pull down Church, King, and Ministers. He assured them that the day was at hand when all who were true to the King, Parliament, and Religion should come forth to oppose these leaders, and draw away their soldiers from them. For himself, he was willing to go back to the army, and labor there until the crisis of which he spoke had arrived. "Whereupon," says he, "they all voted me to go yet longer."

Fortunately for the cause of civil and religious freedom, the great body of the ministers, who disapproved of the ultraism of the victorious army, and sympathized with the defeated King, lacked the courage and devotedness of Baxter. Had they promptly seconded his efforts, although the restoration of the King might have been impossible at that late period, the horrors of civil war must have been greatly protracted. As it was, they preferred to remain at home, and let Baxter have the benefit of their prayers and good wishes. He returned to the army with the settled purpose, of causing its defection from Cromwell; but, by one of those dispensations which the latter used to call "births of Providence," he was stricken down with severe sickness. Baxter's own comments upon this passage in his life are not without interest. He says, God prevented his purposes in his last and chiefest opposition to the army; that he intended to take off or seduce from their officers the regiment with which he was connected, and then to have tried his persuasion upon the others. He says he afterwards found that his sickness was a mercy to himself, "for they were so strong and active, and I had been likely to have had small success in the attempt, and to have lost my life among them in their fury." He was right in this last conjecture; Oliver Cromwell would have had no scruples in making an example of a plotting priest; and "Pitchford's soldiers" might have been called upon to silence, with their muskets, the tough disputant who was proof against their tongues.

After a long and dubious illness, Baxter was so far restored as to be able to go back to his old parish at Kidderminster. Here, under the Protectorate of Cromwell, he remained in the full enjoyment of that religious liberty which he still stoutly condemned in its application to others.

He afterwards candidly admits, that, under the "Usurper," as he styles Cromwell, "he had such liberty and advantage to preach the Gospel with success, as he could not have under a King, to whom he had sworn and performed true subjection and obedience." Yet this did not prevent him from preaching and printing, "seasonably and moderately," against the Protector. "I declared," said he, "Cromwell and his adherents to be guilty of treason and rebellion, aggravated by perfidiousness and hypocrisy. But yet I did not think it my duty to rave against him in the pulpit, or to do this so unseasonably and imprudently as might irritate him to mischief. And the rather, because, as he kept up his approbation of a godly life in general, and of all that was good, except that which the interest of his sinful cause engaged him to be against. So I perceived that it was his design to do good in the main, and to promote the Gospel and the interests of godliness more than any had done before him."

Cromwell, if he heard of his diatribes against him, appears to have cared little for them. Lords Warwick and Broghill, on one occasion, brought him to preach before the Lord Protector. He seized the occasion to preach against the sentries, to condemn all who countenanced them, and to advocate the unity of the Church. Soon after, he was sent for by Cromwell, who made "a long and tedious speech" in the presence of three of his chief men, (one of whom, General Lambert, fell asleep the while,) asserting that God had owned his government in a signal manner. Baxter boldly replied to him, that he and his friends regarded the ancient monarchy as a blessing, and not an evil, and begged to know how that blessing was forfeited to England, and to whom that forfeiture was made. Cromwell, with some heat, made answer that it was no forfeiture, but that God had made the change. They afterwards held a long conference with respect to freedom of conscience, Cromwell defending his liberal policy, and Baxter opposing it. No one can read Baxter's own account of these interviews, without being deeply impressed with the generous and magnanimous spirit of the Lord Protector in tolerating the utmost freedom of speech on the part of one who openly denounced him as a traitor and usurper. Real greatness of mind could alone have risen above personal resentment under such circumstances of peculiar aggravation.

In the death of the Protector, the treachery of Monk, and the restoration of the King, Baxter and his Presbyterian friends believed that they saw the hand of a merciful Providence preparing the way for the best good of

England and the Church. Always royalists, they had acted with the party opposed to the King from necessity rather than choice. Considering all that followed, one can scarcely avoid smiling over the extravagant jubilations of the Presbyterian divines, on the return of the royal debauchee to Whitehall. They hurried up to London with congratulations of formidable length and papers of solemn advice and counsel, to all which the careless monarch listened, with what patience he was master of. Baxter was one of the first to present himself at Court, and it is creditable to his heart rather than his judgment and discrimination that he seized the occasion to offer a long address to the King, expressive of his expectation that his Majesty would discountenance all sin and promote godliness, support the true exercise of Church discipline and cherish and hold up the hands of the faithful ministers of the Church. To all which Charles II. "made as gracious an answer as we could expect," says Baxter, "insomuch that old Mr. Ash burst out into tears of joy." Who doubts that the profligate King avenged himself as soon as the backs of his unwelcome visitors were fairly turned, by coarse jests and ribaldry, directed against a class of men whom he despised and hated, but towards whom reasons of policy dictated a show of civility and kindness?

There is reason to believe that Charles II., had he been able to effect his purpose, would have gone beyond Cromwell himself in the matter of religious toleration; in other words, he would have taken, in the outset of his reign, the very steps which cost his successor his crown, and procured the toleration of Catholics by a declaration of universal freedom in religion. But he was not in a situation to brave the opposition alike of Prelacy and Presbyterianism, and foiled in a scheme to which he was prompted by that vague, superstitious predilection for the Roman Catholic religion which at times struggled with his habitual scepticism, his next object was to rid himself of the importunities of sentries and the trouble of religious controversies by reestablishing the liturgy, and bribing or enforcing conformity to it on the part of the Presbyterians. The history of the successful execution of this purpose is familiar to all the readers of the plausible pages of Clarendon on the one side, or the complaining treatises of Neal and Calamy on the other.

Charles and his advisers triumphed, not so much through their own art, dissimulation, and bad faith as through the blind bigotry, divided counsels, and self-seeking of the Nonconformists. Seduction on one hand and threats on the other, the bribe of bishoprics, hatred of Independents and Quakers, and the terror of penal laws, broke the strength of Presbyterianism.

Baxter's whole conduct, on this occasion, bears testimony to his honesty and sincerity, while it shows him to have been too intolerant to secure his own religious freedom at the price of toleration for Catholics, Quakers, and Anabaptists; and too blind in his loyalty to perceive that pure and undefiled

Christianity had nothing to hope for from a scandalous and depraved King, surrounded by scoffing, licentious courtiers and a haughty, revengeful prelacy. To secure his influence, the Court offered him the bishopric of Hereford. Superior to personal considerations, he declined the honor; but somewhat inconsistently, in his zeal for the interests of his party, he urged the elevation of at least three of his Presbyterian friends to the Episcopal bench, to enforce that very liturgy which they condemned. He was the chief speaker for the Presbyterians at the famous Savoy Conference, summoned to advise and consult upon the Book of Common Prayer. His antagonist was Dr. Gunning, ready, fluent, and impassioned. "They spent," as Gilbert Burnet says, "several days in logical arguing, to the diversion of the town, who looked upon them as a couple of fencers, engaged in a discussion which could not be brought to an end." In themselves considered, many of the points at issue seem altogether too trivial for the zeal with which Baxter contested them,— the form of a surplice, the wording of a prayer, kneeling at sacrament, the sign of the cross, etc. With him, however, they were of momentous interest and importance, as things unlawful in the worship of God. He struggled desperately, but unavailingly. Presbyterianism, in its eagerness for peace and union and a due share of State support, had already made fatal concessions, and it was too late to stand upon non- essentials. Baxter retired from the conference baffled and defeated, amidst murmurs and jests. "If you had only been as fat as Dr. Manton," said Clarendon to him, "you would have done well."

The Act of Conformity, in which Charles II. and his counsellors gave the lie to the liberal declarations of Breda and Whitehall, drove Baxter from his sorrowing parishioners of Kidderminster, and added the evils of poverty and persecution to the painful bodily infirmities under which he was already bowed down. Yet his cup was not one of unalloyed bitterness, and loving lips were prepared to drink it with him.

Among Baxter's old parishioners of Kidderminster was a widowed lady of gentle birth, named Charlton, who, with her daughter Margaret, occupied a house in his neighborhood. The daughter was a brilliant girl, of "strangely vivid wit," and "in early youth," he tells us, "pride, and romances, and company suitable thereunto, did take her up." But erelong, Baxter, who acted in the double capacity of spiritual and temporal physician, was sent for to visit her, on an occasion of sickness. He ministered to her bodily and mental sufferings, and thus secured her gratitude and confidence. On her recovery, under the influence of his warnings and admonitions, the gay young girl became thoughtful and serious, abandoned her light books and companions, and devoted herself to the duties of a Christian profession. Baxter was her counsellor and confidant. She disclosed to him all her doubts, trials, and temptations, and he, in return, wrote her long letters of sympathy, consolation, and encouragement. He began to feel such an unwonted interest in the moral and spiritual growth of his young disciple, that, in his daily walks among his parishioners, he found himself inevitably drawn towards her mother's dwelling. In her presence, the habitual austerity of his manner was softened; his cold, close heart warmed and expanded. He began to repay her confidence with his own, disclosing to her all his plans of benevolence, soliciting her services, and waiting, with deference, for her judgment upon them. A change came over his habits of thought and his literary tastes; the harsh, rude disputant, the tough, dry logician, found himself addressing to his young friend epistles in verse on doctrinal points and matters of casuistry; Westminster Catechism in rhyme; the Solemn League and Covenant set to music. A miracle alone could have made Baxter a poet; the cold, clear light of reason "paled the ineffectual fires" of his imagination; all things presented themselves to his vision "with hard outlines, colorless, and with no surrounding atmosphere." That he did, nevertheless, write verses, so creditable as to justify a judicious modern critic in their citation and approval, can perhaps be accounted for only as one of the phenomena of that subtle and transforming influence to which even his stern nature was unconsciously yielding. Baxter was in love.

Never did the blind god try his archery on a more unpromising subject. Baxter was nearly fifty years of age, and looked still older. His life had been one long fast and penance. Even in youth he had never known a schoolboy's love for cousin or playmate. He had resolutely closed up his heart against emotions which he regarded as the allurements of time and sense. He had made a merit of celibacy, and written and published against the entanglement of godly ministers in matrimonial engagements and family cares. It is questionable whether he now understood his own case, or attributed to its right cause the peculiar interest which he felt in Margaret Charlton. Left to himself, it is more than probable that he might never have discovered the true nature of that interest, or conjectured that anything whatever of earthly passion or sublunary emotion had mingled with his spiritual Platonism. Commissioned and set apart to preach repentance to dying men, penniless and homeless, worn with bodily pain and mental toil, and treading, as he believed, on the very margin of his grave, what had he to do with love? What power had he to inspire that tender sentiment, the appropriate offspring only of youth, and health, and beauty?

> "Could any Beatrice see
>
> A lover in such anchorite!"

But in the mean time a reciprocal feeling was gaining strength in the heart of Margaret. To her grateful appreciation of the condescension of a great and good man—grave, learned, and renowned—to her youth and weakness, and to her enthusiastic admiration of his intellectual powers, devoted to the highest and holiest objects, succeeded naturally enough the tenderly suggestive pity of her woman's heart, as she thought of his lonely home, his unshared sorrows, his lack of those sympathies and kindnesses which make tolerable the hard journey of life. Did she not owe to him, under God, the salvation of body and mind? Was he not her truest and most faithful friend, entering with lively interest into all her joys and sorrows? Had she not seen the cloud of his habitual sadness broken by gleams of sunny warmth and cheerfulness, as they conversed together? Could she do better than devote herself to the pleasing task of making his life happier, of comforting him in seasons of pain and weariness, encouraging him in his vast labors, and throwing over the cold and hard austerities of his nature the warmth and light of domestic affection? Pity, reverence, gratitude, and womanly tenderness, her fervid imagination and the sympathies of a deeply religious nature, combined to influence her decision. Disparity of age and condition rendered it improbable that Baxter would ever venture to address her in any other capacity than that of a friend and teacher; and it was left to herself to give the first intimation of the possibility of a more intimate relation.

It is easy to imagine with what mixed feelings of joy, surprise, and perplexity Baxter must have received the delicate avowal. There was much in the circumstances of the case to justify doubt, misgiving, and close searchings of heart. He must have felt the painful contrast which that fair girl in the bloom of her youth presented to the worn man of middle years, whose very breath was suffering, and over whom death seemed always impending. Keenly conscious of his infirmities of temper, he must have feared for the happiness of a loving, gentle being, daily exposed to their manifestations. From his well-known habit of consulting what he regarded as the divine will in every important step of his life, there can be no doubt that his decision was the result quite as much of a prayerful and patient consideration of duty as of the promptings of his heart. Richard Baxter was no impassioned Abelard; his pupil in the school of his severe and self-denying piety was no Heloise; but what their union lacked in romantic interest was compensated by its purity and disinterestedness, and its sanction by all that can hallow human passion, and harmonize the love of the created with the love and service of the Creator.

Although summoned by a power which it would have been folly to resist, the tough theologian did not surrender at discretion. "From the first thoughts yet many changes and stoppages intervened, and long delays," he tells us. The terms upon which he finally capitulated are perfectly in keeping with his character. "She consented," he says, "to three conditions of our marriage. 1st. That I should have nothing that before our marriage was hers; that I, who wanted no earthly supplies, might not seem to marry her from selfishness. 2d. That she would so alter her affairs that I might be entangled in no lawsuits. 3d. That she should expect none of my time which my ministerial work should require."

As was natural, the wits of the Court had their jokes upon this singular marriage; and many of his best friends regretted it, when they called to mind what he had written in favor of ministerial celibacy, at a time when, as he says, "he thought to live and die a bachelor." But Baxter had no reason to regret the inconsistency of his precept and example. How much of the happiness of the next twenty years of his life resulted from his union with a kind and affectionate woman he has himself testified, in his simple and touching Breviate of the Life of the late Mrs. Baxter. Her affections were so ardent that her husband confesses his fear that he was unable to make an adequate return, and that she must have been disappointed in him in consequence. He extols her pleasant conversation, her active benevolence, her disposition to aid him in all his labors, and her noble forgetfulness of self, in ministering to his comfort, in sickness and imprisonment. "She was the meetest helper I could have had in the world," is his language. "If I spoke harshly or sharply, it offended her. If I carried it (as I am apt) with too much negligence of ceremony or humble compliment to any, she would modestly tell me of it. If my looks seemed not pleasant, she would have me amend them (which my weak, pained state of body indisposed me to do)." He admits she had her failings, but, taken as a whole, the Breviate is an exalted eulogy.

His history from this time is marked by few incidents of a public character. During that most disgraceful period in the annals of England, the reign of the second Charles, his peculiar position exposed him to the persecutions of prelacy and the taunts and abuse of the sentries, standing as he did between these extremes, and pleading for a moderate Episcopacy. He was between the upper millstone of High Church and the nether one of Dissent. To use his own simile, he was like one who seeks to fill with his hand a cleft in a log, and feels both sides close upon him with pain. All parties and sects had, as they thought, grounds of complaint against him. There was in him an almost childish simplicity of purpose, a headlong earnestness and eagerness, which did not allow him to consider how far a present act or opinion harmonized with what he had already done or written. His greatest admirers admit his lack of judgment, his inaptitude for the management of practical matters. His utter incapacity to comprehend rightly the public men and measures of his day is abundantly apparent; and the inconsistencies of his conduct and his writings are too marked to need comment. He suffered persecution for not conforming to some trifling matters of Church usage, while he advocated the doctrine of passive obedience to the King or ruling power, and the right of that power to enforce conformity. He wrote against conformity while himself conforming; seceded from the Church, and yet held stated communion with it; begged for the curacy of Kidderminster, and declined the bishopric of Hereford. His writings were many of them directly calculated to make Dissenters from the Establishment, but he was invariably offended to find others practically influenced by them, and quarrelled with his own converts to Dissent. The High Churchmen of Oxford burned his Holy Commonwealth as seditious and revolutionary; while Harrington and the republican club of Miles's Coffee House condemned it for its hostility to democracy and its servile doctrine of obedience to kings. He made noble pleas for liberty of conscience and bitterly complained of his own suffering from Church courts, yet maintained the necessity of enforcing conformity, and stoutly opposed the tolerant doctrines of Penn and Milton. Never did a great and good man so entangle himself with contradictions and inconsistencies. The witty and wicked Sir Roger L'Estrange compiled from the irreconcilable portions of his works a laughable Dialogue between Richard and Baxter. The Antinomians found him guilty of Socinianism; and one noted controversialist undertook to show, not without some degree of plausibility, that he was by turns a Quaker and a Papist!

Although able to suspend his judgment and carefully weigh evidence, upon matters which he regarded as proper subjects of debate and scrutiny, he possessed the power to shut out and banish at will all doubt and misgiving in respect to whatever tended to prove, illustrate, or enforce his settled opinions and cherished doctrines. His credulity at times seems boundless. Hating the Quakers, and prepared to believe all manner of evil of them, he readily came to the conclusion that their leaders were disguised Papists. He maintained that Lauderdale was a good and pious man, in spite of atrocities in Scotland which entitle him to a place with Claverhouse; and indorsed the character of the infamous Dangerfield, the inventor of the Meal-tub Plot, as a worthy convert from popish errors. To prove the existence of devils and spirits, he collected the most absurd stories and old-wives' fables, of soldiers scared from their posts at night by headless bears, of a young witch pulling the hooks out of Mr. Emlen's breeches and swallowing them, of Mr. Beacham's locomotive tobacco-pipe, and the Rev. Mr. Munn's jumping Bible, and of a drunken man punished for his intemperance by being lifted off his legs by an invisible hand! Cotton Mather's marvellous account of his witch experiments in New England delighted him. He had it republished, declaring that "he must be an obstinate Sadducee who doubted it."

The married life of Baxter, as might be inferred from the state of the times, was an unsettled one. He first took a house at Moorfields, then removed to Acton, where he enjoyed the conversation of his neighbor, Sir Matthew Hale; from thence he found refuge in Rickmansworth, and after that in divers other places. "The women have most of this trouble," he remarks, "but my wife easily bore it all." When unable to preach, his rapid pen was always busy. Huge folios of controversial and doctrinal lore followed each other in quick succession. He assailed Popery and the Establishment, Anabaptists, ultra Calvinists, Antinomians, Fifth Monarchy men, and Quakers. His hatred of the latter was only modified by his contempt. He railed rather than argued against the "miserable creatures," as he styled them. They in turn answered him in like manner. "The Quakers," he says, "in their shops, when I go along London streets, say, 'Alas' poor man, thou art yet in darkness.' They have oft come to the congregation, when I had liberty to preach Christ's Gospel, and cried out against me as a deceiver of the people. They have followed me home, crying out in the streets, 'The day of the Lord is coming, and thou shalt perish as a deceiver.' They have stood in the market-place, and under my window, year after year, crying to the people, 'Take heed of your priests, they deceive your souls;' and if any one wore a lace or neat clothing, they cried out to me, 'These are the fruits of your ministry.'"

At Rickmansworth, he found himself a neighbor of William Penn, whom he calls "the captain of the Quakers." Ever ready for battle, Baxter encountered him in a public discussion, with such fierceness and bitterness as to force from that mild and amiable civilian the remark, that he would rather be Socrates at the final judgment than Richard Baxter. Both lived to know each other better, and to entertain sentiments of mutual esteem. Baxter himself admits that the Quakers, by their perseverance in holding their religious meetings in defiance of penal laws, took upon themselves the burden of persecution which would otherwise have fallen upon himself and his friends; and makes special mention of the noble and successful plea of Penn before the Recorder's Court in London, based on the fundamental liberties of Englishmen and the rights of the Great Charter.

The intolerance of Baxter towards the Separatists was turned against him whenever he appealed to the King and Parliament against the proscription of himself and his friends. "They gathered," he complains, "out of mine and other men's books all that we had said against liberty for Popery and Quakers railing against ministers in open congregation, and applied it as against the toleration of ourselves." It was in vain that he explained that he was only in favor of a gentle coercion of dissent, a moderate enforcement of conformity. His plan for dealing with sentries reminds one of old Isaak Walton's direction to his piscatorial readers, to impale the frog on the hook as gently as if they loved him.

While at Acton, he was complained of by Dr. Ryves, the rector, one of the King's chaplains in ordinary, for holding religious services in his family with more than five strangers present. He was cast into Clerkenwell jail, whither his faithful wife followed him. On his discharge, he sought refuge in the hamlet of Totteridge, where he wrote and published that Paraphrase on the New Testament which was made the ground of his prosecution and trial before Jeffreys.

On the 14th of the sixth month, 1681, he was called to endure the greatest affliction of his life. His wife died on that day, after a brief illness. She who had been his faithful friend, companion, and nurse for twenty years was called away from him in the time of his greatest need of her ministrations. He found consolation in dwelling on her virtues and excellences in the Breviate of her life; "a paper monument," he says, "erected by one who is following her even at the door in some passion indeed of love and grief." In the preface to his poetical pieces he alludes to her in terms of touching simplicity and tenderness: "As these pieces were mostly written in various passions, so passion hath now thrust them out into the world. God having taken away the dear companion of the last nineteen years of my life, as her sorrows and sufferings long ago gave being to some of these poems, for reasons, which the world is not concerned to know; so my grief for her removal, and the revival of the sense of former things, have prevailed upon me to be passionate in the sight of all."

The circumstances of his trial before the judicial monster, Jeffreys, are too well known to justify their detail in this sketch. He was sentenced to pay a fine of five hundred marks. Seventy years of age, and reduced to poverty by former persecutions, he was conveyed to the King's Bench prison. Here for two years he lay a victim to intense bodily suffering. When, through the influence of his old antagonist, Penn, he was restored to freedom, he was already a dying man. But he came forth from prison as he entered it, unsubdued in spirit.

Urged to sign a declaration of thanks to James II., his soul put on the athletic habits of youth, and he stoutly refused to commend an act of toleration which had given freedom not to himself alone, but to Papists and sentries. Shaking off the dust of the Court from his feet, he retired to a dwelling in Charter-House Square, near his friend Sylvester's, and patiently awaited his deliverance. His death was quiet and peaceful. "I have pain," he said to his friend Mather; "there is no arguing against sense; but I have peace. I have peace." On being asked how he did, he answered, in memorable words, "Almost well!"

He was buried in Christ Church, where the remains of his wife and her mother had been placed. An immense concourse attended his funeral, of all ranks and parties. Conformist and Non-conformist forgot the bitterness of the controversialist, and remembered only the virtues and the piety of the man. Looking back on his life of self-denial and faithfulness to apprehended duty, the men who had persecuted him while living wept over his grave. During the last few years of his life, the severity of his controversial tone had been greatly softened; he lamented his former lack of charity, the circle of his sympathies widened, his social affections grew stronger with age, and love for his fellow-men universally, and irrespective of religious differences, increased within him. In his Narrative, written in the long, cool shadows of the evening of life, he acknowledges with extraordinary candor this change in his views and feelings. He confesses his imperfections as a writer and public teacher.

"I wish," he says, "all over-sharp passages were expunged from my writings, and I ask forgiveness of God and man." He tells us that mankind appear more equal to him; the good are not so good as he once thought, nor the bad so evil; and that in all there is more for grace to make advantage of, and more to testify for God and holiness, than he once believed. "I less admire," he continues, "gifts of utterance, and the bare profession of religion, than I once did, and have now much more charity for those who, by want of gifts, do make an obscurer profession."

He laments the effects of his constitutional irritability and impatience upon his social intercourse and his domestic relations, and that his bodily infirmities did not allow him a free expression of the tenderness and love of his heart. Who does not feel the pathos and inconsolable regret which dictated the following paragraph?

"When God forgiveth me, I cannot forgive myself, especially for my rash words and deeds by which I have seemed injurious and less tender and kind than I should have been to my near and dear relations, whose love abundantly obliged me. When such are dead, though we never differed in point of interest or any other matter, every sour or cross or provoking word which I gave them maketh me almost irreconcilable to myself, and tells me how repentance brought some of old to pray to the dead whom they had wronged to forgive them, in the hurry of their passion."

His pride as a logician and skilful disputant abated in the latter and better portion of his life he had more deference to the judgment of others, and more distrust of his own. "You admire," said he to a correspondent who had lauded his character, "one you do not know; knowledge will cure your error." In his Narrative he writes: "I am much more sensible than heretofore of the breadth and length and depth of the radical, universal, odious sin of selfishness, and therefore have written so much against it; and of the excellency and necessity of self-denial and of a public mind, and of loving our neighbors as ourselves." Against many difficulties and discouragements, both within himself and in his outward circumstances, he strove to make his life and conversation an expression of that Christian love whose root, as he has said with equal truth and beauty, "is set

> *In humble self-denial, undertrod,*
>
> *While flower and fruit are growing up to God."*

Of the great mass of his writings, more voluminous than those of any author of his time, it would ill become us to speak with confidence. We are familiar only with some of the best of his practical works, and our estimate of the vast and appalling series of his doctrinal, metaphysical and controversial publications would be entitled to small weight, as the result of very cursory examination. Many of them relate to obsolete questions and issues, monumental of controversies long dead, and of disputatious doctors otherwise forgotten. Yet, in respect to even these, we feel justified in assenting to the opinion of one abundantly capable of appreciating the character of Baxter as a writer. "What works of Mr. Baxter shall I read?" asked Boswell of Dr. Johnson. "Read any of them," was the answer, "for they are all good." He has left upon all the impress of his genius. Many of them contain sentiments which happily find favor with few in our time: philosophical and psychological disquisitions, which look oddly enough in the light of the intellectual progress of nearly two centuries; dissertations upon evil spirits, ghosts, and witches, which provoke smiles at the good man's credulity; but everywhere we find unmistakable evidences of his sincerity and earnest love of truth. He wrote under a solemn impression of duty, allowing neither pain, nor weakness, nor the claims of friendship, nor the social enjoyments of domestic affection, to interfere with his sleepless intensity of purpose. He stipulated with his wife, before marriage, that she should not expect him to relax, even for her society, the severity of his labors. He could ill brook interruption, and disliked the importunity of visitors. "We are afraid, sir, we break in upon your time," said some of his callers to him upon one occasion. "To be sure you do," was his answer. His seriousness seldom forsook him; there is scarce a gleam of gayety in all his one hundred and sixty-eight volumes. He seems to have relished, however, the wit of others, especially when directed against what he looked upon as error. Marvell's inimitable reply to the High-Church pretensions of Parker fairly overcame his habitual gravity, and he several times alludes to it with marked satisfaction; but, for himself, he had no heart for pleasentry. His writings, like his sermons, were the earnest expostulations of a dying man with dying men. He tells us of no other amusement or relaxation than the singing of psalms. "Harmony and melody," said he, "are the pleasure and elevation of my soul. It was not the least comfort that I had in the converse of my late dear wife, that our first act in the morning and last in bed at night was a psalm of praise."

It has been fashionable to speak of Baxter as a champion of civil and religious freedom. He has little claim to such a reputation. He was the stanch advocate of monarchy, and of the right and duty of the State to enforce conformity to what he regarded as the essentials of religious belief and practice. No one regards the prelates who went to the Tower, under James II., on the ground of conscientious scruples against reading the King's declaration of toleration to Dissenters, as martyrs in the cause of universal religious freedom. Nor can Baxter, although he wrote much against the coercion and silencing of godly ministers, and suffered imprisonment himself for the sake of a good conscience, be looked upon in the light of an intelligent and consistent confessor of liberty. He did not deny the abstract right of ecclesiastical coercion, but complained of its exercise upon himself and his friends as unwarranted and unjust.

One of the warmest admirers and ablest commentators of Baxter designates the leading and peculiar trait of his character as unearthliness. In our view, this was its radical defect. He had too little of humanity, he felt too little of the attraction of this world, and lived too exclusively in the spiritual and the unearthly, for a full and healthful development of his nature as a man, or of the graces, charities, and loves of the Christian. He undervalued the common blessings and joys of life, and closed his eyes and ears against the beauty and harmony of outward nature. Humanity, in itself considered, seemed of small moment to him; "passing away" was written alike on its wrongs and its rights, its pleasures and its pains; death would soon level all distinctions; and the sorrows or the joys, the poverty or the riches, the slavery or the liberty, of the brief day of its probation seemed of too little consequence to engage his attention and sympathies. Hence, while he was always ready to minister to temporal suffering wherever it came to his notice, he made no efforts to remove its political or social causes. In this respect he differed widely from some of his illustrious contemporaries. Penn, while preaching up and down the land, and writing theological folios and pamphlets, could yet urge the political rights of Englishmen, mount the hustings for Algernon Sydney, and plead for unlimited religious liberty; and Vane, while dreaming of a coming millennium and reign of the saints, and busily occupied in defending his Antinomian doctrines, could at the same time vindicate, with tongue and pen, the cause of civil and religious freedom. But Baxter overlooked the evils and oppressions which were around him, and forgot the necessities and duties of the world of time and sense in his earnest aspirations towards the world of spirits. It is by no means an uninstructive fact, that with the lapse of years his zeal for proselytism, doctrinal disputations, and the preaching of threats and terrors visibly declined, while love for his fellow-men and catholic charity greatly increased, and he was blessed with a clearer perception of the truth that God is best served through His suffering children, and that love and reverence for visible humanity is an indispensable condition of the appropriate worship of the Unseen God.

But, in taking leave of Richard Baxter, our last words must not be those of censure. Admiration and reverence become us rather. He was an honest man. So far as we can judge, his motives were the highest and best which can influence human action. He had faults and weaknesses, and committed grave errors, but we are constrained to believe that the prayer with which he closes his Saints' Rest and which we have chosen as the fitting termination of our article, was the earnest aspiration of his life:—

"O merciful Father of Spirits! suffer not the soul of thy unworthy servant to be a stranger to the joys which he describes to others, but keep me while I remain on earth in daily breathing after thee, and in a believing affectionate walking with thee! Let those who shall read these pages not merely read the fruits of my studies, but the breathing of my active hope and love; that if my heart were open to their view, they might there read thy love most deeply engraven upon it with a beam from the face of the Son of God; and not find vanity or lust or pride within where the words of life appear without, that so these lines may not witness against me, but, proceeding from the heart of the writer, be effectual through thy grace upon the heart of the reader, and so be the savor of life to both."

WILLIAM LEGGETT

"O Freedom! thou art not, as poets dream,
A fair young girl, with light and delicate limbs,
And wavy tresses, gushing from the cap
With which the Roman master crowned his slave,
When he took off the gyves. A bearded man,
Armed to the teeth, art thou; one mailed hand
Grasps the broad shield, and one the sword; thy brow,
Glorious in beauty though it be, is scarred
With tokens of old wars; thy massive limbs
Are strong with struggling. Power at thee has launched
His bolts, and with his lightnings smitten thee;
They could not quench the life thou hast from Heaven."
BRYANT.

WHEN the noblest woman in all France stood on the scaffold, just before her execution, she is said to have turned towards the statue of Liberty, — which, strangely enough, had been placed near the guillotine, as its patron saint, — with the exclamation, "O Liberty! what crimes have been committed in thy name!" It is with a feeling akin to that which prompted this memorable exclamation of Madame Roland that the sincere lover of human freedom and progress is often compelled to regard American democracy.

For democracy, pure and impartial, — the self-government of the whole; equal rights and privileges, irrespective of birth or complexion; the morality of the Gospel of Christ applied to legislation; Christianity reduced to practice, and showering the blessings of its impartial love and equal protection upon all, like the rain and dews of heaven, — we have the sincerest love and reverence. So far as our own government approaches this standard — and, with all its faults, we believe it does so more nearly than any other — it has our hearty and steadfast allegiance. We complain of and protest against it only where, in its original framework or actual administration, it departs from the democratic principle. Holding, with Novalis, that the Christian religion is the root of all democracy and the highest fact in the rights of man, we regard the New Testament as the true political text-book; and believe that, just in proportion as mankind receive its doctrines and precepts, not merely as matters of faith and relating to another state of being, but as practical rules, designed for the regulation of the present life as well as the future, their institutions, social arrangements, and forms of government will approximate to the democratic model. We believe in the ultimate complete accomplishment of the mission of Him who came "to preach deliverance to the captive, and the opening of prison doors to them that are bound." We look forward to the universal dominion of His benign humanity; and, turning from the strife and blood, the slavery, and social and political wrongs of the past and present, anticipate the realization in the distant future of that state when the song of the angels at His advent shall be no longer a prophecy, but the jubilant expression of a glorious reality,— "Glory to God in the highest! Peace on earth, and good will to man!"

For the party in this country which has assumed the name of Democracy, as a party, we have had, we confess, for some years past, very little respect. It has advocated many salutary measures, tending to equalize the advantages of trade and remove the evils of special legislation. But if it has occasionally lopped some of the branches of the evil tree of oppression, so far from striking at its root, it has suffered itself to be made the instrument of nourishing and protecting it. It has allowed itself to be called, by its Southern flatterers, "the natural ally of slavery." It has spurned the petitions of the people in behalf of freedom under its feet, in Congress and State legislatures. Nominally the advocate of universal suffrage, it has wrested from the colored citizens of Pennsylvania that right of citizenship which they had enjoyed under a Constitution framed by Franklin and Rush. Perhaps the most shameful exhibition of its spirit was made in the late Rhode Island struggle, when the free suffrage convention, solemnly calling heaven and earth to witness its readiness to encounter all the horrors of civil war, in defence of the holy principle of equal and universal suffrage, deliberately excluded colored Rhode Islanders from the privilege of voting. In the Constitutional Conventions of Michigan and Iowa, the same party declared all men equal, and then provided an exception to this rule in the case of the colored inhabitants. Its course on the question of excluding slavery from Texas is a matter of history, known and read of all.

After such exhibitions of its practice, its professions have lost their power. The cant of democracy upon the lips of men who are living down its principles is, to an earnest mind, well nigh insufferable. Pertinent were the queries of Eliphaz the Temanite, "Shall a man utter vain knowledge, and fill his belly with the east wind? Shall he reason with unprofitable talk, or with speeches wherewith he can do no good?" Enough of wearisome talk we have had about "progress," the rights of "the masses," the "dignity of labor," and "extending the area of freedom"! "Clear your mind of cant, sir," said Johnson to Boswell; and no better advice could be now given to a class of our democratic politicians. Work out your democracy; translate your words into deeds; away with your sentimental generalizations, and come down to the practical details of your duty as men and Christians. What avail your abstract theories, your hopeless virginity of democracy, sacred from the violence of meanings? A democracy which professes to hold, as by divine right, the doctrine of human equality in its special keeping, and which at the same time gives its direct countenance and support to the vilest system of oppression on which the sun of heaven looks, has no better title to the name it disgraces than the apostate Son of the Morning has to his old place in heaven. We are using strong language, for we feel strongly on this subject. Let those whose hypocrisy we condemn, and whose sins against humanity we expose, remember that they are the publishers of their own shame, and that they have gloried in their apostasy. There is a cutting severity in the answer which Sophocles puts in the mouth of Electra, in justification of her indignant rebuke of her wicked mother:—

> "'Tis you that say it, not I
> You do the unholy deeds which find rue words."

Yet in that party calling itself democratic we rejoice to recognize true, generous, and thoroughly sincere men,—lovers of the word of democracy, and doers of it also, honest and hearty in their worship of liberty, who are still hoping that the antagonism which slavery presents to democracy will be perceived by the people, in spite of the sophistry and appeals to prejudice by which interested partisans have hitherto succeeded in deceiving them. We believe with such that the mass of the democratic voters of the free States are in reality friends of freedom, and hate slavery in all its forms; and that, with a full understanding of the matter, they could never consent to be sold to presidential aspirants, by political speculators, in lots to suit purchasers, and warranted to be useful in putting down free discussion, perpetuating oppression, and strengthening the hands of modern feudalism. They are beginning already to see that, under the process whereby men of easy virtue obtain offices from the general government, as the reward of treachery to free principles, the strength and vitality of the party are rapidly declining. To them, at least, democracy means something more than collectorships, consulates, and governmental contracts. For the sake of securing a monopoly of these to a few selfish and heartless party managers, they are not prepared to give up the distinctive principles of democracy, and substitute in their place the doctrines of the Satanic school of politics. They will not much longer consent to stand before the world as the slavery party of the United States, especially when policy and expediency, as well as principle, unite in recommending a position more congenial to the purposes of their organization, the principles of the fathers of their political faith, the spirit of the age, and the obligations of Christianity.

The death-blow of slavery in this country will be given by the very power upon which it has hitherto relied with so much confidence. Abused and insulted Democracy will, erelong, shake off the loathsome burden under which it is now staggering. In the language of the late Theodore Sedgwiek, of Massachusetts, a consistent democrat of the old school: "Slavery, in all its forms, is anti-democratic,—an old poison left in the veins, fostering the worst principles of aristocracy, pride, and aversion to labor; the natural enemy of the poor man, the laboring man, the oppressed man. The question is, whether absolute dominion over any creature in the image of man be a wholesome power in a free country; whether this is a school in which to train the young republican mind; whether slave blood and free blood can course healthily together in the same body politic. Whatever may be present appearances, and by whatever name party may choose to call things, this question must finally be settled by the democracy of the country."

This prediction was made eight years ago, at a time when all the facts in the case seemed against the probability of its truth, and when only here and there the voice of an indignant freeman protested against the exulting claims of the slave power upon the democracy as its "natural ally." The signs of the times now warrant the hope of its fulfilment. Over the hills of the East, and over the broad territory of the Empire State, a new spirit is moving. Democracy, like Balaam upon Zophim, has felt the divine *afflatus*, and is blessing that which it was summoned to curse.

The present hopeful state of things is owing, in no slight degree, to the self-sacrificing exertions of a few faithful and clear-sighted men, foremost among whom was the late William Leggett; than whom no one has labored more perseveringly, or, in the end, more successfully, to bring the practice of American democracy into conformity with its professions.

William Leggett! Let our right hand forget its cunning, when that name shall fail to awaken generous emotions and aspirations for a higher and worthier manhood! True man and true democrat; faithful always to Liberty, following wherever she led, whether the storm beat in his face or on his back; unhesitatingly counting her enemies his own, whether in the guise of Whig monopoly and selfish expediency, or democratic servility north of Mason and Dixon's line towards democratic slaveholding south of it; poor, yet incorruptible; dependent upon party favor, as a party editor, yet risking all in condemnation of that party, when in the wrong; a man of the people, yet never stooping to flatter the people's prejudices,—he is the politician, of all others, whom we would hold up to the admiration and imitation of the young men of our country. What Fletcher of Saltoun is to Scotland, and the brave spirits of the old Commonwealth time—

"Hands that penned
And tongues that uttered wisdom, better none
The later Sydney, Marvell, Harrington,
Young Vane, and others, who called Milton friend—"

are to England, should Leggett be to America. His character was formed on these sturdy democratic models. Had he lived in their day, he would have scraped with old Andrew Marvell the bare blade-bone of poverty, or even laid his head on the block with Vane, rather than forego his independent thought and speech.

Of the early life of William Leggett we have no very definite knowledge. Born in moderate circumstances; at first a woodsman in the Western wilderness, then a midshipman in the navy, then a denizen of New York; exposed to sore hardships and perilous temptations, he worked his way by the force of his genius to the honorable position of associate editor of the Evening Post, the leading democratic journal of our great commercial metropolis. Here he became early distinguished for his ultraism in democracy. His whole soul revolted against oppression. He was for liberty everywhere and in all things, in thought, in speech, in vote, in religion, in government, and in trade; he was for throwing off all restraints upon the right of suffrage; regarding all men as brethren, he looked with disapprobation upon attempts to exclude foreigners from the rights of citizenship; he was for entire freedom of commerce; he denounced a national bank; he took the lead in opposition to the monopoly of incorporated banks; he argued in favor of direct taxation, and advocated a free post-office, or a system by which letters should be transported, as goods and passengers now are, by private enterprise. In all this he was thoroughly in earnest. That he often erred through passion and prejudice cannot be doubted; but in no instance was he found turning aside from the path which he believed to be the true one, from merely selfish considerations. He was honest alike to himself and the public. Every question which was thrown up before him by the waves of political or moral agitation he measured by his standard of right and truth, and condemned or advocated it in utter disregard of prevailing opinions, of its effect upon his pecuniary interest, or of his standing with his party. The vehemence of his passions sometimes betrayed him into violence of language and injustice to his opponents; but he had that rare and manly trait which enables its possessor, whenever he becomes convinced of error, to make a prompt acknowledgment of the conviction.

In the summer of 1834, a series of mobs, directed against the Abolitionists, who had organized a national society, with the city of New York as its central point, followed each other in rapid succession. The houses of the leading men in the society were sacked and pillaged; meeting-houses broken into and defaced; and the unoffending colored inhabitants of the city treated with the grossest indignity, and subjected, in some instances, to shameful personal outrage. It was emphatically a "Reign of Terror." The press of both political parties and of the leading religious sects, by appeals to prejudice and passion, and by studied misrepresentation of the designs and measures of the Abolitionists, fanned the flame of excitement, until the fury of demons possessed the misguided populace. To advocate emancipation, or defend those who did so, in New York, at that period, was like preaching democracy in Constantinople or religious toleration in Paris on the eve of St. Bartholomew. Law was prostrated in the dust; to be suspected of abolitionism was to incur a liability to an indefinite degree of insult and indignity; and the few and hunted friends of the slave who in those nights of terror laid their heads upon the pillow did so with the prayer of the Psalmist on their lips, "Defend me from them that rise up against me; save me from bloody men."

At this period the New York Evening Post spoke out strongly in condemnation of the mob. William Leggett was not then an Abolitionist; he had known nothing of the proscribed class, save through the cruel misrepresentations of their enemies; but, true to his democratic faith, he maintained the right to discuss the question of slavery. The infection of cowardly fear, which at that time sealed the lips of multitudes who deplored the excesses of the mob and sympathized with its victims, never reached him. Boldly, indignantly, he demanded that the mob should be put down at once by the civil authorities. He declared the Abolitionists, even if guilty of all that had been charged upon them, fully entitled to the privileges and immunities of American citizens. He sternly reprimanded the board of aldermen of the city for rejecting with contempt the memorial of the Abolitionists to that body, explanatory of their principles and the measures by which they had sought to disseminate them. Referring to the determination, expressed by the memorialists in the rejected document, not to recant or relinquish any principle which they had adopted, but to live and die by their faith, he said: "In this, however mistaken, however mad, we may consider their opinions in relation to the blacks, what honest, independent mind can blame them? Where is the man so poor of soul, so white-livered, so base, that he would do less in relation to any important doctrine in which he religiously believed? Where is the man who would have his tenets drubbed into him by the clubs of ruffians, or hold his conscience at the dictation of a mob?"

In the summer of 1835, a mob of excited citizens broke open the post-office at Charleston, South Carolina, and burnt in the street such papers and pamphlets as they judged to be "incendiary;" in other words, such as advocated the application of the democratic principle to the condition of the slaves of the South. These papers were addressed, not to the slave, but to the master. They contained nothing which had not been said and written by Southern men themselves, the Pinkneys, Jeffersons, Henrys, and Martins, of Maryland and Virginia. The example set at Charleston did not lack imitators. Every petty postmaster south of Mason and Dixon's line became ex officio a censor of the press. The Postmaster-General, writing to his subordinate at Charleston, after stating that the post-office department had "no legal right to exclude newspapers from the mail, or prohibit their carriage or delivery, on account of their character or tendency, real or supposed," declared that he would, nevertheless, give no aid, directly or indirectly, in circulating publications of an incendiary or inflammatory character; and assured the perjured functionary, who had violated his oath of office, that, while he could not sanction, he would not condemn his conduct. Against this virtual encouragement of a flagrant infringement of a constitutional right, this licensing of thousands of petty government officials to sit in their mail offices — to use the figure of Milton — cross-legged, like so many envious Junos, in judgment upon the daily offspring of the press, taking counsel of passion, prejudice, and popular excitement as to what was "incendiary" or "inflammatory," the Evening Post spoke in tones of manly protest.

While almost all the editors of his party throughout the country either openly approved of the conduct of the Postmaster-General or silently acquiesced in it, William Leggett, who, in the absence of his colleague, was at that time sole editor of the Post, and who had everything to lose, in a worldly point of view, by assailing a leading functionary of the government, who was a favorite of the President and a sharer of his popularity, did not hesitate as to the course which consistency and duty required at his hands. He took his stand for unpopular truth, at a time when a different course on his part could not have failed to secure him the favor and patronage of his party. In the great struggle with the Bank of the United States, his services had not been unappreciated by the President and his friends. Without directly approving the course of the administration on the question of the rights of the Abolitionists, by remaining silent in respect to it, he might have avoided all suspicion of mental and moral independence incompatible with party allegiance. The impracticable honesty of Leggett, never bending from the erectness of truth for the sake of that "thrift which follows fawning," dictated a most severe and scorching review of the letter of the Postmaster-General. "More monstrous, more detestable doctrines we have never heard promulgated," he exclaimed in one of his leading editorials. "With what face, after this, can the Postmaster-General punish a postmaster for any exercise of the fearfully dangerous power of stopping and destroying any portion of the mails?" "The Abolitionists do not deserve to be placed on the same footing with a foreign enemy, nor their publications as the secret despatches of a spy. They are American citizens, in the exercise of their undoubted right of citizenship; and however erroneous their views, however fanatic their conduct, while they act within the limits of the law, what official functionary, be he merely a subordinate or the head of the post-office department, shall dare to abridge them of their rights as citizens, and deny them those facilities of intercourse which were instituted for the equal accommodation of all? If the American people will submit to this, let us expunge all written codes, and resolve society into its original elements, where the might of the strong is better than the right of the weak."

A few days after the publication of this manly rebuke, he wrote an indignantly sarcastic article upon the mobs which were at this time everywhere summoned to "put down the Abolitionists." The next day, the 4th of the ninth month, 1835, he received a copy of the Address of the American Anti-Slavery Society to the public, containing a full and explicit avowal of all the principles and designs of the association. He gave it a candid perusal, weighed its arguments, compared its doctrines with those at the foundation of his own political faith, and rose up from its examination an Abolitionist. He saw that he himself, misled by the popular clamor, had done injustice to benevolent and self-sacrificing men; and he took the earliest occasion, in an article of great power and eloquence, to make the amplest atonement. He declared his entire concurrence with the views of the American Anti-Slavery Society, with the single exception of a doubt which rested, on his mind as to the abolition of slavery in the District of Columbia. We quote from the concluding paragraph of this article:—

"We assert without hesitation, that, if we possessed the right, we should not scruple to exercise it for the speedy annihilation of servitude and chains. The impression made in boyhood by the glorious exclamation of Cato,

"'A day, an hour, of virtuous liberty
Is worth a whole eternity of bondage!'

has been worn deeper, not effaced, by time; and we eagerly and ardently trust that the day will yet arrive when the clank of the bondman's fetters will form no part of the multitudinous sounds which our country sends up to Heaven, mingling, as it were, into a song of praise for our national prosperity. We yearn with strong desire for the day when freedom shall no longer wave

"Her fustian flag in mockery over slaves.'"

A few days after, in reply to the assaults made upon him from all quarters, he calmly and firmly reiterated his determination to maintain the right of free discussion of the subject of slavery.

"The course we are pursuing," said he, "is one which we entered upon after mature deliberation, and we are not to be turned from it by a species of opposition, the inefficacy of which we have seen displayed in so many former instances. It is Philip Van Artevelde who says:—

> "'All my life long,
> I have beheld with most respect the man
> Who knew himself, and knew the ways before him;
> And from among them chose considerately,
> With a clear foresight, not a blindfold courage;
> And, having chosen, with a steadfast mind.
> Pursued his purpose.'

"This is the sort of character we emulate. If to believe slavery a deplorable evil and curse, in whatever light it is viewed; if to yearn for the day which shall break the fetters of three millions of human beings, and restore to them their birthright of equal freedom; if to be willing, in season and out of season, to do all in our power to promote so desirable a result, by all means not inconsistent with higher duty: if these sentiments constitute us Abolitionists, then are we such, and glory in the name."

"The senseless cry of 'Abolitionist' shall never deter us, nor the more senseless attempt of puny prints to read us out of the democratic party. The often-quoted and beautiful saying of the Latin historian, Homo sum: humani nihil a me alienum puto, we apply to the poor slave as well as his master, and shall endeavor to fulfil towards both the obligations of an equal humanity."

The generation which, since the period of which we are speaking, have risen into active life can have but a faint conception of the boldness of this movement on the part of William Leggett. To be an Abolitionist then was to abandon all hope of political preferment or party favor; to be marked and branded as a social outlaw, under good society's interdict of food and fire; to hold property, liberty, and life itself at the mercy of lawless mobs. All this William Leggett clearly saw. He knew how rugged and thorny was the path upon which, impelled by his love of truth and the obligations of humanity, he was entering. From hunted and proscribed Abolitionists and oppressed and spirit-broken colored men, the Pariahs of American democracy, he could alone expect sympathy. The Whig journals, with a few honorable exceptions, exulted over what they regarded as the fall of a formidable opponent; and after painting his abolitionism in the most hideous colors, held him up to their Southern allies as a specimen of the radical disorganizers and democratic levellers of the North. His own party, in consequence, made haste to proscribe him. Government advertising was promptly withdrawn from his paper. The official journals of Washington and Albany read him out of the pale of democracy. Father Ritchie scolded and threatened. The democratic committee issued its bull against him from Tammany Hall. The resolutions of that committee were laid before him when he was sinking under a severe illness. Rallying his energies, he dictated from his sick-bed an answer marked by all his accustomed vigor and boldness. Its tone was calm, manly, self-relying; the language of one who, having planted his feet hard down on the rock of principle, stood there like Luther at Worms, because he "could not otherwise." Exhausted nature sunk under the effort. A weary sickness of nearly a year's duration followed. In this sore affliction, deserted as he was by most of his old political friends, we have reason to know that he was cheered by the gratitude of those in whose behalf he had well-nigh made a martyr's sacrifice; and that from the humble hearths of his poor colored fellow-citizens fervent prayers went up for his restoration.

His work was not yet done. Purified by trial, he was to stand forth once more in vindication of the truths of freedom. As soon as his health was sufficiently reestablished, he commenced the publication of an independent political and literary journal, under the expressive title of The Plaindealer. In his first number he stated, that, claiming the right of absolute freedom of discussion, he should exercise it with no other limitations than those of his own judgment. A poor man, he admitted that he established the paper in the expectation of deriving from it a livelihood, but that even for that object he could not trim its sails to suit the varying breeze of popular prejudice. "If," said he, "a paper which makes the Right, and not the Expedient, its cardinal object, will not yield its conductor a support, there are honest vocations that will, and better the humblest of them than to be seated at the head of an influential press, if its influence is not exerted to promote the cause of truth." He was true to his promise. The free soul of a free, strong man spoke out in his paper. How refreshing was it, after listening to the inanities, the dull, witless vulgarity, the wearisome commonplace of journalists, who had no higher aim than to echo, with parrot-like exactness, current prejudices and falsehoods, to turn to the great and generous thoughts, the chaste and vigorous diction, of the Plaindealer! No man ever had a clearer idea of the duties and responsibilities of a conductor of the public press than William Leggett, and few have ever combined so many of the qualifications for their perfect discharge: a nice sense of justice, a warm benevolence, inflexible truth, honesty defying temptation, a mind stored with learning, and having at command the treasures of the best thoughts of the best authors. As was said of Fletcher of Saltoun, he was "a gentleman steady in his principles; of nice honor, abundance of learning; bold as a lion; a sure friend; a man who would lose his life to serve his country, and would not do a base thing to save it."

He had his faults: his positive convictions sometimes took the shape of a proud and obstinate dogmatism; he who could so well appeal to the judgment and the reason of his readers too often only roused their passions by invective and vehement declamation. Moderate men were startled and pained by the fierce energy of his language; and he not unfrequently made implacable enemies of opponents whom he might have conciliated and won over by mild expostulation and patient explanation. It must be urged in extenuation, that, as the champion of unpopular truths, he was assailed unfairly on all sides, and indecently misrepresented and calumniated to a degree, as his friend Sedgwick justly remarks, unprecedented even in the annals of the American press; and that his errors in this respect were, in the main, errors of retaliation.

In the Plaindealer, in common with the leading moral and political subjects of the day, that of slavery was freely discussed in all its bearings. It is difficult, in a single extract, to convey an adequate idea of the character of the editorial columns of a paper, where terse and concentrated irony and sarcasm alternate with eloquent appeal and diffuse commentary and labored argument. We can only offer at random the following passages from a long review of a speech of John C. Calhoun, in which that extraordinary man, whose giant intellect has been shut out of its appropriate field of exercise by the very slavery of which he is the champion, undertook to maintain, in reply to a Virginia senator, that chattel slavery was not an evil, but "a great good."

"We have Mr. Calhoun's own warrant for attacking his position with all the fervor which a high sense of duty can give, for we do hold, from the bottom of our soul, that slavery is an evil,—a deep, detestable, damnable evil; evil in all its aspects to the blacks, and a greater evil to the whites; an evil moral, social, and political; an evil which shows itself in the languishing condition of agriculture where it exists, in paralyzed commerce, and in the prostration of the mechanic arts; an evil which stares you in the face from uncultivated fields, and howls in your ears through tangled swamps and morasses. Slavery is such an evil that it withers what it touches. Where it is once securely established the land becomes desolate, as the tree inevitably perishes which the sea-hawk chooses for its nest; while freedom, on the contrary, flourishes like the tannen, 'on the loftiest and least sheltered rocks,' and clothes with its refreshing verdure what, without it, would frown in naked and incurable sterility.

"If any one desires an illustration of the opposite influences of slavery and freedom, let him look at the two sister States of Kentucky and Ohio. Alike in soil and climate, and divided only by a river, whose translucent waters reveal, through nearly the whole breadth, the sandy bottom over which they sparkle, how different are they in all the respects over which man has control! On the one hand the air is vocal with the mingled tumult of a vast and prosperous population. Every hillside smiles with an abundant harvest, every valley shelters a thriving village, the click of a busy mill drowns the prattle of every rivulet, and all the multitudinous sounds of business denote happy activity in every branch of social occupation.

"This is the State which, but a few years ago, slept in the unbroken solitude of nature. The forest spread an interminable canopy of shade over the dark soil on which the fat and useless vegetation rotted at ease, and through the dusky vistas of the wood only savage beasts and more savage men prowled in quest of prey. The whole land now blossoms like a garden. The tall and interlacing trees have unlocked their hold, and bowed before the woodman's axe. The soil is disencumbered of the mossy trunks which had reposed upon it for ages. The rivers flash in the sunlight, and the fields smile with waving harvests. This is Ohio, and this is what freedom has done for it.

"Now, let us turn to Kentucky, and note the opposite influences of slavery. A narrow and unfrequented path through the close and sultry canebrake conducts us to a wretched hovel. It stands in the midst of an unweeded field, whose dilapidated enclosure scarcely protects it from the lowing and hungry kine. Children half clad and squalid, and destitute of the buoyancy natural to their age, lounge in the sunshine, while their parent saunters apart, to watch his languid slaves drive the ill- appointed team afield. This is not a fancy picture. It is a true copy of one of the features which make up the aspect 'of the State, and of every State where the moral leprosy of slavery covers the people with its noisome scales; a deadening lethargy benumbs the limbs of the body politic; a stupor settles on the arts of life; agriculture reluctantly drags the plough and harrow to the field, only when scourged by necessity; the axe drops from the woodman's nerveless hand the moment his fire is scantily supplied with fuel; and the fen, undrained, sends up its noxious exhalations, to rack with cramps and agues the frame already too much enervated by a moral epidemic to creep beyond the sphere of the material miasm."

The Plaindealer was uniformly conducted with eminent ability; but its editor was too far in advance of his contemporaries to find general acceptance, or even toleration. In addition to pecuniary embarrassments, his health once more failed, and in the autumn of 1837 he was compelled to suspend the publication of his paper. One of the last articles which he wrote for it shows the extent to which he was sometimes carried by the intensity and depth of his abhorrence of oppression, and the fervency of his adoration of liberty. Speaking of the liability of being called upon to aid the master in the subjection of revolted slaves, and in replacing their cast-off fetters, he thus expresses himself: "Would we comply with such a requisition? No! Rather would we see our right arm lopped from our body, and the mutilated trunk itself gored with mortal wounds, than raise a finger in opposition to men struggling in the holy cause of freedom. The obligations of citizenship are strong, but those of justice, humanity, and religion, stronger. We earnestly trust that the great contest of opinion which is now going on in this country may terminate in the enfranchisement of the slaves, without recourse to the strife of blood; but should the oppressed bondmen, impatient of the tardy progress of truth, urged only in discussion, attempt to burst their chains by a more violent and shorter process, they should never encounter our arm nor hear our voice in the ranks of their opponents. We should stand a sad spectator of the conflict; and, whatever commiseration we might feel for the discomfiture of the oppressors, we should pray that the battle might end in giving freedom to the oppressed."

With the Plain dealer, his connection with the public, in a great measure, ceased. His steady and intimate friend, personal as well as political, Theodore Sedgwick, Jun., a gentleman who has, on many occasions, proved himself worthy of his liberty-loving ancestry, thus speaks of him in his private life at this period: "Amid the reverses of fortune, harassed by pecuniary embarrassments, during the tortures of a disease which tore away his life piecemeal, hee ever maintained the same manly and unaltered front, the same cheerfulness of disposition, the same dignity of conduct. No humiliating solicitation, no weak complaint, escaped him." At the election in the fall of 1838, the noble-spirited democrat was not wholly forgotten. A strenuous effort, which was well- nigh successful, was made to secure his nomination as a candidate for Congress. It was at this juncture that he wrote to a friend in the city, from his residence at New Rochelle, one of the noblest letters ever penned by a candidate for popular favor. The following extracts will show how a true man can meet the temptations of political life:—

"What I am most afraid of is, that some of my friends, in their too earnest zeal, will place me in a false position on the subject of slavery. I am an Abolitionist. I hate slavery in all its forms, degrees, and influences; and I deem myself bound, by the highest moral and political obligations, not to let that sentiment of hate lie dormant and smouldering in my own breast, but to give it free vent, and let it blaze forth, that it may kindle equal ardor through the whole sphere of my influence. I would not have this fact disguised or mystified for any office the people have it in their power to give. Rather, a thousand times rather, would I again meet the denunciations of Tammany Hall, and be stigmatized with all the foul epithets with which the anti-abolition vocabulary abounds, than recall or deny one tittle of my creed. Abolition is, in my sense, a necessary and a glorious part of democracy; and I hold the right and duty to discuss the subject of slavery, and to expose its hideous evils in all their bearings,—moral, social, and political,—as of infinitely higher importance than to carry fifty sub- treasury bills. That I should discharge this duty temperately; that I should not let it come in collision with other duties; that I should not let my hatred of slavery transcend the express obligations of the Constitution, or violate its clear spirit, I hope and trust you think sufficiently well of me to believe. But what I fear is, (not from you, however,) that some of my advocates and champions will seek to recommend me to popular support by representing me as not an Abolitionist, which is false. All that I have written gives the lie to it. All I shall write will give the lie to it.

"And here, let me add, (apart from any consideration already adverted to,) that, as a matter of mere policy, I would not, if I could, have my name disjoined from abolitionism. To be an Abolitionist now is to be an incendiary; as, three years ago, to be an anti-monopolist was to be a leveller and a Jack Cade. See what three short years have done in effecting the anti-monopoly reform; and depend upon it that the next three years, or, if not three, say three times three, if you please, will work a greater revolution on the slavery question. The stream of public opinion now sets against us; but it is about to turn, and the regurgitation will be tremendous. Proud in that day may well be the man who can float in triumph on the first refluent wave, swept onward by the deluge which he himself, in advance of his fellows, has largely shared in occasioning. Such be my fate; and, living or dead, it will, in some measure, be mine! I have written my name in ineffaceable letters on the abolition record; and whether the reward ultimately come in the shape of honors to the living man, or a tribute to the memory of a departed one, I would not forfeit my right to it for as many offices as has in his gift, if each of them was greater than his own."

_ After mentioning that he had understood that some of his friends had endeavored to propitiate popular prejudice by representing him as no Abolitionist, he says:—

"Keep them, for God's sake, from committing any such fooleries for the sake of getting me into Congress. Let others twist themselves into what shapes they please, to gratify the present taste of the people; as for me, I am not formed of such pliant materials, and choose to retain, undisturbed, the image of my God! I do not wish to cheat the people of their votes. I would not get their support, any more than their money, under false pretences. I am what I am; and if that does not suit them, I am content to stay at home."

God be praised for affording us, even in these latter days, the sight of an honest man! Amidst the heartlessness, the double-dealing, the evasions, the prevarications, the shameful treachery and falsehood, of political men of both parties, in respect to the question of slavery, how refreshing is it to listen to words like these! They renew our failing faith in human nature. They reprove our weak misgivings. We rise up from their perusal stronger and healthier. With something of the spirit which dictated them, we renew our vows to freedom, and, with manlier energy, gird up our souls for the stern struggle before us.

As might have been expected, and as he himself predicted, the efforts of his friends to procure his nomination failed; but the same generous appreciators of his rare worth were soon after more successful in their exertions in his behalf. He received from President Van Buren the appointment of the mission to Guatemala,—an appointment which, in addition to honorable employment in the service of his country, promised him the advantages of a sea voyage and a change of climate, for the restoration of his health. The course of Martin Van Buren on the subject of slavery in the District of Columbia forms, in the estimation of many of his best friends, by no means the most creditable portion of his political history; but it certainly argues well for his magnanimity and freedom from merely personal resentment that he gave this appointment to the man who had animadverted upon that course with the greatest freedom, and whose rebuke of the veto pledge, severe in its truth and justice, formed the only discord in the paean of partisan flattery which greeted his inaugural. But, however well intended, it came too late. In the midst of the congratulations of his friends on the brightening prospect before him, the still hopeful and vigorous spirit of William Leggett was summoned away by death. Universal regret was awakened. Admiration of his intellectual power, and that generous and full appreciation of his high moral worth which had been in too many instances withheld from the living man by party policy and prejudice, were now freely accorded to the dead. The presses of both political parties vied with each other in expressions of sorrow at the loss of a great and true man. The Democracy, through all its organs, hastened to canonize him as one of the saints of its calendar. The general committee, in New York, expunged their resolutions of censure. The Democratic Review, at that period the most respectable mouthpiece of the democratic party, made him the subject of exalted eulogy. His early friend and co-editor, William Cullen Bryant, laid upon his grave the following tribute, alike beautiful and true:—

> "The earth may ring, from shore to shore,
> With echoes of a glorious name,
> But he whose loss our tears deplore
> Has left behind him more than fame.

> "For when the death-frost came to lie
> On Leggett's warm and mighty heart,
> And quenched his bold and friendly eye,
> His spirit did not all depart.

"The words of fire that from his pen
He flung upon the lucid page
Still move, still shake the hearts of men,
Amid a cold and coward age.

"His love of Truth, too warm, too strong,
For Hope or Fear to chain or chill,
His hate of tyranny and wrong,
Burn in the breasts they kindled still."

So lived and died William Leggett. What a rebuke of party perfidy, of political meanness, of the common arts and stratagems of demagogues, comes up from his grave! How the cheek of mercenary selfishness crimsons at the thought of his incorruptible integrity! How heartless and hollow pretenders, who offer lip service to freedom, while they give their hands to whatever work their slaveholding managers may assign them; who sit in chains round the crib of governmental patronage, putting on the spaniel, and putting off the man, and making their whole lives a miserable lie, shrink back from a contrast with the proud and austere dignity of his character! What a comment on their own condition is the memory of a man who could calmly endure the loss of party favor, the reproaches of his friends, the malignant assaults of his enemies, and the fretting evils of poverty, in the hope of bequeathing, like the dying testator of Ford,

"A fame by scandal untouched,
To Memory and Time's old daughter, Truth."

The praises which such men are now constrained to bestow upon him are their own condemnation. Every stone which they pile upon his grave is written over with the record of their hypocrisy.

We have written rather for the living than the dead. As one of that proscribed and hunted band of Abolitionists, whose rights were so bravely defended by William Leggett, we should, indeed, be wanting in ordinary gratitude not to do honor to his memory; but we have been actuated at the present time mainly by a hope that the character, the lineaments of which we have so imperfectly sketched, may awaken a generous emulation in the hearts of the young democracy of our country. Democracy such as William Leggett believed and practised, democracy in its full and all- comprehensive significance, is destined to be the settled political faith of this republic. Because the despotism of slavery has usurped its name, and offered the strange incense of human tears and blood on its profaned altars, shall we, therefore, abandon the only political faith which coincides with the Gospel of Jesus, and meets the aspirations and wants of humanity? No. The duty of the present generation in the United States is to reduce this faith to practice, to make the beautiful ideal a fact.

"Every American," says Leggett, "who in any way countenances slavery is derelict to his duty, as a Christian, a patriot, a man; and every one does countenance and authorize it who suffers any opportunity of expressing his deep abhorrence of its manifold abominations to pass unimproved." The whole world has an interest in this matter. The influence of our democratic despotism is exerted against the liberties of Europe. Political reformers in the Old World, who have testified to their love of freedom by serious sacrifices, hold but one language on this point. They tell us that American slavery furnishes kings and aristocracies with their most potent arguments; that it is a perpetual drag on the wheel of political progress.

We have before us, at this time, a letter from Seidensticker, one of the leaders of the patriotic movement in behalf of German liberty in 1831. It was written from the prison of Celle, where he had been confined for eight years. The writer expresses his indignant astonishment at the speeches of John C. Calhoun, and others in Congress, on the slavery question, and deplores the disastrous influence of our great inconsistency upon the cause of freedom throughout the world, — an influence which paralyzes the hands of the patriotic reformer, while it strengthens those of his oppressor, and deepens around the living martyrs and confessors of European democracy the cold shadow of their prisons.

Joseph Sturge, of Birmingham, the President of the British Free Suffrage Union, and whose philanthropy and democracy have been vouched for by the Democratic Review in this country, has the following passage in an address to the citizens of the United States: "Although an admirer of the institutions of your country, and deeply lamenting the evils of my own government, I find it difficult to reply to those who are opposed to any extension of the political rights of Englishmen, when they point to America, and say that where all have a control over the legislation but those who are guilty of a dark skin, slavery and the slave trade remain, not only unmitigated, but continue to extend; and that while there is an onward movement in favor of its extinction, not only in England and France, but in Cuba and Brazil, American legislators cling to this enormous evil, without attempting to relax or mitigate its horrors."

How long shall such appeals, from such sources, be wasted upon us? Shall our baleful example enslave the world? Shall the tree of democracy, which our fathers intended for "the healing of the nations," be to them like the fabled upas, blighting all around it?

The men of the North, the pioneers of the free West, and the non-slaveholders of the South must answer these questions. It is for them to say whether the present wellnigh intolerable evil shall continue to increase its boundaries, and strengthen its hold upon the government, the political parties, and the religious sects of our country. Interest and honor, present possession and future hope, the memory of fathers, the prospects of children, gratitude, affection, the still call of the dead, the cry of oppressed nations looking hitherward for the result of all their hopes, the voice of God in the soul, in revelation, and in His providence, all appeal to them for a speedy and righteous decision. At this moment, on the floor of Congress, Democracy and Slavery have met in a death-grapple. The South stands firm; it allows no party division on the slave question. One of its members has declared that "the slave States have no traitors." Can the same be said of the free? Now, as in the time of the fatal Missouri Compromise, there are, it is to be feared, political peddlers among our representatives, whose souls are in the market, and whose consciences are vendible commodities. Through their means, the slave power may gain a temporary triumph; but may not the very baseness of the treachery arouse the Northern heart? By driving the free States to the wall, may it not compel them to turn and take an aggressive attitude, clasp hands over the altar of their common freedom, and swear eternal hostility to slavery?

Be the issue of the present contest what it may, those who are faithful to freedom should allow no temporary reverse to shake their confidence in the ultimate triumph of the right. The slave will be free. Democracy in America will yet be a glorious reality; and when the topstone of that temple of freedom which our fathers left unfinished shall be brought forth with shoutings and cries of grace unto it, when our now drooping- Liberty lifts up her head and prospers, happy will be he who can say, with John Milton, "Among those who have something more than wished her welfare, I too have my charter and freehold of rejoicing to me and my heirs."

NATHANIEL PEABODY ROGERS

"And Lamb, the frolic and the gentle,
Has vanished from his kindly hearth."

So, in one of the sweetest and most pathetic of his poems touching the loss of his literary friends, sang Wordsworth. We well remember with what freshness and vividness these simple lines came before us, on hearing, last autumn, of the death of the warm-hearted and gifted friend whose name heads this article; for there was much in his character and genius to remind us of the gentle author of Elia. He had the latter's genial humor and quaintness; his nice and delicate perception of the beautiful and poetic; his happy, easy diction, not the result, as in the case of that of the English essayist, of slow and careful elaboration, but the natural, spontaneous language in which his conceptions at once embodied themselves, apparently without any consciousness of effort. As Mark Antony talked, he wrote, "right on," telling his readers often what "they themselves did know," yet imparting to the simplest commonplaces of life interest and significance, and throwing a golden haze of poetry over the rough and thorny pathways of every-day duty. Like Lamb, he loved his friends without stint or limit. The "old familiar faces" haunted him. Lamb loved the streets and lanes of London—the places where he oftenest came in contact with the warm, genial heart of humanity—better than the country. Rogers loved the wild and lonely hills and valleys of New Hampshire none the less that he was fully alive to the enjoyments of society, and could enter with the heartiest sympathy into all the joys and sorrows of his friends and neighbors.

In another point of view, he was not unlike Elia. He had the same love of home, and home friends, and familiar objects; the same fondness for common sights and sounds; the same dread of change; the same shrinking from the unknown and the dark. Like him, he clung with a child's love to the living present, and recoiled from a contemplation of the great change which awaits us. Like him, he was content with the goodly green earth and human countenances, and would fain set up his tabernacle here. He had less of what might be termed self-indulgence in this feeling than Lamb. He had higher views; he loved this world not only for its own sake, but for the opportunities it afforded of doing good. Like the Persian seer, he beheld the legions of

Ormuzd and Ahriman, of Light and Darkness, contending for mastery over the earth, as the sunshine and shadow of a gusty, half-cloudy day struggled on the green slopes of his native mountains; and, mingled with the bright host, he would fain have fought on until its banners waved in eternal sunshine over the last hiding-place of darkness. He entered into the work of reform with the enthusiasm and chivalry of a knight of the crusades. He had faith in human progress,—in the ultimate triumph of the good; millennial lights beaconed up all along his horizon. In the philanthropic movements of the day; in the efforts to remove the evils of slavery, war, intemperance, and sanguinary laws; in the humane and generous spirit of much of our modern poetry and literature; in the growing demand of the religious community, of all sects, for the preaching of the gospel of love and humanity, he heard the low and tremulous prelude of the great anthem of universal harmony. "The world," said he, in a notice of the music of the Hutchinson family, "is out of tune now. But it will be tuned again, and all will become harmony." In this faith he lived and acted; working, not always, as it seemed to some of his friends, wisely, but bravely, truthfully, earnestly, cheering on his fellow-laborers, and imparting to the dullest and most earthward looking of them something of his own zeal and loftiness of purpose.

"Who was he?" does the reader ask? Naturally enough, too, for his name has never found its way into fashionable reviews; it has never been associated with tale, or essay, or poem, to our knowledge. Our friend Griswold, who, like another Noah, has launched some hundreds of American poets and prose writers on the tide of immortality in his two huge arks of rhyme and reason, has either overlooked his name, or deemed it unworthy of preservation. Then, too, he was known mainly as the editor of a proscribed and everywhere-spoken-against anti-slavery paper. It had few readers of literary taste and discrimination; plain, earnest men and women, intent only upon the thought itself, and caring little for the clothing of it, loved the *Herald of Freedom* for its honestness and earnestness, and its bold rebukes of the wrong, its all-surrendering homage to what its editor believed to be right. But the literary world of authors and critics saw and heard little or nothing of him or his writings. "I once had a bit of scholar-craft," he says of himself on one occasion, "and had I attempted it in some pitiful sectarian or party or literary sheet, I should have stood a chance to get quoted into the periodicals. Now, who dares quote from the *Herald of Freedom*?" He wrote for humanity, as his biographer justly says, not for fame. "He wrote because he had something to say, and true to nature, for to him nature was truth; he spoke right on, with the artlessness and simplicity of a child."

He was born in Plymouth, New Hampshire, in the sixth month of 1794, — a lineal descendant from John Rogers, of martyr-memory. Educated at Dartmouth College, he studied law with Hon. Richard Fletcher, of Salisbury, New Hampshire, now of Boston, and commenced the practice of it in 1819, in his native village. He was diligent and successful in his profession, although seldom known as a pleader. About the year 1833, he became interested in the anti-slavery movement. His was one of the few voices of encouragement and sympathy which greeted the author of this sketch on the publication of a pamphlet in favor of immediate emancipation. He gave us a kind word of approval, and invited us to his mountain home, on the banks of the Pemigewasset, — an invitation which, two years afterwards, we accepted. In the early autumn, in company with George Thompson, (the eloquent reformer, who has since been elected a member of the British Parliament from the Tower Hamlets,) we drove up the beautiful valley of the White Mountain tributary of the Merrimac, and, just as a glorious sunset was steeping river, valley, and mountain in its hues of heaven, were welcomed to the pleasant home and family circle of our friend Rogers. We spent two delightful evenings with him. His cordiality, his warm-hearted sympathy in our object, his keen wit, inimitable humor, and childlike and simple mirthfulness, his full appreciation of the beautiful in art and nature, impressed us with the conviction that we were the guests of no ordinary man; that we were communing with unmistakable genius, such an one as might have added to the wit and eloquence of Ben Jonson's famous club at the *Mermaid*, or that which Lamb and Coleridge and Southey frequented at the *Salutation and Cat*, of Smithfield. "The most brilliant man I have met in America!" said George Thompson, as we left the hospitable door of our friend.

In 1838, he gave up his law practice, left his fine outlook at Plymouth upon the mountains of the North, Moosehillock and the Haystacks, and took up his residence at Concord, for the purpose of editing the *Herald of Freedom*, an anti-slavery paper which had been started some three or four years before. John Pierpont, than whom there could not be a more competent witness, in his brief and beautiful sketch of the life and writings of Rogers, does not overestimate the ability with which the Herald was conducted, when he says of its editor: "As a newspaper writer, we think him unequalled by any living man; and in the general strength, clearness, and quickness of his intellect, we think all who knew him well will agree with us that he was not excelled by any editor in the country." He was not a profound reasoner: his imagination and brilliant fancy played the wildest tricks with his logic; yet, considering the way by which he reached them, it is remarkable that his conclusions were so often correct. The tendency of his mind was to extremes. A zealous Calvinistic church-member, he became an equally zealous opponent of churches and priests; a warm politician, he became an ultra non-resistant and no-government man. In all this, his sincerity was manifest. If, in the indulgence of his remarkable powers of sarcasm, in the free antics of a humorous fancy, upon whose graceful neck he had flung loose the reins, he sometimes did injustice to individuals, and touched, in irreverent sport, the hem of sacred garments, it had the excuse, at least, of a generous and honest motive. If he sometimes exaggerated, those who best, knew him can testify that he "set down naught in malice."

We have before us a printed collection of his writings,—hasty editorials, flung off without care or revision, the offspring of sudden impulse frequently; always free, artless, unstudied; the language transparent as air, exactly expressing the thought. He loved the common, simple dialect of the people,—the "beautiful strong old Saxon,—the talk words." He had an especial dislike of learned and "dictionary words." He used to recommend Cobbett's Works to "every young man and woman who has been hurt in his or her talk and writing by going to school."

Our limits will not admit of such extracts from the Collection of his writings as would convey to our readers an adequate idea of his thought and manner. His descriptions of natural scenery glow with life. One can almost see the sunset light flooding the Franconia Notch, and glorifying the peaks of Moosehillock, and hear the murmur of the west wind in the pines, and the light, liquid voice of Pemigewasset sounding up from its rocky channel, through its green hem of maples, while reading them. We give a brief extract from an editorial account of an autumnal trip to Vermont:

"We have recently journeyed through a portion of this, free State; and it is not all imagination in us that sees, in its bold scenery, its uninfected inland position, its mountainous but fertile and verdant surface, the secret of the noble predisposition of its people. They are located for freedom. Liberty's home is on their Green Mountains. Their farmer republic nowhere touches the ocean, the highway of the world's crimes, as well as its nations. It has no seaport for the importation of slavery, or the exportation of its own highland republicanism. Should slavery ever prevail over this nation, to its utter subjugation, the last lingering footsteps of retiring Liberty will be seen, not, as Daniel Webster said, in the proud old Commonwealth of Massachusetts, about Bunker Hill and Faneuil Hall; but she will be found wailing, like Jephthah's daughter, among the 'hollows' and along the sides of the Green Mountains.

"Vermont shows gloriously at this autumn season. Frost has gently laid hands on her exuberant vegetation, tinging her rock-maple woods without abating the deep verdure of her herbage. Everywhere along her peopled hollows and her bold hillslopes and summits the earth is alive with green, while her endless hard-wood forests are uniformed with all the hues of early fall, richer than the regimentals of the kings that glittered in the train of Napoleon on the confines of Poland, when he lingered there, on the last outposts of summer, before plunging into the snow-drifts of the North; more gorgeous than the array of Saladin's life- guard in the wars of the Crusaders, or of 'Solomon in all his glory,' decked in, all colors and hues, but still the hues of life. Vegetation touched, but not dead, or, if killed, not bereft yet of 'signs of life.' 'Decay's effacing fingers' had not yet 'swept the hills' 'where beauty lingers.' All looked fresh as growing foliage. Vermont frosts don't seem to be 'killing frosts.' They only change aspects of beauty. The mountain pastures, verdant to the peaks, and over the peaks of the high, steep hills, were covered with the amplest feed, and clothed with countless sheep; the hay-fields heavy with second crop, in some partly cut and abandoned, as if in very weariness and satiety, blooming with honeysuckle, contrasting strangely with the colors on the woods; the fat cattle and the long-tailed colts and close-built Morgans wallowing in it up to the eyes, or the cattle down to rest, with full bellies, by ten in the morning. Fine but narrow roads wound along among the hills, free almost entirely of stone, and so smooth as to be safe for the most rapid driving, made of their rich, dark, powder-looking soil. Beautiful villages or scattered settlements breaking upon the delighted view, on the meandering way, making the ride a continued scene of excitement and admiration. The air fresh, free, and wholesome; the road almost dead level for miles and miles, among mountains that lay over the land like the great swells of the sea, and looking in the prospect as though there could be no passage."

To this autumnal limning, the following spring picture may be a fitting accompaniment:—

"At last Spring is here in full flush. Winter held on tenaciously and mercilessly, but it has let go. The great sun is high on his northern journey, and the vegetation, and the bird-singing, and the loud frog- chorus, the tree budding and blowing, are all upon us; and the glorious grass—super-best of earth's garniture—with its ever-satisfying green. The king-birds have come, and the corn-planter, the scolding bob-o-link. 'Plant your corn, plant your corn,' says he, as he scurries athwart the ploughed ground, hardly lifting his crank wings to a level with his back, so self-important is he in his admonitions. The earlier birds have gone to housekeeping, and have disappeared from the spray. There has been brief period for them, this spring, for scarcely has the deep snow gone, but the dark-green grass has come, and first we shall know, the ground will be yellow with dandelions.

"I incline to thank Heaven this glorious morning of May 16th for the pleasant home from which we can greet the Spring. Hitherto we have had to await it amid a thicket of village houses, low down, close together, and awfully white. For a prospect, we had the hinder part of an ugly meeting-house, which an enterprising neighbor relieved us of by planting a dwelling-house, right before our eyes, (on his own land, and he had a right to,) which relieved us also of all prospect whatever. And the revival spirit of habitation which has come over Concord is clapping up a house between every two in the already crowded town; and the prospect is, it will be soon all buildings. They are constructing, in quite good taste though, small, trim, cottage-like. But I had rather be where I can breathe air, and see beyond my own features, than be smothered among the prettiest houses ever built. We are on the slope of a hill; it is all sand, be sure, on all four sides of us, but the air is free, (and the sand, too, at times,) and our water, there is danger of hard drinking to live by it. Air and water, the two necessaries of life, and high, free play-ground for the small ones. There is a sand precipice hard by, high enough, were it only rock and overlooked the ocean, to be as sublime as any of the Nahant cliffs. As it is, it is altogether a safer haunt for daring childhood, which could hardly break its neck by a descent of some hundreds of feet.

"A low flat lies between us and the town, with its State-house, and body- guard of well-proportioned steeples standing round. It was marshy and wet, but is almost all redeemed by the translation into it of the high hills of sand. It must have been a terrible place for frogs, judging from what remains of it. Bits of water from the springs hard by lay here and there about the low ground, which are peopled as full of singers as ever the gallery of the old North Meeting-house was, and quite as melodious ones. Such performers I never heard, in marsh or pool. They are not the great, stagnant, bull-paddocks, fat and coarse-noted like Parson, but clear-water frogs, green, lively, and sweet-voiced. I passed their orchestra going home the other evening, with a small lad, and they were at it, all parts, ten thousand peeps, shrill, ear-piercing, and incessant, coming up from every quarter, accompanied by a second, from some larger swimmer with his trombone, and broken in upon, every now and then, but not discordantly, with the loud, quick hallo, that resembles the cry of the tree-toad. 'There are the Hutchinsons,' cried the lad. 'The Rainers,' responded I, glad to remember enough of my ancient Latin to know that Rana, or some such sounding word, stood for frog. But it was a 'band of music,' as the Miller friends say. Like other singers, (all but the Hutchinsons,) these are apt to sing too much, all the time they are awake, constituting really too much of a good thing. I have wondered if the little reptiles were singing in concert, or whether every one peeped on his own hook, their neighbor hood only making it a chorus. I incline to the opinion that they are performing together, that they know the tune, and each carries his part, self- selected, in free meeting, and therefore never discordant. The hour rule of Congress might be useful, though far less needed among the frogs than among the profane croakers of the fens at Washington."

Here is a sketch of the mountain scenery of New Hampshire, as seen from the Holderness Mountain, or North Hill, during a visit which he made to his native valley in the autumn of 1841:—

"The earth sphered up all around us, in every quarter of the horizon, like the crater of a vast volcano, and the great hollow within the mountain circle was as smoky as Vesuvius or Etna in their recess of eruption. The little village of Plymouth lay right at our feet, with its beautiful expanse of intervale opening on the eye like a lake among the woods and hills, and the Pemigewasset, bordered along its crooked way with rows of maples, meandering from upland to upland through the meadows. Our young footsteps had wandered over these localities. Time had cast it all far back that Pemigewasset, with its meadows and border trees; that little village whitening in the margin of its inter vale; and that one house which we could distinguish, where the mother that watched over and endured our wayward childhood totters at fourscore!

"To the south stretched a broken, swelling upland country, but champaign from the top of North Hill, patched all over with grain-fields and green wood-lots, the roofs of the farm-houses shining in the sun. Southwest, the Cardigan Mountain showed its bald forehead among the smokes of a thousand fires, kindled in the woods in the long drought. Westward, Moosehillock heaved up its long back, black as a whale; and turning the eye on northward, glancing down the while on the Baker's River valley, dotted over with human dwellings like shingle-bunches for size, you behold the great Franconia Range, its Notch and its Haystacks, the Elephant Mountain on the left, and Lafayette (Great Haystack) on the right, shooting its peak in solemn loneliness high up into the desert sky, and overtopping all the neighboring Alps but Mount Washington itself. The prospect of these is most impressive and satisfactory. We don't believe the earth presents a finer mountain display. The Haystacks stand there like the Pyramids on the wall of mountains. One of them eminently has this Egyptian shape. It is as accurate a pyramid to the eye as any in the old valley of the Nile, and a good deal bigger than any of those hoary monuments of human presumption, of the impious tyranny of monarchs and priests, and of the appalling servility of the erecting multitude. Arthur's Seat in Edinburgh does not more finely resemble a sleeping lion than the huge mountain on the left of the Notch does an elephant, with his great, overgrown rump turned uncivilly toward the gap where the people have to pass. Following round the panorama, you come to the Ossipees and the Sandwich Mountains, peaks innumerable and nameless, and of every variety of fantastic shape. Down their vast sides are displayed the melancholy-looking slides, contrasting with the fathomless woods.

"But the lakes,—you see lakes, as well as woods and mountains, from the top of North Hill. Newfound Lake in Hebron, only eight miles distant, you can't see; it lies too deep among the hills. Ponds show their small blue mirrors from various quarters of the great picture. Worthen's Mill- Pond and the Hardhack, where we used to fish for trout in truant, barefooted days, Blair's Mill-Pond, White Oak Pond, and Long Pond, and the Little Squam, a beautiful dark sheet of deep, blue water, about two miles long, stretched an id the green hills and woods, with a charming little beach at its eastern end, and without an island. And then the Great Squam, connected with it on the east by a short, narrow stream, the very queen of ponds, with its fleet of islands, surpassing in beauty all the foreign waters we have seen, in Scotland or elsewhere,—the islands covered with evergreens, which impart their hue to the mass of the lake, as it stretches seven miles on east from its smaller sister, towards the peerless Winnipesaukee. Great Squam is as beautiful as water and island can be. But Winnipesaukee, it is the very 'Smile of the Great Spirit.' It looks as if it had a thousand islands; some of them large enough for little towns, and others not bigger than a swan or a wild duck swimming on its surface of glass."

His wit and sarcasm were generally too good-natured to provoke even their unfortunate objects, playing all over his editorials like the thunderless lightnings which quiver along the horizon of a night of summer calmness; but at times his indignation launched them like bolts from heaven. Take the following as a specimen. He is speaking of the gag rule of Congress, and commending Southern representatives for their skilful selection of a proper person to do their work:—

"They have a quick eye at the South to the character, or, as they would say, the points of a slave. They look into him shrewdly, as an old jockey does into a horse. They will pick him out, at rifle-shot distance, among a thousand freemen. They have a nice eye to detect shades of vassalage. They saw in the aristocratic popinjay strut of a counterfeit Democrat an itching aspiration to play the slaveholder. They beheld it in 'the cut of his jib,' and his extreme Northern position made him the very tool for their purpose. The little creature has struck at the right of petition. A paltrier hand never struck at a noble right. The Eagle Right of Petition, so loftily sacred in the eyes of the Constitution that Congress can't begin to 'abridge' it, in its pride of place, is hawked at by this crested jay-bird. A 'mousing owl' would have seen better at midnoon than to have done it. It is an idiot blue-jay, such as you see fooling about among the shrub oaks and dwarf pitch pines in the winter. What an ignominious death to the lofty right, were it to die by such a hand; but it does not die. It is impalpable to the 'malicious mockery' of such vain blows.' We are glad it is done—done by the South—done proudly, and in slaveholding style, by the hand of a vassal. What a man does by another he does by himself, says the maxim. But they will disown the honor of it, and cast it on the despised 'free nigger' North."

Or this description—not very flattering to the "Old Commonwealth"—of the treatment of the agent of Massachusetts in South Carolina:—

"Slavery may perpetrate anything, and New England can't see it. It can horsewhip the old Commonwealth of Massachusetts, and spit in her governmental face, and she will not recognize it as an offence. She sent her agent to Charleston on a State embassy. Slavery caught him, and sent him ignominiously home. The solemn great man came back in a hurry. He returned in a most undignified trot. He ran; he scampered,—the stately official. The Old Bay State actually pulled foot, cleared, dug, as they say, like any scamp with a hue and cry after him. Her grave old Senator, who no more thought of having to break his stately walk than he had of being flogged at school for stealing apples, came back from Carolina upon the full run, out of breath and out of dignity. Well, what's the result? Why, nothing. She no more thinks of showing resentment about it than she would if lightning had struck him. He was sent back 'by the visitation of God;' and if they had lynched him to death, and stained the streets of Charleston with his blood, a Boston jury, if they could have held inquest over him, would have found that he 'died by the visitation of God.' And it would have been crowner's quest law, Slavery's crowners."

Here is a specimen of his graceful blending of irony and humor. He is expostulating with his neighbor of the New Hampshire Patriot, assuring him that he cannot endure the ponderous weight of his arguments, begging for a little respite, and, as a means of obtaining it, urging the editor to travel. He advises him to go South, to the White Sulphur Springs, and thinks that, despite of his dark complexion, he would be safe there from being sold for jail fees, as his pro-slavery merits would more than counterbalance his colored liabilities, which, after all, were only prima facie evidence against him. He suggests Texas, also, as a place where "patriots" of a certain class "most do congregate," and continues as follows:—

"There is Arkansas, too, all glorious in new-born liberty, fresh and unsullied, like Venus out of the ocean,—that newly discovered star, in the firmament banner of this Republic. Sister Arkansas, with her bowie- knife graceful at her side, like the huntress Diana with her silver bow, —oh it would be refreshing and recruiting to an exhausted patriot to go and replenish his soul at her fountains. The newly evacuated lands of the Cherokee, too, a sweet place now for a lover of his country to visit, to renew his self-complacency by wandering among the quenched hearths of the expatriated Indians; a land all smoking with the red man's departing curse,—a malediction that went to the centre. Yes, and Florida,— blossoming and leafy Florida, yet warm with the life-blood of Osceola and his warriors, shed gloriously under flag of truce. Why should a patriot of such a fancy for nature immure himself in the cells of the city, and forego such an inviting and so broad a landscape? Ite viator. Go forth, traveller, and leave this mouldy editing to less elastic fancies. We would respectfully invite our Colonel to travel. What signifies? Journey—wander—go forth—itinerate—exercise—perambulate—roam."

He gives the following ludicrous definition of Congress:—

"But what is Congress? It is the echo of the country at home,—the weathercock, that denotes and answers the shifting wind,—a thing of tail, nearly all tail, moved by the tail and by the wind, with small heading, and that corresponding implicitly in movement with the broad sail-like stern, which widens out behind to catch the rum-fraught breath of 'the Brotherhood.' As that turns, it turns; when that stops, it stops; and in calmish weather looks as steadfast and firm as though it was riveted to the centre. The wind blows, and the little popularity-hunting head dodges this way and that, in endless fluctuation. Such is Congress, or a great portion of it. It will point to the northwest heavens of Liberty, whenever the breezes bear down irresistibly upon it, from the regions of political fair weather. It will abolish slavery at the Capitol, when it has already been doomed to abolition and death everywhere else in the country. 'It will be in at the death.'"

Replying to the charge that the Abolitionists of the North were "secret" in their movements and designs, he says:—

"'In secret!' Why, our movements have been as prominent and open as the house-tops from the beginning. We have striven from the outset to write the whole matter cloud-high in the heavens, that the utmost South might read it. We have cast an arc upon the horizon, like the semicircle of the polar lights, and upon it have bent our motto, 'Immediate Emancipation,' glorious as the rainbow. We have engraven it there, on the blue table of the cold vault, in letters tall enough for the reading of the nations. And why has the far South not read and believed before this? Because a steam has gone up—a fog—from New England's pulpit and her degenerate press, and hidden the beaming revelation from its vision. The Northern hierarchy and aristocracy have cheated the South."

He spoke at times with severity of slaveholders, but far oftener of those who, without the excuse of education and habit, and prompted only by a selfish consideration of political or sectarian advantage, apologized for the wrong, and discountenanced the anti-slavery movement. "We have nothing to say," said he, "to the slave. He is no party to his own enslavement,—he is none to his disenthralment. We have nothing to say to the South. The real holder of slaves is not there. He is in the North, the free North. The South alone has not the power to hold the slave. It is the character of the nation that binds and holds him. It is the Republic that does it, the efficient force of which is north of Mason and Dixon's line. By virtue of the majority of Northern hearts and voices, slavery lives in the South!"

In 1840, he spent a few weeks in England, Ireland, and Scotland. He has left behind a few beautiful memorials of his tour. His Ride over the Border, Ride into Edinburgh, Wincobank hall, Ailsa Craig, gave his paper an interest in the eyes of many who had no sympathy with his political and religious views.

Scattered all over his editorials, like gems, are to be found beautiful images, sweet touches of heartfelt pathos,—thoughts which the reader pauses over with surprise and delight. We subjoin a few specimens, taken almost at random from the book before us:—

"A thunder-storm,—what can match it for eloquence and poetry? That rush from heaven of the big drops, in what multitude and succession, and how they sound as they strike! How they play on the old home roof and the thick tree-tops! What music to go to sleep by, to the tired boy, as he lies under the naked roof! And the great, low bass thunder, as it rolls off over the hills, and settles down behind them to the very centre, and you can feel the old earth jar under your feet!"

"There was no oratory in the speech of the *Learned Blacksmith*, in the ordinary sense of that word, no grace of elocution, but mighty thoughts radiating off from his heated mind, like sparks from the glowing steel of his own anvil."

"The hard hands of Irish labor, with nothing in them,—they ring like slabs of marble together, in response to the wild appeals of O'Connell, and the British stand conquered before them, with shouldered arms. Ireland is on her feet, with nothing in her hands, impregnable, unassailable, in utter defencelessness,—the first time that ever a nation sprung to its feet unarmed. The veterans of England behold them, and forbear to fire. They see no mark. It will not do to fire upon men; it will do only to fire upon soldiers. They are the proper mark of the murderous gun, but men cannot be shot."

"It is coming to that (abolition of war) the world over; and when it does come to it, oh what a long breath of relief the tired world will draw, as it stretches itself for the first time out upon earth's greensward, and learns the meaning of repose and peaceful sleep!"

"He who vests his labor in the faithful ground is dealing directly with God; human fraud or weakness do not intervene between him and his requital. No mechanic has a set of customers so trustworthy as God and the elements. No savings bank is so sure as the old earth."

"Literature is the luxury of words. It originates nothing, it does nothing. It talks hard words about the labor of others, and is reckoned more meritorious for it than genius and labor for doing what learning can only descant upon. It trades on the capital of unlettered minds. It struts in stolen plumage, and it is mere plumage. A learned man resembles an owl in more respects than the matter of wisdom. Like that solemn bird, he is about all feathers."

"Our Second Advent friends contemplate a grand conflagration about the first of April next. I should be willing there should be one, if it could be confined to the productions of the press, with which the earth is absolutely smothered. Humanity wants precious few books to read, but the great living, breathing, immortal volume of Providence. Life,—real life,—how to live, how to treat one another, and how to trust God in matters beyond our ken and occasion,—these are the lessons to learn, and you find little of them in libraries."

"That accursed drum and fife! How they have maddened mankind! And the deep bass boom of the cannon, chiming in in the chorus of battle, that trumpet and wild charging bugle,—how they set the military devil in a man, and make him into a soldier! Think of the human family falling upon one another at the inspiration of music! How must God feel at it, to see those harp-strings he meant should be waked to a love bordering on divine, strung and swept to mortal hate and butchery!"

"Leave off being Jews," (he is addressing Major Noah with regard to his appeal to his brethren to return to Judaea,) "and turn mankind. The rocks and sands of Palestine have been worshipped long enough. Connecticut River or the Merrimac are as good rivers as any Jordan that ever run into a dead or live sea, and as holy, for that matter. In Humanity, as in Christ Jesus, as Paul says, 'there is neither Jew nor Greek.' And there ought to be none. Let Humanity be reverenced with the tenderest devotion; suffering, discouraged, down-trodden, hard-handed, haggard-eyed, care-worn mankind! Let these be regarded a little. Would to God I could alleviate all their sorrows, and leave them a chance to laugh! They are, miserable now. They might be as happy as the blackbird on the spray, and as full of melody."

"I am sick as death at this miserable struggle among mankind for a living. Poor devils! were they born to run such a gauntlet after the means of life? Look about you, and see your squirming neighbors, writhing and twisting like so many angleworms in a fisher's bait-box, or the wriggling animalculae seen in the vinegar drop held to the sun. How they look, how they feel, how base it makes them all!"

"Every human being is entitled to the means of life, as the trout is to his brook or the lark to the blue sky. Is it well to put a human 'young one' here to die of hunger, thirst, and nakedness, or else be preserved as a pauper? Is this fair earth but a poor-house by creation and intent? Was it made for that?—and these other round things we see dancing in the firmament to the music of the spheres, are they all great shining poor-houses?"

"The divines always admit things after the age has adopted them. They are as careful of the age as the weathercock is of the wind. You might as well catch an old experienced weathercock, on some ancient Orthodox steeple, standing all day with its tail east in a strong out wind, as the divines at odds with the age."

But we must cease quoting. The admirers of Jean Paul Richter might find much of the charm and variety of the "Flower, Fruit, and Thorn Pieces" in this newspaper collection. They may see, perhaps, as we do, some things which they cannot approve of, the tendency of which, however intended, is very questionable. But, with us, they will pardon something to the spirit of liberty, much to that of love and humanity which breathes through all.

Disgusted and heart-sick at the general indifference of Church and clergy to the temporal condition of the people,—at their apologies for and defences of slavery, war, and capital punishment,—Rogers turned Protestant, in the full sense of the term. He spoke of priests and "pulpit wizards" as freely as John Milton did two centuries ago, although with far less bitterness and rasping satire. He could not endure to see Christianity and Humanity divorced. He longed to see the beautiful life of Jesus—his sweet humanities, his brotherly love, his abounding sympathies—made the example of all men. Thoroughly democratic, in his view all men were equal. Priests, stripped of their sacerdotal tailoring, were in his view but men, after all. He pitied them, he said, for they were in a wrong position,—above life's comforts and sympathies,—"up in the unnatural cold, they had better come down among men, and endure and enjoy with them." "Mankind," said he, "want the healing influences of humanity. They must love one another more. Disinterested good will make the world as it should be."

His last visit to his native valley was in the autumn of 1845. In a familiar letter to a friend, he thus describes his farewell view of the mountain glories of his childhood's home:—

"I went a jaunt, Thursday last, about twenty miles north of this valley, into the mountain region, where what I beheld, if I could tell it as I saw it, would make your outlawed sheet sought after wherever our Anglo-Saxon tongue is spoken in the wide world. I have been many a time among those Alps, and never without a kindling of wildest enthusiasm in my woodland blood. But I never saw them till last Thursday. They never loomed distinctly to my eye before, and the sun never shone on them from heaven till then. They were so near me, I could seem to hear the voice of their cataracts, as I could count their great slides, streaming adown their lone and desolate sides,—old slides, some of them overgrown with young woods, like half-healed scars on the breast of a giant. The great rains had clothed the valleys of the upper Pemigewasset in the darkest and deepest green. The meadows were richer and more glorious in their thick 'fall feed' than Queen Anne's Garden, as I saw it from the windows of Windsor Castle. And the dark hemlock and hackmatack woods were yet darker after the wet season, as they lay, in a hundred wildernesses, in the mighty recesses of the mountains. But the peaks,—the eternal, the solitary, the beautiful, the glorious and dear mountain peaks, my own Moosehillock and my native Haystacks,—these were the things on which eye and heart gazed and lingered, and I seemed to see them for the last time. It was on my way back that I halted and turned to look at them from a high point on the Thornton road. It was about four in the afternoon. It had rained among the hills about the Notch, and cleared off. The sun, there sombred at that early hour, as towards his setting, was pouring his most glorious light upon the naked peaks, and they casting their mighty shadows far down among the inaccessible woods that darken the hollows that stretch between their bases. A cloud was creeping up to perch and rest awhile on the highest top of Great Haystack. Vulgar folks have called it Mount Lafayette, since the visit of that brave old Frenchman in 1825 or 1826. If they had asked his opinion, he would have told them the names of mountains couldn't be altered, and especially names like that, so appropriate, so descriptive, and so picturesque. A little hard white cloud, that looked like a hundred fleeces of wool rolled into one, was climbing rapidly along up the northwestern ridge, that ascended to the lonely top of Great Haystack. All the others were bare. Four or five of them,—as distinct and shapely as so many pyramids; some topped out with naked cliff, on which the sun lay in melancholy glory; others clothed thick all the way up with the old New Hampshire hemlock or the daring hackmatack,— Pierpont's hackmatack. You could see their shadows stretching many and many a mile, over Grant and Location, away beyond the invading foot of Incorporation,—where the timber-hunter has scarcely explored, and where the moose browses now, I suppose, as undisturbed as he did before the settlement of the State. I wish our young friend and genius, Harrison Eastman, had been with me, to see the sunlight as it glared on the tops of those woods, and to see the purple of the mountains. I looked at it myself almost with the eye of a painter. If a painter looked with mine, though, he never could look off upon his canvas long enough to make a picture; he would gaze forever at the original.

"But I had to leave it, and to say in my heart, Farewell! And as I travelled on down, and the sun sunk lower and lower towards the summit of the western ridge, the clouds came up and formed an Alpine range in the evening heavens above it,—like other Haystacks and Moosehillocks,—so dark and dense that fancy could easily mistake them for a higher Alps. There were the peaks and the great passes; the Franconia Notches among the cloudy cliffs, and the great White Mountain Gap."

His health, never robust, had been gradually failing for some time previous to his death. He needed more repose and quiet than his duties as an editor left him; and to this end he purchased a small and pleasant farm in his loved Pennigewasset valley, in the hope that he might there recruit his wasted energies. In the sixth month of the year of his death, in a letter to us, he spoke of his prospects in language which even then brought moisture to our eyes:—

"I am striving to get me an asylum of a farm. I have a wife and seven children, every one of them with a whole spirit. I don't want to be separated from any of them, only with a view to come together again. I have a beautiful little retreat in prospect, forty odd miles north, where I imagine I can get potatoes and repose,—a sort of haven or port. I am among the breakers, and 'mad for land.' If I get this home,—it is a mile or two in among the hills from the pretty domicil once visited by yourself and glorious Thompson,—I am this moment indulging the fancy that I may see you at it before we die. Why can't I have you come and see me? You see, dear W., I don't want to send you anything short of a full epistle. Let me end as I begun, with the proffer of my hand in grasp of yours extended. My heart I do not proffer,—it was yours before,—it shall be yours while I am N. P. ROGERS."

Alas! the haven of a deeper repose than he had dreamed of was close at hand. He lingered until the middle of the tenth month, suffering much, yet calm and sensible to the last. Just before his death, he desired his children to sing at his bedside that touching song of Lover's, *The Angel's Whisper*. Turning his eyes towards the open window, through which the leafy glory of the season he most loved was visible, he listened to the sweet melody. In the words of his friend Pierpont,—

> "The angel's whisper stole in song upon his closing ear;
> From his own daughter's lips it came, so musical and clear,
> That scarcely knew the dying man what melody was there—
> The last of earth's or first of heaven's pervading all the air."

He sleeps in the Concord burial-ground, under the shadow of oaks; the very spot he would have chosen, for he looked upon trees with something akin to human affection. "They are," he said, "the beautiful handiwork and architecture of God, on which the eye never tires. Every one is a feather in the earth's cap, a plume in her bonnet, a tress on her forehead,—a comfort, a refreshing, and an ornament to her." Spring has hung over him her buds, and opened beside him her violets. Summer has laid her green oaken garland on his grave, and now the frost-blooms of autumn drop upon it. Shall man cast a nettle on that mound? He loved humanity,—shall it be less kind to him than Nature? Shall the bigotry of sect, and creed, and profession, drive its condemnatory stake into his grave? God forbid. The doubts which he sometimes unguardedly expressed had relation, we are constrained to believe, to the glosses of commentators and creed-makers and the inconsistency of professors, rather than to those facts and precepts of Christianity to which he gave the constant assent of his practice. He sought not his own. His heart yearned with pity and brotherly affection for all the poor and suffering in the universe. Of him, the angel of Leigh Hunt's beautiful allegory might have written, in the golden book of remembrance, as he did of the good Abou Ben Adhem, "He loved his fellow-men."

ROBERT DINSMORE

The great charm of Scottish poetry consists in its simplicity, and genuine, unaffected sympathy with the common joys and sorrows of daily life. It is a home-taught, household melody. It calls to mind the pastoral bleat on the hillsides, the kirkbells of a summer Sabbath, the song of the lark in the sunrise, the cry of the quail in the corn-land, the low of cattle, and the blithe carol of milkmaids "when the kye come hame" at gloaming. Meetings at fair and market, blushing betrothments, merry weddings, the joy of young maternity, the lights and shades of domestic life, its bereavements and partings, its chances and changes, its holy death-beds, and funerals solemnly beautiful in quiet kirkyards, — these furnish the hints of the immortal melodies of Burns, the sweet ballads of the Ettrick Shepherd and Allan Cunningham, and the rustic drama of Ramsay. It is the poetry of home, of nature, and the affections.

All this is sadly wanting in our young literature. We have no songs; American domestic life has never been hallowed and beautified by the sweet and graceful and tender associations of poetry. We have no Yankee pastorals. Our rivers and streams turn mills and float rafts, and are otherwise as commendably useful as those of Scotland; but no quaint ballad or simple song reminds us that men and women have loved, met, and parted on their banks, or that beneath each roof within their valleys the tragedy and comedy of life have been enacted. Our poetry is cold and imitative; it seems more the product of over-strained intellects than the spontaneous outgushing of hearts warm with love, and strongly sympathizing with human nature as it actually exists about us, with the joys and griefs of the men and women whom we meet daily. Unhappily, the opinion prevails that a poet must be also a philosopher, and hence it is that much of our poetry is as indefinable in its mysticism as an Indian Brahmin's commentary on his sacred books, or German metaphysics subjected to homeopathic dilution. It assumes to be prophetical, and its utterances are oracular. It tells of strange, vague emotions and yearnings, painfully suggestive of spiritual "groanings which cannot be uttered." If it "babbles o' green fields" and the common sights and sounds of nature, it is only for the purpose of finding some vague analogy between them and its internal experiences and longings. It leaves the warm and comfortable fireside of actual knowledge and human comprehension, and goes wailing and gibbering like a ghost about the impassable doors of mystery:—

> "It fain would be resolved
> How things are done,
> And who the tailor is
> That works for the man I' the sun."

How shall we account for this marked tendency in the literature of a shrewd, practical people? Is it that real life in New England lacks those conditions of poetry and romance which age, reverence, and superstition have gathered about it in the Old World? Is it that

> "Ours are not Tempe's nor Arcadia's vales,"

but are more famous for growing Indian corn and potatoes, and the manufacture of wooden ware and pedler notions, than for romantic associations and legendary interest? That our huge, unshapely shingle structures, blistering in the sun and glaring with windows, were evidently never reared by the spell of pastoral harmonies, as the walls of Thebes rose at the sound of the lyre of Amphion? That the habits of our people are too cool, cautious, undemonstrative, to furnish the warp and woof of song and pastoral, and that their dialect and figures of speech, however richly significant and expressive in the autobiography of Sam Slick, or the satire of Hosea Biglow and Ethan Spike, form a very awkward medium of sentiment and pathos? All this may be true. But the Yankee, after all, is a man, and as such his history, could it be got at, must have more or less of poetic material in it; moreover, whether conscious of it or not, he also stands relieved against the background of Nature's beauty or sublimity. There is a poetical side to the commonplace of his incomings and outgoings; study him well, and you may frame an idyl of some sort from his apparently prosaic existence. Our poets, we must needs think, are deficient in that shiftiness, ready adaptation to circumstances, and ability of making the most of things, for which, as a people, we are proverbial. Can they make nothing of our Thanksgiving, that annual gathering of long-severed friends? Do they find nothing to their purpose in our apple-bees, buskings, berry- pickings, summer picnics, and winter sleigh-rides? Is there nothing available in our peculiarities of climate, scenery, customs, and political institutions? Does the Yankee leap into life, shrewd, hard, and speculating, armed, like Pallas, for a struggle with fortune? Are there not boys and girls, school loves and friendship, courtings and match-makings, hope and fear, and all the varied play of human passions, —the keen struggles of gain, the mad grasping of ambition,—sin and remorse, tearful repentance and holy aspirations? Who shall say that we have not all the essentials of the poetry of human life and simple nature, of the hearth and the farm-field? Here, then, is a mine unworked, a harvest ungathered. Who shall sink the shaft and thrust in the sickle?

And here let us say that the mere dilettante and the amateur ruralist may as well keep their hands off. The prize is not for them. He who would successfully strive for it must be himself what he sings,—part and parcel of the rural life of New England,—one who has grown strong amidst its healthful influences, familiar with all its details, and capable of detecting whatever of beauty, humor, or pathos pertain to it,—one who has added to his book-lore the large experience of an active participation in the rugged toil, the hearty amusements, the trials, and the pleasures he describes.

We have been led to these reflections by an incident which has called up before us the homespun figure of an old friend of our boyhood, who had the good sense to discover that the poetic element existed in the simple home life of a country farmer, although himself unable to give a very creditable expression of it. He had the "vision," indeed, but the "faculty divine" was wanting; or, if he possessed it in any degree, as Thersites says of the wit of Ajax, "it would not out, but lay coldly in him like fire in the flint."

While engaged this morning in looking over a large exchange list of newspapers, a few stanzas of poetry in the Scottish dialect attracted our attention. As we read them, like a wizard's rhyme they seemed to have the power of bearing us back to the past. They had long ago graced the columns of that solitary sheet which once a week diffused happiness over our fireside circle, making us acquainted, in our lonely nook, with the goings-on of the great world. The verses, we are now constrained to admit, are not remarkable in themselves, truth and simple nature only; yet how our young hearts responded to them! Twenty years ago there were fewer verse-makers than at present; and as our whole stock of light literature consisted of Ellwood's *Davideis* and the selections of *Lindley Murray's English Reader*, it is not improbable that we were in a condition to overestimate the contributions to the poet's corner of our village newspaper. Be that as it may, we welcome them as we would the face of an old friend, for they somehow remind us of the scent of haymows, the breath of cattle, the fresh greenery by the brookside, the moist earth broken by the coulter and turned up to the sun and winds of May. This particular piece, which follows, is entitled *The Sparrow*, and was occasioned by the crushing of a bird's-nest by the author while ploughing among his corn. It has something of the simple tenderness of Burns.

> "*Poor innocent and hapless Sparrow*
> *Why should my mould-board gie thee sorrow!*
> *This day thou'll chirp and mourn the morrow*
> *Wi' anxious breast;*
> *The plough has turned the mould'ring furrow*
> *Deep o'er thy nest!*

"Just I' the middle o' the hill
Thy nest was placed wi' curious skill;
There I espied thy little bill
Beneath the shade.
In that sweet bower, secure frae ill,
Thine eggs were laid.

"Five corns o' maize had there been drappit,
An' through the stalks thy head was pappit,
The drawing nowt could na be stappit
I quickly foun';
Syne frae thy cozie nest thou happit,
Wild fluttering roun'.

"The sklentin stane beguiled the sheer,
In vain I tried the plough to steer;
A wee bit stumpie I' the rear
Cam' 'tween my legs,
An' to the jee-side gart me veer
An' crush thine eggs.

"Alas! alas! my bonnie birdie!
Thy faithful mate flits round to guard thee.
Connubial love! —a pattern worthy
The pious priest!
What savage heart could be sae hardy
As wound thy breast?

"Ah me! it was nae fau't o' mine;
It gars me greet to see thee pine.
It may be serves His great design
Who governs all;
Omniscience tents wi' eyes divine
The Sparrow's fall!

"How much like thine are human dools,
Their sweet wee bairns laid I' the mools?
The Sovereign Power who nature rules
Hath said so be it
But poor blip' mortals are sic fools
They canna see it.

"Nae doubt that He who first did mate us
Has fixed our lot as sure as fate is,
An' when He wounds He disna hate us,
But anely this,
He'll gar the ills which here await us
Yield lastin' bliss."

In the early part of the eighteenth century a considerable number of Presbyterians of Scotch descent, from the north of Ireland, emigrated to the New World. In the spring of 1719, the inhabitants of Haverhill, on the Merrimac, saw them passing up the river in several canoes, one of which unfortunately upset in the rapids above the village. The following fragment of a ballad celebrating this event has been handed down to the present time, and may serve to show the feelings even then of the old English settlers towards the Irish emigrants:—

"They began to scream and bawl,
As out they tumbled one and all,
And, if the Devil had spread his net,
He could have made a glorious haul!"

The new-comers proceeded up the river, and, landing opposite to the Uncanoonuc Hills, on the present site of Manchester, proceeded inland to Beaver Pond. Charmed with the appearance of the country, they resolved here to terminate their wanderings. Under a venerable oak on the margin of the little lake, they knelt down with their minister, Jamie McGregore, and laid, in prayer and thanksgiving, the foundation of their settlement. In a few years they had cleared large fields, built substantial stone and frame dwellings and a large and commodious meeting-house; wealth had accumulated around them, and they had everywhere the reputation of a shrewd and thriving community. They were the first in New England to cultivate the potato, which their neighbors for a long time regarded as a pernicious root, altogether unfit for a Christian stomach. Every lover of that invaluable esculent has reason to remember with gratitude the settlers of Londonderry.

Their moral acclimation in Ireland had not been without its effect upon their character. Side by side with a Presbyterianism as austere as that of John Knox had grown up something of the wild Milesian humor, love of convivial excitement and merry-making. Their long prayers and fierce zeal in behalf of orthodox tenets only served, in the eyes of their Puritan neighbors, to make more glaring still the scandal of their marked social irregularities. It became a common saying in the region round about that "the Derry Presbyterians would never give up a pint of doctrine or a pint of rum." Their second minister was an old scarred fighter, who had signalized himself in the stout defence of Londonderry, when James II. and his Papists were thundering at its gates. Agreeably to his death-bed directions, his old fellow-soldiers, in their leathern doublets and battered steel caps, bore him to his grave, firing over him the same rusty muskets which had swept down rank after rank of the men of Amalek at the Derry siege.

Erelong the celebrated Derry fair was established, in imitation of those with which they had been familiar in Ireland. Thither annually came all manner of horse-jockeys and pedlers, gentlemen and beggars, fortune-tellers, wrestlers, dancers and fiddlers, gay young farmers and buxom maidens. Strong drink abounded. They who had good-naturedly wrestled and joked together in the morning not unfrequently closed the day with a fight, until, like the revellers of Donnybrook,

> "Their hearts were soft with whiskey,
> And their heads were soft with blows."

A wild, frolicking, drinking, fiddling, courting, horse-racing, riotous merry-making,—a sort of Protestant carnival, relaxing the grimness of Puritanism for leagues around it.

In the midst of such a community, and partaking of all its influences, Robert Dinsmore, the author of the poem I have quoted, was born, about the middle of the last century. His paternal ancestor, John, younger son of a Laird of Achenmead, who left the banks of the Tweed for the green fertility of Northern Ireland, had emigrated to New England some forty years before, and, after a rough experience of Indian captivity in the wild woods of Maine, had settled down among his old neighbors in Londonderry. Until nine years of age, Robert never saw a school. He was a short time under the tuition of an old British soldier, who had strayed into the settlement after the French war, "at which time," he says in a letter to a friend, "I learned to repeat the shorter and larger catechisms. These, with the Scripture proofs annexed to them, confirmed me in the orthodoxy of my forefathers, and I hope I shall ever remain an evidence of the truth of what the wise man said, 'Train up a child in the way he should go, and when he is old he will not depart from it.'" He afterwards took lessons with one Master McKeen, who used to spend much of his time in hunting squirrels with his pupils. He learned to read and write; and the old man always insisted that he should have done well at ciphering also, had he not fallen in love with Molly Park. At the age of eighteen he enlisted in the Revolutionary army, and was at the battle of Saratoga. On his return he married his fair Molly, settled down as a farmer in Windham, formerly a part of Londonderry, and before he was thirty years of age became an elder in the church, of the creed and observances of which he was always a zealous and resolute defender. From occasional passages in his poems, it is evident that the instructions which he derived from the pulpit were not unlike those which Burns suggested as needful for the unlucky lad whom he was commending to his friend Hamilton:—

> "Ye 'll catechise him ilka quirk,
>
> An' shore him weel wi' hell."

In a humorous poem, entitled Spring's Lament, he thus describes the consternation produced in the meeting-house at sermon time by a dog, who, in search of his mistress, rattled and scraped at the "west porch door:"—

> "The vera priest was scared himsel',
>
> His sermon he could hardly spell;
>
> Auld carlins fancied they could smell
>
> The brimstone matches;
>
> They thought he was some imp o' hell,
>
> In quest o' wretches."

He lived to a good old age, a home-loving, unpretending farmer, cultivating his acres with his own horny hands, and cheering the long rainy days and winter evenings with homely rhyme. Most of his pieces were written in the dialect of his ancestors, which was well understood by his neighbors and friends, the only audience upon which he could venture to calculate. He loved all old things, old language, old customs, old theology. In a rhyming letter to his cousin Silas, he says:—

> "Though Death our ancestors has cleekit,
>
> An' under clods then closely steekit,
>
> We'll mark the place their chimneys reekit,
>
> Their native tongue we yet wad speak it,
>
> Wi' accent glib."

He wrote sometimes to amuse his neighbors, often to soothe their sorrow under domestic calamity, or to give expression to his own. With little of that delicacy of taste which results from the attrition of fastidious and refined society, and altogether too truthful and matter-of-fact to call in the aid of imagination, he describes in the simplest and most direct terms the circumstances in which he found himself, and the impressions which these circumstances had made on his own mind. He calls things by their right names; no euphuism or transcendentalism,—the plainer and commoner the better. He tells us of his farm life, its joys and sorrows, its mirth and care, with no embellishment, with no concealment of repulsive and ungraceful features. Never having seen a nightingale, he makes no attempt to describe the fowl; but he has seen the night-hawk, at sunset, cutting the air above him, and he tells of it. Side by side with his waving corn-fields and orchard-blooms we have the barn-yard and pigsty. Nothing which was necessary to the comfort and happiness of his home and avocation was to him "common or unclean." Take, for instance, the following, from a poem written at the close of autumn, after the death of his wife:—

"No more may I the Spring Brook trace,
No more with sorrow view the place
Where Mary's wash-tub stood;
No more may wander there alone,
And lean upon the mossy stone
Where once she piled her wood.
'T was there she bleached her linen cloth,
By yonder bass-wood tree
From that sweet stream she made her broth,
Her pudding and her tea.
That stream, whose waters running,
O'er mossy root and stone,
Made ringing and singing,
Her voice could match alone."

We envy not the man who can sneer at this simple picture. It is honest as Nature herself. An old and lonely man looks back upon the young years of his wedded life. Can we not look with him? The sunlight of a summer morning is weaving itself with the leafy shadows of the bass-tree, beneath which a fair and ruddy-checked young woman, with her full, rounded arms bared to the elbow, bends not ungracefully to her task, pausing ever and anon to play with the bright-eyed child beside her, and mingling her songs with the pleasant murmurings of gliding water! Alas! as the old man looks, he hears that voice, which perpetually sounds to us all from the past—no more!

Let us look at him in his more genial mood. Take the opening lines of his Thanksgiving Day. What a plain, hearty picture of substantial comfort!

"When corn is in the garret stored,
And sauce in cellar well secured;
When good fat beef we can afford,
And things that 're dainty,
With good sweet cider on our board,
And pudding plenty;

> "When stock, well housed, may chew the cud,
> And at my door a pile of wood,
> A rousing fire to warm my blood,
> Blest sight to see!
> It puts my rustic muse in mood
> To sing for thee."

If he needs a simile, he takes the nearest at hand. In a letter to his daughter he says:—

> "That mine is not a longer letter,
> The cause is not the want of matter,—
> Of that there's plenty, worse or better;
> But like a mill
> Whose stream beats back with surplus water,
> The wheel stands still."

Something of the humor of Burns gleams out occasionally from the sober decorum of his verses. In an epistle to his friend Betton, high sheriff of the county, who had sent to him for a peck of seed corn, he says:—

> "Soon plantin' time will come again,
> Syne may the heavens gie us rain,
> An' shining heat to bless ilk plain
> An' fertile hill,
> An' gar the loads o' yellow grain,
> Our garrets fill.
>
> "As long as I has food and clothing,
> An' still am hale and fier and breathing,
> Ye 's get the corn—and may be aething
> Ye'll do for me;
> (Though God forbid)—hang me for naething
> An' lose your fee."

And on receiving a copy of some verses written by a lady, he talks in a sad way for a Presbyterian deacon:—

> "Were she some Aborigine squaw,
> Wha sings so sweet by nature's law,
> I'd meet her in a hazle shaw,
> Or some green loany,
> And make her tawny phiz and 'a
> My welcome crony."

The practical philosophy of the stout, jovial rhymer was but little affected by the sour-featured asceticism of the elder. He says:—

> "We'll eat and drink, and cheerful take
>
> Our portions for the Donor's sake,
>
> For thus the Word of Wisdom spake—
>
> Man can't do better;
>
> Nor can we by our labors make
>
> The Lord our debtor!"

A quaintly characteristic correspondence in rhyme between the Deacon and Parson McGregore, evidently "birds o' ane feather," is still in existence. The minister, in acknowledging the epistle of his old friend, commences his reply as follows:—

> "Did e'er a cuif tak' up a quill,
>
> Wha ne'er did aught that he did well,
>
> To gar the muses rant and reel,
>
> An' flaunt and swagger,
>
> Nae doubt ye 'll say 't is that daft chiel
>
> Old Dite McGregore!"

The reply is in the same strain, and may serve to give the reader some idea of the old gentleman as a religious controversialist:—

> "My reverend friend and kind McGregore,
>
> Although thou ne'er was ca'd a bragger,
>
> Thy muse I'm sure nave e'er was glegger
>
> Thy Scottish lays
>
> Might gar Socinians fa' or stagger,
>
> E'en in their ways.
>
> "When Unitarian champions dare thee,
>
> Goliah like, and think to scare thee,
>
> Dear Davie, fear not, they'll ne'er waur thee;
>
> But draw thy sling,
>
> Weel loaded frae the Gospel quarry,
>
> An' gie 't a fling."

The last time I saw him, he was chaffering in the market-place of my native village, swapping potatoes and onions and pumpkins for tea, coffee, molasses, and, if the truth be told, New England rum. Threescore years and ten, to use his own words,

> "Hung o'er his back,
>
> And bent him like a muckle pack,"

yet he still stood stoutly and sturdily in his thick shoes of cowhide, like one accustomed to tread independently the soil of his own acres,— his broad, honest face seamed by care and darkened by exposure to "all the airts that blow," and his white hair flowing in patriarchal glory beneath his felt hat. A genial, jovial, large-hearted old man, simple as a child, and betraying, neither in look nor manner, that he was accustomed to

> "Feed on thoughts which voluntary move
>
> Harmonious numbers."

Peace to him! A score of modern dandies and sentimentalists could ill supply the place of this one honest man. In the ancient burial-ground of Windham, by the side of his "beloved Molly," and in view of the old meeting-house, there is a mound of earth, where, every spring, green grasses tremble in the wind and the warm sunshine calls out the flowers. There, gathered like one of his own ripe sheaves, the farmer poet sleeps with his fathers.

PLACIDO, THE SLAVE POET (1845.)

I have been greatly interested in the fate of Juan Placido, the black revolutionist of Cuba, who was executed in Havana, as the alleged instigator and leader of an attempted revolt on the part of the slaves in that city and its neighborhood.

Juan Placido was born a slave on the estate of Don Terribio de Castro. His father was an African, his mother a mulatto. His mistress treated him with great kindness, and taught him to read. When he was twelve years of age she died, and he fell into other and less compassionate hands. At the age of eighteen, on seeing his mother struck with a heavy whip, he for the first time turned upon his tormentors. To use his own words, "I felt the blow in my heart. To utter a loud cry, and from a downcast boy, with the timidity of one weak as a lamb, to become all at office like a raging lion, was a thing of a moment." He was, however, subdued, and the next morning, together with his mother, a tenderly nurtured and delicate woman, severely scourged. On seeing his mother rudely stripped and thrown down upon the ground, he at first with tears implored the overseer to spare her; but at the sound of the first blow, as it cut into her naked flesh, he sprang once more upon the ruffian, who, having superior strength, beat him until he was nearer dead than alive.

After suffering all the vicissitudes of slavery,—hunger, nakedness, stripes; after bravely and nobly bearing up against that slow, dreadful process which reduces the man to a thing, the image of God to a piece of merchandise, until he had reached his thirty-eighth year, he was unexpectedly released from his bonds. Some literary gentlemen in Havana, into whose hands two or three pieces of his composition had fallen, struck with the vigor, spirit, and natural grace which they manifested, sought out the author, and raised a subscription to purchase his freedom. He came to Havana, and maintained himself by house-painting, and such other employments as his ingenuity and talents placed within his reach. He wrote several poems, which have been published in Spanish at Havana, and translated by Dr. Madden, under the title of *Poems by a Slave*.

It is not too much to say of these poems that they will bear a comparison with most of the productions of modern Spanish literature. The style is bold, free, energetic. Some of the pieces are sportive and graceful; such is the address to *The Cucuya*, or Cuban firefly. This beautiful insect is sometimes fastened in tiny nets to the light dresses of the Cuban ladies, a custom to which the writer gallantly alludes in the following lines:—

> "Ah!—still as one looks on such brightness and bloom,
> On such beauty as hers, one might envy the doom
> Of a captive Cucuya that's destined, like this,
> To be touched by her hand and revived by her kiss!
> In the cage which her delicate hand has prepared,
> The beautiful prisoner nestles unscared,
> O'er her fair forehead shining serenely and bright,
> In beauty's own bondage revealing its light!
> And when the light dance and the revel are done,
> She bears it away to her alcove alone,
> Where, fed by her hand from the cane that's most choice,
> In secret it gleans at the sound of her voice!
> O beautiful maiden! may Heaven accord
> Thy care of the captive a fitting reward,
> And never may fortune the fetters remove
> Of a heart that is thine in the bondage of love!"

In his Dream, a fragment of some length, Placido dwells in a touching manner upon the scenes of his early years. It is addressed to his brother Florence, who was a slave near Matanzas, while the author was in the same condition at Havana. There is a plaintive and melancholy sweetness in these lines, a natural pathos, which finds its way to the heart:—

> "Thou knowest, dear Florence, my sufferings of old,
> The struggles maintained with oppression for years;
> We shared them together, and each was consoled
> With the love which was nurtured by sorrow and tears.

> "But now far apart, the sad pleasure is gone,
> We mingle our sighs and our sorrows no more;
> The course is a new one which each has to run,
> And dreary for each is the pathway before.

> "But in slumber our spirits at least shall commune,
> We will meet as of old in the visions of sleep,
> In dreams which call back early days, when at noon
> We stole to the shade of the palm-tree to weep!

"For solitude pining, in anguish of late
The heights of Quintana I sought for repose;
And there, in the cool and the silence, the weight
Of my cares was forgotten, I felt not any woes.

"Exhausted and weary, the spell of the place
Sank down on my eyelids, and soft slumber stole
So sweetly upon me, it left not a trace
Of sorrow o'ercasting the light of the soul."

The writer then imagines himself borne lightly through the air to the place of his birth. The valley of Matanzas lies beneath him, hallowed by the graves of his parents. He proceeds:—

"I gazed on that spot where together we played,
Our innocent pastimes came fresh to my mind,
Our mother's caress, and the fondness displayed
In each word and each look of a parent so kind.

"I looked on the mountain, whose fastnesses wild
The fugitives seek from the rifle and hound;
Below were the fields where they suffered and toiled,
And there the low graves of their comrades are found.

"The mill-house was there, and the turmoil of old;
But sick of these scenes, for too well were they known,
I looked for the stream where in childhood I strolled
When a moment of quiet and peace was my own.

"With mingled emotions of pleasure and pain,
Dear Florence, I sighed to behold thee once more;
I sought thee, my brother, embraced thee again,
But I found thee a slave as I left thee before!"

Some of his devotional pieces evince the fervor and true feeling of the Christian poet. His *Ode to Religion* contains many admirable lines. Speaking of the martyrs of the early days of Christianity, he says finely:—

"Still in that cradle, purpled with their blood,
The infant Faith waxed stronger day by day."

I cannot forbear quoting the last stanza of this poem:—

"O God of mercy, throned in glory high,

On earth and all its misery look down:
Behold the wretched, hear the captive's cry,
And call Thy exiled children round Thy throne!
There would I fain in contemplation gaze
On Thy eternal beauty, and would make
Of love one lasting canticle of praise,
And every theme but Thee henceforth forsake!"

His best and noblest production is an ode   *To Cuba,* written on the occasion of Dr. Madden's departure from the island, and presented to that gentleman. It was never published in Cuba, as its sentiments would have subjected the author to persecution. It breathes a lofty spirit of patriotism, and an indignant sense of the wrongs inflicted upon his race. Withal, it has something of the grandeur and stateliness of the old Spanish muse.

"Cuba!—of what avail that thou art fair,
Pearl of the Seas, the pride of the Antilles,
If thy poor sons have still to see thee share
The pangs of bondage and its thousand ills?
Of what avail the verdure of thy hills,
The purple bloom thy coffee-plain displays;
The cane's luxuriant growth, whose culture fills
More graves than famine, or the sword finds ways
To glut with victims calmly as it slays?

"Of what avail that thy clear streams abound
With precious ore, if wealth there's, none to buy
Thy children's rights, and not one grain is found
For Learning's shrine, or for the altar nigh
Of poor, forsaken, downcast Liberty?
Of what avail the riches of thy port,
Forests of masts and ships from every sea,
If Trade alone is free, and man, the sport
And spoil of Trade, bears wrongs of every sort?

"Cuba! O Cuba!—-when men call thee fair,
And rich, and beautiful, the Queen of Isles,
Star of the West, and Ocean's gem most rare,
Oh, say to those who mock thee with such wiles:

Take off these flowers; and view the lifeless spoils
Which wait the worm; behold their hues beneath
The pale, cold cheek; and seek for living smiles
Where Beauty lies not in the arms of Death,
And Bondage taints not with its poison breath!"

The disastrous result of the last rising of the slaves—in Cuba is well known. Betrayed, and driven into premature collision with their oppressors, the insurrectionists were speedily crushed into subjection. Placido was arrested, and after a long hearing was condemned to be executed, and consigned to the Chapel of the Condemned.

How far he was implicated in the insurrectionary movement it is now perhaps impossible to ascertain. The popular voice at Havana pronounced him its leader and projector, and as such he was condemned. His own bitter wrongs; the terrible recollections of his life of servitude; the sad condition of his relatives and race, exposed to scorn, contumely, and the heavy hand of violence; the impunity with which the most dreadful outrages upon the persons of slaves were inflicted,—acting upon a mind fully capable of appreciating the beauty and dignity of freedom,— furnished abundant incentives to an effort for the redemption of his race and the humiliation of his oppressors. The Heraldo, of Madrid speaks of him as "the celebrated poet, a man of great natural genius, and beloved and appreciated by the most respectable young men of Havana." It accuses him of wild and ambitious projects, and states that he was intended to be the chief of the black race after they had thrown off the yoke of bondage.

He was executed at Havana in the seventh month, 1844. According to the custom in Cuba with condemned criminals, he was conducted from prison to the Chapel of the Doomed. He passed thither with singular composure, amidst a great concourse of people, gracefully saluting his numerous acquaintances. The chapel was hung with black cloth, and dimly lighted. He was seated beside his coffin. Priests in long black robes stood around him, chanting in sepulchral voices the service of the dead. It is an ordeal under which the stoutest-hearted and most resolute have been found to sink. After enduring it for twenty-four hours he was led out to execution. He came forth calm and undismayed; holding a crucifix in his hand, he recited in a loud, clear voice a solemn prayer in verse, which he had composed amidst the horrors of the Chapel. The following is an imperfect rendering of a poem which thrilled the hearts of all who heard it:—

"God of unbounded love and power eternal,
To Thee I turn in darkness and despair!
Stretch forth Thine arm, and from the brow infernal
Of Calumny the veil of Justice tear;

And from the forehead of my honest fame
Pluck the world's brand of infamy and shame!

"O King of kings! — my fathers' God! — who only
Art strong to save, by whom is all controlled,
Who givest the sea its waves, the dark and lonely
Abyss of heaven its light, the North its cold,
The air its currents, the warm sun its beams,
Life to the flowers, and motion to the streams!

"All things obey Thee, dying or reviving
As thou commandest; all, apart from Thee,
From Thee alone their life and power deriving,
Sink and are lost in vast eternity!
Yet doth the void obey Thee; since from naught
This marvellous being by Thy hand was wrought.

"O merciful God! I cannot shun Thy presence,
For through its veil of flesh Thy piercing eye
Looketh upon my spirit's unsoiled essence,
As through the pure transparence of the sky;
Let not the oppressor clap his bloody hands,
As o'er my prostrate innocence he stands!

"But if, alas, it seemeth good to Thee
That I should perish as the guilty dies,
And that in death my foes should gaze on me
With hateful malice and exulting eyes,
Speak Thou the word, and bid them shed my blood,
Fully in me Thy will be done, O God!"

On arriving at the fatal spot, he sat down as ordered, on a bench, with his back to the soldiers. The multitude recollected that in some affecting lines, written by the conspirator in prison, he had said that it would be useless to seek to kill him by shooting his body, — that his heart must be pierced ere it would cease its throbbings. At the last moment, just as the soldiers were about to fire, he rose up and gazed for an instant around and above him on the beautiful capital of his native land and its sail-flecked bay, on the dense crowds about him, the blue mountains in the distance, and the sky glorious with summer sunshine. "Adios, mundo!" (Farewell, world!) he said calmly, and sat down. The word was given, and five balls entered his body. Then it was that, amidst the groans and murmurs of the horror-stricken spectators, he rose up once more, and turned his head to the shuddering soldiers, his face wearing an expression of superhuman courage. "Will no one pity me?" he said, laying his hand over his heart. "Here, fire here!" While he yet spake, two balls entered his heart, and he fell dead.

Thus perished the hero poet of Cuba. He has not fallen in vain. His genius and his heroic death will doubtless be regarded by his race as precious legacies. To the great names of L'Ouverture and Petion the colored man can now add that of Juan Placido.

PERSONAL SKETCHES AND TRIBUTES

THE FUNERAL OF TORREY

Charles T. Torrey, an able young Congregational clergyman, died May
9, 1846, in the state's prison of Maryland, for the offence of
aiding slaves to escape from bondage. His funeral in Boston,
attended by thousands, was a most impressive occasion. The
following is an extract from an article written for the Essex
Transcript:—

Some seven years ago, we saw Charles T. Torrey for the first time. His wife was leaning on his arm,—young, loving, and beautiful; the heart that saw them blessed them. Since that time, we have known him as a most energetic and zealous advocate of the anti-slavery cause. He had fine talents, improved by learning and observation, a clear, intensely active intellect, and a heart full of sympathy and genial humanity. It was with strange and bitter feelings that we bent over his coffin and looked upon his still face. The pity which we had felt for him in his long sufferings gave place to indignation against his murderers. Hateful beyond the power of expression seemed the tyranny which had murdered him with the slow torture of the dungeon. May God forgive us, if for the moment we felt like grasping His dread prerogative of vengeance. As we passed out of the hall, a friend grasped our hand hard, his eye flashing through its tears, with a stern reflection of our own emotions, while he whispered through his pressed lips: "It is enough to turn every anti- slavery heart into steel." Our blood boiled; we longed to see the wicked apologists of slavery—the blasphemous defenders of it in Church and State—led up to the coffin of our murdered brother, and there made to feel that their hands had aided in riveting the chain upon those still limbs, and in shutting out from those cold lips the free breath of heaven.

A long procession followed his remains to their resting-place at Mount Auburn. A monument to his memory will be raised in that cemetery, in the midst of the green beauty of the scenery which he loved in life, and side by side with the honored dead of Massachusetts. Thither let the friends of humanity go to gather fresh strength from the memory of the martyr. There let the slaveholder stand, and as he reads the record of the enduring marble commune with his own heart, and feel that sorrow which worketh repentance.

The young, the beautiful, the brave!—he is safe now from the malice of his enemies. Nothing can harm him more. His work for the poor and helpless was well and nobly done. In the wild woods of Canada, around many a happy fireside and holy family altar, his name is on the lips of God's poor. He put his soul in their souls' stead; he gave his life for those who had no claim on his love save that of human brotherhood. How poor, how pitiful and paltry, seem our labors! How small and mean our trials and sacrifices! May the spirit of the dead be with us, and infuse into our hearts something of his own deep sympathy, his hatred of injustice, his strong faith and heroic endurance. May that spirit be gladdened in its present sphere by the increased zeal and faithfulness of the friends he has left behind.

EDWARD EVERETT

A letter to Robert C. Waterston

Amesbury, 27th 1st Month, 1865.

I acknowledge through thee the invitation of the standing committee of the Massachusetts Historical Society to be present at a special meeting of the Society for the purpose of paying a tribute to the memory of our late illustrious associate, Edward Everett.

It is a matter of deep regret to me that the state of my health will not permit me to be with you on an occasion of so much interest.

It is most fitting that the members of the Historical Society of Massachusetts should add their tribute to those which have been already offered by all sects, parties, and associations to the name and fame of their late associate. He was himself a maker of history, and part and parcel of all the noble charities and humanizing influences of his State and time.

When the grave closed over him who added new lustre to the old and honored name of Quincy, all eyes instinctively turned to Edward Everett as the last of that venerated class of patriotic civilians who, outliving all dissent and jealousy and party prejudice, held their reputation by the secure tenure of the universal appreciation of its worth as a common treasure of the republic. It is not for me to pronounce his eulogy. Others, better qualified by their intimate acquaintance with him, have done and will do justice to his learning, eloquence, varied culture, and social virtues. My secluded country life has afforded me few opportunities of personal intercourse with him, while my pronounced radicalism on the great question which has divided popular feeling rendered our political paths widely divergent. Both of us early saw the danger which threatened the country. In the language of the prophet, we "saw the sword coming upon the land," but while he believed in the possibility of averting it by concession and compromise, I, on the contrary, as firmly believed that such a course could only strengthen and confirm what I regarded as a gigantic conspiracy against the rights and liberties, the union and the life, of the nation.

Recent events have certainly not tended to change this belief on my part; but in looking over the past, while I see little or nothing to retract in the matter of opinion, I am saddened by the reflection that through the very intensity of my convictions I may have done injustice to the motives of those with whom I differed. As respects Edward Everett, it seems to me that only within the last four years I have truly known him.

In that brief period, crowded as it is with a whole life-work of consecration to the union, freedom, and glory of his country, he not only commanded respect and reverence, but concentrated upon himself in a most remarkable degree the love of all loyal and generous hearts. We have seen, in these years of trial, very great sacrifices offered upon the altar of patriotism, —wealth, ease, home, love, life itself. But Edward Everett did more than this: he laid on that altar not only his time, talents, and culture, but his pride of opinion, his long-cherished views of policy, his personal and political predilections and prejudices, his constitutional fastidiousness of conservatism, and the carefully elaborated symmetry of his public reputation. With a rare and noble magnanimity, he met, without hesitation, the demand of the great occasion. Breaking away from all the besetments of custom and association, he forgot the things that are behind, and, with an eye single to present duty, pressed forward towards the mark of the high calling of Divine Providence in the events of our time. All honor to him! If we mourn that he is now beyond the reach of our poor human praise, let us reverently trust that he has received that higher plaudit: "Well done, thou good and faithful servant!"

When I last met him, as my colleague in the Electoral College of Massachusetts, his look of health and vigor seemed to promise us many years of his wisdom and usefulness. On greeting him I felt impelled to express my admiration and grateful appreciation of his patriotic labors; and I shall never forget how readily and gracefully he turned attention from himself to the great cause in which we had a common interest, and expressed his thankfulness that he had still a country to serve.

To keep green the memory of such a man is at once a privilege and a duty. That stainless life of seventy years is a priceless legacy. His hands were pure. The shadow of suspicion never fell on him. If he erred in his opinions (and that he did so he had the Christian grace and courage to own), no selfish interest weighed in the scale of his judgment against truth.

As our thoughts follow him to his last resting-place, we are sadly reminded of his own touching lines, written many years ago at Florence. The name he has left behind is none the less "pure" that instead of being "humble," as he then anticipated, it is on the lips of grateful millions, and written ineffaceable on the record of his country's trial and triumph: —

> "Yet not for me when I shall fall asleep
> Shall Santa Croce's lamps their vigils keep.
> Beyond the main in Auburn's quiet shade,
> With those I loved and love my couch be made;
> Spring's pendant branches o'er the hillock wave,
> And morning's dewdrops glisten on my grave,
> While Heaven's great arch shall rise above my bed,
> When Santa Croce's crumbles on her dead, —
> Unknown to erring or to suffering fame,
> So may I leave a pure though humble name."

Congratulating the Society on the prospect of the speedy consummation of the great objects of our associate's labors, — the peace and permanent union of our country, —

I am very truly thy friend.

LEWIS TAPPAN (1873.)

One after another, those foremost in the antislavery conflict of the last half century are rapidly passing away. The grave has just closed over all that was mortal of Salmon P. Chase, the kingliest of men, a statesman second to no other in our history, too great and pure for the Presidency, yet leaving behind him a record which any incumbent of that station might envy,—and now the telegraph brings us the tidings of the death of Lewis Tappan, of Brooklyn, so long and so honorably identified with the anti- slavery cause, and with every philanthropic and Christian enterprise. He was a native of Massachusetts, born at Northampton in 1788, of Puritan lineage,—one of a family remarkable for integrity, decision of character, and intellectual ability. At the very outset, in company with his brother Arthur, he devoted his time, talents, wealth, and social position to the righteous but unpopular cause of Emancipation, and became, in consequence, a mark for the persecution which followed such devotion. His business was crippled, his name cast out as evil, his dwelling sacked, and his furniture dragged into the street and burned. Yet he never, in the darkest hour, faltered or hesitated for a moment. He knew he was right, and that the end would justify him; one of the cheerfullest of men, he was strong where others were weak, hopeful where others despaired. He was wise in counsel, and prompt in action; like Tennyson's Sir Galahad,

> "His strength was as the strength of ten,
> Because his heart was pure."

I met him for the first time forty years ago, at the convention which formed the American Anti-Slavery Society, where I chanced to sit by him as one of the secretaries. Myself young and inexperienced, I remember how profoundly I was impressed by his cool self-possession, clearness of perception, and wonderful executive ability. Had he devoted himself to party politics with half the zeal which he manifested in behalf of those who had no votes to give and no honors to bestow, he could have reached the highest offices in the land. He chose his course, knowing all that he renounced, and he chose it wisely. He never, at least, regretted it.

And now, at the ripe age of eighty-five years, the brave old man has passed onward to the higher life, having outlived here all hatred, abuse, and misrepresentation, having seen the great work of Emancipation completed, and white men and black men equal before the law. I saw him for the last time three years ago, when he was preparing his valuable biography of his beloved brother Arthur. Age had begun to tell upon his constitution, but his intellectual force was not abated. The old, pleasant laugh and playful humor remained. He looked forward to the close of life hopefully, even cheerfully, as he called to mind the dear friends who had passed on before him, to await his coming.

Of the sixty-three signers of the Anti-Slavery Declaration at the Philadelphia Convention in 1833, probably not more than eight or ten are now living.

> "As clouds that rake the mountain summits,
> As waves that know no guiding hand,
> So swift has brother followed brother
> From sunshine to the sunless land."

Yet it is a noteworthy fact that the oldest member of that convention, David Thurston, D. D., of Maine, lived to see the slaves emancipated, and to mingle his voice of thanksgiving with the bells that rang in the day of universal freedom

BAYARD TAYLOR

Read at the memorial meeting in Tremont Temple, Boston, January 10, 1879.

I am not able to attend the memorial meeting in Tremont Temple on the 10th instant, but my heart responds to any testimonial appreciative of the intellectual achievements and the noble and manly life of Bayard Taylor. More than thirty years have intervened between my first meeting him in the fresh bloom of his youth and hope and honorable ambition, and my last parting with him under the elms of Boston Common, after our visit to Richard H. Dana, on the occasion of the ninetieth anniversary of that honored father of American poetry, still living to lament the death of his younger disciple and friend. How much he has accomplished in these years! The most industrious of men, slowly, patiently, under many disadvantages, he built up his splendid reputation. Traveller, editor, novelist, translator, diplomatist, and through all and above all poet, what he was he owed wholly to himself. His native honesty was satisfied with no half tasks. He finished as he went, and always said and did his best.

It is perhaps too early to assign him his place in American literature. His picturesque books of travel, his Oriental lyrics, his Pennsylvanian idyls, his Centennial ode, the pastoral beauty and Christian sweetness of Lars, and the high argument and rhythmic marvel of Deukalion are sureties of the permanence of his reputation. But at this moment my thoughts dwell rather upon the man than the author. The calamity of his death, felt in both hemispheres, is to me and to all who intimately knew and loved him a heavy personal loss. Under the shadow of this bereavement, in the inner circle of mourning, we sorrow most of all that we shall see his face no more, and long for "the touch of a vanished hand, and the sound of a voice that is still."

WILLIAM ELLERY CHANNING

Read at the dedication of the Channing Memorial Church at Newport, R. I.

DANVERS, MASS., 3d Mo., 13, 1880.

I scarcely need say that I yield to no one in love and reverence for the great and good man whose memory, outliving all prejudices of creed, sect, and party, is the common legacy of Christendom. As the years go on, the value of that legacy will be more and more felt; not so much, perhaps, in doctrine as in spirit, in those utterances of a devout soul which are above and beyond the affirmation or negation of dogma.

His ethical severity and Christian tenderness; his hatred of wrong and oppression, with love and pity for the wrong-doer; his noble pleas for self-culture, temperance, peace, and purity; and above all, his precept and example of unquestioning obedience to duty and the voice of God in his soul, can never become obsolete. It is very fitting that his memory should be especially cherished with that of Hopkins and Berkeley in the beautiful island to which the common residence of those worthies has lent additional charms and interest.

DEATH OF PRESIDENT GARFIELD

A letter written to W. H. B. Currier, of Amesbury, Mass.

DANVERS, MASS., 9th Mo., 24, 1881.

I regret that it is not in my power to join the citizens of Amesbury and Salisbury in the memorial services on the occasion of the death of our lamented President. But in heart and sympathy I am with you. I share the great sorrow which overshadows the land; I fully appreciate the irretrievable loss. But it seems to me that the occasion is one for thankfulness as well as grief.

Through all the stages of the solemn tragedy which has just closed with the death of our noblest and best, I have felt that the Divine Providence was overruling the mighty affliction, — that the patient sufferer at Washington was drawing with cords of sympathy all sections and parties nearer to each other. And now, when South and North, Democrat and Republican, Radical and Conservative, lift their voices in one unbroken accord of lamentation; when I see how, in spite of the greed of gain, the lust of office, the strifes and narrowness of party politics, the great heart of the nation proves sound and loyal, I feel a new hope for the republic, I have a firmer faith in its stability. It is said that no man liveth and no man dieth to himself; and the pure and noble life of Garfield, and his slow, long martyrdom, so bravely borne in view of all, are, I believe, bearing for us as a people "the peaceable fruits of righteousness." We are stronger, wiser, better, for them.

With him it is well. His mission fulfilled, he goes to his grave by the Lakeside honored and lamented as man never was before. The whole world mourns him. There is no speech nor language where the voice of his praise is not heard. About his grave gather, with heads uncovered, the vast brotherhood of man.

And with us it is well, also. We are nearer a united people than ever before. We are at peace with all; our future is full of promise; our industrial and financial condition is hopeful. God grant that, while our material interests prosper, the moral and spiritual influence of the occasion may be permanently felt; that the solemn sacrament of Sorrow, whereof we have been made partakers, may be blest to the promotion of the righteousness which exalteth a nation.

LYDIA MARIA CHILD

In 1882 a collection of the Letters of Lydia Maria Child was
published, for which I wrote the following sketch, as an
introduction:—

In presenting to the public this memorial volume, its compilers deemed that a brief biographical introduction was necessary; and as a labor of love I have not been able to refuse their request to prepare it.

Lydia Maria Francis was born in Medford, Massachusetts, February 11, 1802. Her father, Convers Francis, was a worthy and substantial citizen of that town. Her brother, Convers Francis, afterwards theological professor in Harvard College, was some years older than herself, and assisted her in her early home studies, though, with the perversity of an elder brother, he sometimes mystified her in answering her questions. Once, when she wished to know what was meant by Milton's "raven down of darkness," which was made to smile when smoothed, he explained that it was only the fur of a black cat, which sparkled when stroked! Later in life this brother wrote of her, "She has been a dear, good sister to me would that I had been half as good a brother to her." Her earliest teacher was an aged spinster, known in the village as "Marm Betty," painfully shy, and with many oddities of person and manner, the never- forgotten calamity of whose life was that Governor Brooks once saw her drinking out of the nose of her tea-kettle. Her school was in her bedroom, always untidy, and she was a constant chewer of tobacco but the children were fond of her, and Maria and ¬her father always carried her a good Sunday dinner. Thomas W. Higginson, in *Eminent Women of the Age*, mentions in this connection that, according to an established custom, on the night before Thanksgiving "all the humble friends of the Francis household—Marm Betty, the washerwoman, wood-sawyer, and journeymen, some twenty or thirty in all—were summoned to a preliminary entertainment. They there partook of an immense chicken pie, pumpkin pie made in milk- pans, and heaps of doughnuts. They feasted in the large, old-fashioned kitchen, and went away loaded with crackers and bread and pies, not forgetting 'turnovers' for the children. Such plain application of the doctrine that it is more blessed to give than receive may have done more to mould the character of Lydia Maria Child of maturer years than all the faithful labors of good Dr. Osgood, to whom she and her brother used to repeat the Assembly's catechism once a month."

Her education was limited to the public schools, with the exception of one year at a private seminary in her native town. From a note by her brother, Dr. Francis, we learn that when twelve years of age she went to Norridgewock, Maine, where her married sister resided. At Dr. Brown's, in Skowhegan, she first read *Waverley*. She was greatly excited, and exclaimed, as she laid down the book, "Why cannot I write a novel?" She remained in Norridgewock and vicinity for several years, and on her return to Massachusetts took up her abode with her brother at Watertown. He encouraged her literary tastes, and it was in his study that she commenced her first story, *Hobomok*, which she published in the twenty- first year of her age. The success it met with induced her to give to the public, soon after, *The Rebels: a Tale of the Revolution*, which was at once received into popular favor, and ran rapidly through several editions. Then followed in close succession *The Mother's Book*, running through eight American editions, twelve English, and one German, *The Girl's Book*, the *History of Women*, and the *Frugal Housewife*, of which thirty-five editions were published. Her *Juvenile Miscellany* was commenced in 1826.

It is not too much to say that half a century ago she was the most popular literary woman in the United States. She had published historical novels of unquestioned power of description and characterization, and was widely and favorably known as the editor of the *Juvenile Miscellany*, which was probably the first periodical in the English tongue devoted exclusively to children, and to which she was by far the largest contributor. Some of the tales and poems from her pen were extensively copied and greatly admired. It was at this period that the *North American Review*, the highest literary authority of the country, said of her, "We are not sure that any woman of our country could outrank Mrs. Child. This lady has been long before the public as an author with much success. And she well deserves it, for in all her works nothing can be found which does not commend itself, by its tone of healthy morality and good sense. Few female writers, if any, have done more or better things for our literature in the lighter or graver departments."

Comparatively young, she had placed herself in the front rank of American authorship. Her books and her magazine had a large circulation, and were affording her a comfortable income, at a time when the rewards of authorship were uncertain and at the best scanty.

In 1828 she married David Lee Child, Esq., a young and able lawyer, and took up her residence in Boston. In 1831-32 both became deeply interested in the subject of slavery, through the writings and personal influence of William Lloyd Garrison. Her husband, a member of the Massachusetts legislature and editor of the *Massachusetts Journal*, had, at an earlier date, denounced the project of the dismemberment of Mexico for the purpose of strengthening and extending American slavery. He was one of the earliest members of the New England Anti-Slavery Society, and his outspoken hostility to the peculiar institution greatly and unfavorably affected his interests as a lawyer. In 1832 he addressed a series of able letters on slavery and the slave-trade to Edward S. Abdy, a prominent English philanthropist. In 1836 he published in Philadelphia ten strongly written articles on the same subject. He visited England and France in 1837, and while in Paris addressed an elaborate memoir to the Societe pour l'Abolition d'Esclavage, and a paper on the same subject to the editor of the *Eclectic Review*, in London. To his facts and arguments John Quincy Adams was much indebted in the speeches which he delivered in Congress on the Texas question.

In 1833 the American Anti-Slavery Society was formed by a convention in Philadelphia. Its numbers were small, and it was everywhere spoken against. It was at this time that Lydia Maria Child startled the country by the publication of her noble *Appeal in Behalf of that Class of Americans called Africans*. It is quite impossible for any one of the present generation to imagine the popular surprise and indignation which the book called forth, or how entirely its author cut herself off from the favor and sympathy of a large number of those who had previously delighted to do her honor. Social and literary circles, which had been proud of her presence, closed their doors against her. The sale of her books, the subscriptions to her magazine, fell off to a ruinous extent. She knew all she was hazarding, and made the great sacrifice, prepared for all the consequences which followed. In the preface to her book she says, "I am fully aware of the unpopularity of the task I have undertaken; but though I expect ridicule and censure, I do not fear them. A few years hence, the opinion of the world will be a matter in which I have not even the most transient interest; but this book will be abroad on its mission of humanity long after the hand that wrote it is mingling with the dust. Should it be the means of advancing, even one single hour, the inevitable progress of truth and justice, I would not exchange the consciousness for all Rothschild's wealth or Sir Walter's fame."

Thenceforth her life was a battle; a constant rowing hard against the stream of popular prejudice and hatred. And through it all—pecuniary privation, loss of friends and position, the painfulness of being suddenly thrust from "the still air of delightful studies" into the bitterest and sternest controversy of the age—she bore herself with patience, fortitude, and unshaken reliance upon the justice and ultimate triumph of the cause she had espoused. Her pen was never idle. Wherever there was a brave word to be spoken, her voice was heard, and never without effect. It is not exaggeration to say that no man or woman at that period rendered more substantial service to the cause of freedom, or made such a "great renunciation" in doing it.

A practical philanthropist, she had the courage of her convictions, and from the first was no mere closet moralist or sentimental bewailer of the woes of humanity. She was the Samaritan stooping over the wounded Jew. She calmly and unflinchingly took her place by the side, of the despised slave and free man of color, and in word and act protested against the cruel prejudice which shut out its victims from the rights and privileges of American citizens. Her philanthropy had no taint of fanaticism; throughout the long struggle, in which she was a prominent actor, she kept her fine sense of humor, good taste, and sensibility to the beautiful in art and nature.

The opposition she met with from those who had shared her confidence
and friendship was of course keenly felt, but her kindly and genial
disposition remained unsoured. She rarely spoke of her personal
trials, and never posed as a martyr. The nearest approach to
anything like complaint is in the following lines, the date of which
I have not been able to ascertain: —

THE WORLD THAT I AM PASSING THROUGH.

Few in the days of early youth
Trusted like me in love and truth.
I've learned sad lessons from the years,
But slowly, and with many tears;
For God made me to kindly view
The world that I am passing through.

Though kindness and forbearance long
Must meet ingratitude and wrong,
I still would bless my fellow-men,
And trust them though deceived again.
God help me still to kindly view
The world that I am passing through.

From all that fate has brought to me
I strive to learn humility,
And trust in Him who rules above,
Whose universal law is love.
Thus only can I kindly view
The world that I am passing through.

When I approach the setting sun,
And feel my journey well-nigh done,
May Earth be veiled in genial light,
And her last smile to me seem bright.
Help me till then to kindly view
The world that I am passing through.

And all who tempt a trusting heart
From faith and hope to drift apart,
May they themselves be spared the pain
Of losing power to trust again.
God help us all to kindly view
The world that we are passing through.

While faithful to the great duty which she felt was laid upon her in an especial manner, she was by no means a reformer of one idea, but her interest was manifested in every question affecting the welfare of humanity. Peace, temperance, education, prison reform, and equality of civil rights, irrespective of sex, engaged her attention. Under all the disadvantages of her estrangement from popular favor, her charming Greek romance of *Philothea* and her *Lives of Madame Roland* and the *Baroness de Stael* proved that her literary ability had lost nothing of its strength, and that the hand which penned such terrible rebukes had still kept its delicate touch, and gracefully yielded to the inspiration of fancy and art. While engaged with her husband in the editorial supervision of the *Anti-Slavery Standard*, she wrote her admirable *Letters from New York*; humorous, eloquent, and picturesque, but still humanitarian in tone, which extorted the praise of even a pro-slavery community. Her great work, in three octavo volumes, *The Progress of Religious Ideas*, belongs, in part, to that period. It is an attempt to represent in a candid, unprejudiced manner the rise and progress of the great religions of the world, and their ethical relations to each other. She availed herself of, and carefully studied, the authorities at that time accessible, and the result is creditable to her scholarship, industry, and conscientiousness. If, in her desire to do justice to the religions of Buddha and Mohammed, in which she has been followed by Maurice, Max Muller, and Dean Stanley, she seems at times to dwell upon the best and overlook the darker features of those systems, her concluding reflections should vindicate her from the charge of undervaluing the Christian faith, or of lack of reverent appreciation of its founder. In the closing chapter of her work, in which the large charity and broad sympathies of her nature are manifest, she thus turns with words of love, warm from the heart, to Him whose Sermon on the Mount includes most that is good and true and vital in the religions and philosophies of the world:—

"It was reserved for Him to heal the brokenhearted, to preach a gospel to the poor, to say, 'Her sins, which are many, are forgiven, for she loved much.' Nearly two thousand years have passed away since these words of love and pity were uttered, yet when I read them my eyes fill with tears. I thank Thee, O Heavenly Father, for all the messengers thou hast sent to man; but, above all, I thank Thee for Him, thy beloved Son! Pure lily blossom of the centuries, taking root in the lowliest depths, and receiving the light and warmth of heaven in its golden heart! All that the pious have felt, all that poets have said, all that artists have done, with their manifold forms of beauty, to represent the ministry of Jesus, are but feeble expressions of the great debt we owe Him who is even now curing the lame, restoring sight to the blind, and raising the dead in that spiritual sense wherein all miracle is true."

During her stay in New York, as editor of the *Anti-Slavery Standard*, she found a pleasant home at the residence of the genial philanthropist, Isaac T. Hopper, whose remarkable life she afterwards wrote. Her portrayal of this extraordinary man, so brave, so humorous, so tender and faithful to his convictions of duty, is one of the most readable pieces of biography in English literature. Thomas Wentworth Higginson, in a discriminating paper published in 1869, speaks of her eight years' sojourn in New York as the most interesting and satisfactory period of her whole life. "She was placed where her sympathetic nature found abundant outlet and occupation. Dwelling in a house where disinterestedness and noble labor were as daily breath, she had great opportunities. There was no mere alms-giving; but sin and sorrow must be brought home to the fireside and the heart; the fugitive slave, the drunkard, the outcast woman, must be the chosen guests of the abode,— must be taken, and held, and loved into reformation or hope."

It would be a very imperfect representation of Maria Child which regarded her only from a literary point of view. She was wise in counsel; and men like Charles Sumner, Henry Wilson, Salmon P. Chase, and Governor Andrew availed themselves of her foresight and sound judgment of men and measures. Her pen was busy with correspondence, and whenever a true man or a good cause needed encouragement, she was prompt to give it. Her donations for benevolent causes and beneficent reforms were constant and liberal; and only those who knew her intimately could understand the cheerful and unintermitted self-denial which alone enabled her to make them. She did her work as far as possible out of sight, without noise or pretension. Her time, talents, and money were held not as her own, but a trust from the Eternal Father for the benefit of His suffering children. Her plain, cheap dress was glorified by the generous motive for which she wore it. Whether in the crowded city among the sin-sick and starving, or among the poor and afflicted in the neighborhood of her country home, no story of suffering and need, capable of alleviation, ever reached her without immediate sympathy and corresponding action. Lowell, one of her warmest admirers, in his *Fable for Critics* has beautifully portrayed her abounding benevolence:—

"There comes Philothea, her face all aglow:
She has just been dividing some poor creature's woe,
And can't tell which pleases her most, to relieve
His want, or his story to hear and believe.
No doubt against many deep griefs she prevails,
For her ear is the refuge of destitute tales;
She knows well that silence is sorrow's best food,
And that talking draws off from the heart its black blood."

"The pole, science tells us, the magnet controls,
But she is a magnet to emigrant Poles,
And folks with a mission that nobody knows
Throng thickly about her as bees round a rose.
She can fill up the carets in such, make their scope
Converge to some focus of rational hope,
And, with sympathies fresh as the morning, their gall
Can transmute into honey,—but this is not all;
Not only for those she has solace; O, say,
Vice's desperate nursling adrift in Broadway,
Who clingest, with all that is left of thee human,
To the last slender spar from the wreck of the woman,
Hast thou not found one shore where those tired, drooping feet
Could reach firm mother-earth, one full heart on whose beat
The soothed head in silence reposing could hear
The chimes of far childhood throb back on the ear?"

"Ah, there's many a beam from the fountain of day
That, to reach us unclouded, must pass, on its way,
Through the soul of a woman, and hers is wide ope
To the influence of Heaven as the blue eyes of Hope;
Yes, a great heart is hers, one that dares to go in
To the prison, the slave-hut, the alleys of sin,

And to bring into each, or to find there, some line
Of the never completely out-trampled divine;
If her heart at high floods swamps her brain now and then,
'T is but richer for that when the tide ebbs again,
As, after old Nile has subsided, his plain
Overflows with a second broad deluge of grain;
What a wealth would it bring to the narrow and sour,
Could they be as a Child but for one little hour!"

After leaving New York, her husband and herself took up their residence in the rural town of Wayland, Mass. Their house, plain and unpretentious, had a wide and pleasant outlook; a flower garden, carefully tended by her own hands, in front, and on the side a fruit orchard and vegetable garden, under the special care of her husband. The house was always neat, with some appearance of unostentatious decoration, evincing at once the artistic taste of the hostess and the conscientious economy which forbade its indulgence to any great extent. Her home was somewhat apart from the lines of rapid travel, and her hospitality was in a great measure confined to old and intimate friends, while her visits to the city were brief and infrequent. A friend of hers, who had ample opportunities for a full knowledge of her home-life, says, "The domestic happiness of Mr. and Mrs. Child seemed to me perfect. Their sympathies, their admiration of all things good, and their hearty hatred of all things mean and evil were in entire unison. Mr. Child shared his wife's enthusiasms, and was very proud of her. Their affection, never paraded, was always manifest. After Mr. Child's death, Mrs. Child, in speaking of the future life, said, 'I believe it would be of small value to me if I were not united to him.'"

In this connection I cannot forbear to give an extract from some reminiscences of her husband, which she left among her papers, which, better than any words of mine, will convey an idea of their simple and beautiful home-life: —

"In 1852 we made a humble home in Wayland, Mass., where we spent twenty- two pleasant years entirely alone, without any domestic, mutually serving each other, and dependent upon each other for intellectual companionship. I always depended on his richly stored mind, which was able and ready to furnish needed information on any subject. He was my walking dictionary of many languages, my Universal Encyclopaedia.

"In his old age he was as affectionate and devoted as when the lover of my youth; nay, he manifested even more tenderness. He was often singing, —

"'There's nothing half so sweet in life
As Love's old dream.'

"Very often, when he passed by me, he would lay his hand softly on my head and murmur, 'Carum caput.' . . . But what I remember with the most tender gratitude is his uniform patience and forbearance with my faults. . . . He never would see anything but the bright side of my character. He always insisted upon thinking that whatever I said was the wisest and the wittiest, and that whatever I did was the best. The simplest little jeu d'esprit of mine seemed to him wonderfully witty. Once, when he said, 'I wish for your sake, dear, I were as rich as Croesus,' I answered, 'You are Croesus, for you are king of Lydia.' How often he used to quote that!

"His mind was unclouded to the last. He had a passion for philology, and only eight hours before he passed away he was searching out the derivation of a word."

Her well-stored mind and fine conversational gifts made her company always desirable. No one who listened to her can forget the earnest eloquence with which she used to dwell upon the evidences, from history, tradition, and experience, of the superhuman and supernatural; or with what eager interest she detected in the mysteries of the old religions of the world the germs of a purer faith and a holier hope. She loved to listen, as in St. Pierre's symposium of *The Coffee-House of Surat*, to the confessions of faith of all sects and schools of philosophy, Christian and pagan, and gather from them the consoling truth that our Father has nowhere left his children without some witness of Himself. She loved the old mystics, and lingered with curious interest and sympathy over the writings of Bohme, Swedenborg, Molinos, and Woolman. Yet this marked speculative tendency seemed not in the slightest degree to affect her practical activities. Her mysticism and realism ran in close parallel lines without interfering with each other.

With strong rationalistic tendencies from education and conviction, she found herself in spiritual accord with the pious introversion of Thomas a Kempis and Madame Guion. She was fond of Christmas Eve stories, of warnings, signs, and spiritual intimations, her half belief in which sometimes seemed like credulity to her auditors. James Russell Lowell, in his tender tribute to her, playfully alludes to this characteristic:—

> *"She has such a musical taste that she 'll go*
> *Any distance to hear one who draws a long bow.*
> *She will swallow a wonder by mere might and main."*

In 1859 the descent of John Brown upon Harper's Ferry, and his capture, trial, and death, startled the nation. When the news reached her that the misguided but noble old man lay desperately wounded in prison, alone and unfriended, she wrote him a letter, under cover of one to Governor Wise, asking permission to go and nurse and care for him. The expected arrival of Captain Brown's wife made her generous offer unnecessary. The prisoner wrote her, thanking her, and asking her to help his family, a request with which she faithfully complied. With his letter came one from Governor Wise, in courteous reproval of her sympathy for John Brown. To this she responded in an able and effective manner. Her reply found its way from Virginia to the New York Tribune, and soon after Mrs. Mason, of King George's County, wife of Senator Mason, the author of the infamous Fugitive Slave Law, wrote her a vehement letter, commencing with threats of future damnation, and ending with assuring her that "no Southerner, after reading her letter to Governor Wise, ought to read a line of her composition, or touch a magazine which bore her name in its list of contributors." To this she wrote a calm, dignified reply, declining to dwell on the fierce invectives of her assailant, and wishing her well here and hereafter. She would not debate the specific merits or demerits of a man whose body was in charge of the courts, and whose reputation was sure to be in charge of posterity. "Men," she continues, "are of small consequence in comparison with principles, and the principle for which John Brown died is the question at issue between us." These letters were soon published in pamphlet form, and had the immense circulation of 300,000 copies.

In 1867 she published *A Romance of the Republic*, a story of the days of slavery; powerful in its delineation of some of the saddest as well as the most dramatic conditions of master and slave in the Southern States. Her husband, who had been long an invalid, died in 1874. After his death her home, in winter especially, became a lonely one, and in 1877 she began to spend the cold months in Boston.

Her last publication was in 1878, when her *Aspirations of the World*, a book of selections, on moral and religious subjects, from the literature of all nations and times, was given to the public. The introduction, occupying fifty pages, shows, at threescore and ten, her mental vigor unabated, and is remarkable for its wise, philosophic tone and felicity of diction. It has the broad liberality of her more elaborate work on the same subject, and in the mellow light of life's sunset her words seem touched with a tender pathos and beauty. "All we poor mortals," she says, "are groping our way through paths that are dim with shadows; and we are all striving, with steps more or less stumbling, to follow some guiding star. As we travel on, beloved companions of our pilgrimage vanish from our sight, we know not whither; and our bereaved hearts utter cries of supplication for more light. We know not where Hermes Trismegistus lived, or who he was; but his voice sounds plaintively human, coming up from the depths of the ages, calling out, 'Thou art God! and thy man crieth these things unto Thee!' Thus closely allied in our sorrows and limitations, in our aspirations and hopes, surely we ought not to be separated in our sympathies. However various the names by which we call the Heavenly Father, if they are set to music by brotherly love, they can all be sung together."

Her interest in the welfare of the emancipated class at the South and of the ill-fated Indians of the West remained unabated, and she watched with great satisfaction the experiment of the education of both classes in General Armstrong's institution at Hampton, Va. She omitted no opportunity of aiding the greatest social reform of the age, which aims to make the civil and political rights of women equal to those of men. Her sympathies, to the last, went out instinctively to the wronged and weak. She used to excuse her vehemence in this respect by laughingly quoting lines from a poem entitled *The Under Dog in the Fight*:—

> "*I know that the world, the great big world,*
>
> *Will never a moment stop*
>
> *To see which dog may be in the wrong,*
>
> *But will shout for the dog on top.*
>
> "*But for me, I never shall pause to ask*
>
> *Which dog may be in the right;*
>
> *For my heart will beat, while it beats at all,*
>
> *For the under dog in the fight.*"

I am indebted to a gentleman who was at one time a resident of Wayland, and who enjoyed her confidence and warm friendship, for the following impressions of her life in that place:—

"On one of the last beautiful Indian summer afternoons, closing the past year, I drove through Wayland, and was anew impressed with the charm of our friend's simple existence there. The tender beauty of the fading year seemed a reflection of her own gracious spirit; the lovely autumn of her life, whose golden atmosphere the frosts of sorrow and advancing age had only clarified and brightened.

"My earliest recollection of Mrs. Child in Wayland is of a gentle face leaning from the old stage window, smiling kindly down on the childish figures beneath her; and from that moment her gracious motherly presence has been closely associated with the charm of rural beauty in that village, which until very lately has been quite apart from the line of travel, and unspoiled by the rush and worry of our modern steam-car mode of living.

"Mrs. Child's life in the place made, indeed, an atmosphere of its own, a benison of peace and good-will, which was a noticeable feature to all who were acquainted with the social feeling of the little community, refined, as it was too, by the elevating influence of its distinguished pastor, Dr. Sears. Many are the acts of loving kindness and maternal care which could be chronicled of her residence there, were we permitted to do so; and numberless are the lives that have gathered their onward impulse from her helping hand. But it was all a confidence which she hardly betrayed to her inmost self, and I will not recall instances which might be her grandest eulogy. Her monument is builded in the hearts which knew her benefactions, and it will abide with 'the power that makes for righteousness.'

"One of the pleasantest elements of her life in Wayland was the high regard she won from the people of the village, who, proud of her literary attainment, valued yet more the noble womanhood of the friend who dwelt so modestly among them. The grandeur of her exalted personal character had, in part, eclipsed for them the qualities which made her fame with the world outside.

"The little house on the quiet by-road overlooked broad green meadows. The pond behind it, where bloom the lilies whose spotless purity may well symbolize her gentle spirit, is a sacred pool to her townsfolk. But perhaps the most fitting similitude of her life in Wayland was the quiet flow of the river, whose gentle curves make green her meadows, but whose powerful energy, joining the floods from distant mountains, moves, with resistless might, the busy shuttles of a hundred mills. She was too truthful to affect to welcome unwarrantable invaders of her peace, but no weary traveller on life's hard ways ever applied to her in vain. The little garden plot before her door was a sacred enclosure, not to be rudely intruded upon; but the flowers she tended with maternal care were no selfish possession, for her own enjoyment only, and many are the lives their sweetness has gladdened forever. So she lived among a singularly peaceful and intelligent community as one of themselves, industrious, wise, and happy; with a frugality whose motive of wider benevolence was in itself a homily and a benediction."

In my last interview with her, our conversation, as had often happened before, turned upon the great theme of the future life. She spoke, as I remember, calmly and not uncheerfully, but with the intense earnestness and reverent curiosity of one who felt already the shadow of the unseen world resting upon her.

Her death was sudden and quite unexpected. For some months she had been troubled with a rheumatic affection, but it was by no means regarded as serious. A friend, who visited her a few days before her departure, found her in a comfortable condition, apart from lameness. She talked of the coming election with much interest, and of her plans for the winter. On the morning of her death (October 20, 1880) she spoke of feeling remarkably well. Before leaving her chamber she complained of severe pain in the region of the heart. Help was called by her companion, but only reached her to witness her quiet passing away.

The funeral was, as befitted one like her, plain and simple. Many of her old friends were present, and Wendell Phillips paid an affecting and eloquent tribute to his old friend and anti-slavery coadjutor. He referred to the time when she accepted, with serene self-sacrifice, the obloquy which her *Appeal* had brought upon her, and noted, as one of the many ways in which popular hatred was manifested, the withdrawal from her of the privileges of the Boston Athenaeum. Her pallbearers were elderly, plain farmers in the neighborhood; and, led by the old white-haired undertaker, the procession wound its way to the not distant burial- ground, over the red and gold of fallen leaves, and tinder the half- clouded October sky. A lover of all beautiful things, she was, as her intimate friends knew, always delighted by the sight of rainbows, and used to so arrange prismatic glasses as to throw the colors on the walls of her room. Just after her body was consigned to the earth, a magnificent rainbow spanned with its are of glory the eastern sky.

> The incident at her burial is alluded to in a sonnet written by
> William P. Andrews: —

> "Freedom! she knew thy summons, and obeyed
> That clarion voice as yet scarce heard of men;
> Gladly she joined thy red-cross service when
> Honor and wealth must at thy feet be laid
> Onward with faith undaunted, undismayed
> By threat or scorn, she toiled with hand and brain
> To make thy cause triumphant, till the chain
> Lay broken, and for her the freedmen prayed.
> Nor yet she faltered; in her tender care
> She took us all; and wheresoe'er she went,
> Blessings, and Faith, and Beauty followed there,
> E'en to the end, where she lay down content;
> And with the gold light of a life more fair,
> Twin bows of promise o'er her grave were blest."

The letters in this collection constitute but a small part of her large correspondence. They have been gathered up and arranged by the hands of dear relatives and friends as a fitting memorial of one who wrote from the heart as well as the head, and who held her literary reputation subordinate always to her philanthropic aim to lessen the sum of human suffering, and to make the world better for her living. If they sometimes show the heat and impatience of a zealous reformer, they may well be pardoned in consideration of the circumstances under which they were written, and of the natural indignation of a generous nature in view of wrong and oppression. If she touched with no very reverent hand the garment hem of dogmas, and held to the spirit of Scripture rather than its letter, it must be remembered that she lived in a time when the Bible was cited in defence of slavery, as it is now in Utah in support of polygamy; and she may well be excused for some degree of impatience with those who, in the tithing of mint and anise and cummin, neglected the weightier matters of the law of justice and mercy.

Of the men and women directly associated with the beloved subject of this sketch, but few are now left to recall her single-hearted devotion to apprehended duty, her unselfish generosity, her love of all beauty and harmony, and her trustful reverence, free from pretence and cant. It is not unlikely that the surviving sharers of her love and friendship may feel the inadequateness of this brief memorial, for I close it with the consciousness of having failed to fully delineate the picture which my memory holds of a wise and brave, but tender and loving woman, of whom it might well have been said, in the words of the old Hebrew text, "Many, daughters have done virtuously, but thou excellest them all."

OLIVER WENDELL HOLMES

On the occasion of the seventy-fifth birthday of Dr. Holmes The
Critic of New York collected personal tributes from friends and
admirers of that author. My own contribution was as follows:—

Poet, essayist, novelist, humorist, scientist, ripe scholar, and wise philosopher, if Dr. Holmes does not, at the present time, hold in popular estimation the first place in American literature, his rare versatility is the cause. In view of the inimitable prose writer, we forget the poet; in our admiration of his melodious verse, we lose sight of *Elsie Venner* and *The Autocrat of the Breakfast Table.* We laugh over his wit and humor, until, to use his own words,

"We suspect the azure blossom that unfolds upon a shoot,
As if Wisdom's old potato could not flourish at its root;"

and perhaps the next page melts us into tears by a pathos only equalled by that of Sterne's sick Lieutenant. He is Montaigne and Bacon under one hat. His varied qualities would suffice for the mental furnishing of half a dozen literary specialists.

To those who have enjoyed the privilege of his intimate acquaintance, the man himself is more than the author. His genial nature, entire freedom from jealousy or envy, quick tenderness, large charity, hatred of sham, pretence, and unreality, and his reverent sense of the eternal and permanent have secured for him something more and dearer than literary renown,— the love of all who know him. I might say much more: I could not say less. May his life be long in the land.

Amesbury, Mass., 8th Month, 18, 1884.

LONGFELLOW

Written to the chairman of the committee of arrangements for unveiling the bust of Longfellow at Portland, Maine, on the poet's birthday, February 27, 1885.

I am sorry it is not in my power to accept the invitation of the committee to be present at the unveiling of the bust of Longfellow on the 27th instant, or to write anything worthy of the occasion in metrical form.

The gift of the Westminster Abbey committee cannot fail to add another strong tie of sympathy between two great English-speaking peoples. And never was gift more fitly bestowed. The city of Portland—the poet's birthplace, "beautiful for situation," looking from its hills on the scenery he loved so well, Deering's Oaks, the many-islanded bay and far inland mountains, delectable in sunset—needed this sculptured representation of her illustrious son, and may well testify her joy and gratitude at its reception, and repeat in so doing the words of the Hebrew prophet: "O man, greatly beloved! thou shalt stand in thy place."

OLD NEWBURY

Letter to Samuel J. Spalding, D. D., on the occasion of the
celebration of the 250th anniversary of the settlement of Newbury.

MY DEAR FRIEND,—I am sorry that I cannot hope to be with you on the 250th anniversary of the settlement of old Newbury. Although I can hardly call myself a son of the ancient town, my grandmother, Sarah Greenleaf, of blessed memory, was its daughter, and I may therefore claim to be its grandson. Its genial and learned historian, Joshua Coffin, was my first school-teacher, and all my life I have lived in sight of its green hills and in hearing of its Sabbath bells. Its wealth of natural beauty has not been left unsung by its own poets, Hannah Gould, Mrs. Hopkins, George Lunt, and Edward A. Washburn, while Harriet Prescott Spofford's Plum Island Sound is as sweet and musical as Tennyson's Brook. Its history and legends are familiar to me. I seem to have known all its old worthies, whose descendants have helped to people a continent, and who have carried the name and memories of their birthplace to the Mexican gulf and across the Rocky Mountains to the shores of the Pacific. They were the best and selectest of Puritanism, brave, honest, God-fearing men and women; and if their creed in the lapse of time has lost something of its vigor, the influence of their ethical righteousness still endures. The prophecy of Samuel Sewall that Christians should be found in Newbury so long as pigeons shall roost on its oaks and Indian corn grows in Oldtown fields remains still true, and we trust will always remain so. Yet, as of old, the evil personage sometimes intrudes himself into company too good for him. It was said in the witchcraft trials of 1692 that Satan baptized his converts at Newbury Falls, the scene, probably, of one of Hawthorne's weird *Twice Told Tales*; and there is a tradition that, in the midst of a heated controversy between one of Newbury's painful ministers and his deacon, who (anticipating Garrison by a century) ventured to doubt the propriety of clerical slaveholding, the Adversary made his appearance in the shape of a black giant stalking through Byfield. It was never, I believe, definitely settled whether he was drawn there by the minister's zeal in defence of slavery or the deacon's irreverent denial of the minister's right and duty to curse Canaan in the person of his negro.

Old Newbury has sometimes been spoken of as ultra-conservative and hostile to new ideas and progress, but this is not warranted by its history. More than two centuries ago, when Major Pike, just across the river, stood up and denounced in open town meeting the law against freedom of conscience and worship, and was in consequence fined and outlawed, some of Newbury's best citizens stood bravely by him. The town took no part in the witchcraft horror, and got none of its old women and town charges hanged for witches, "Goody" Morse had the spirit rappings in her house two hundred years earlier than the Fox girls did, and somewhat later a Newbury minister, in wig and knee-buckles, rode, Bible in hand, over to Hampton to lay a ghost who had materialized himself and was stamping up and down stairs in his military boots.

Newbury's ingenious citizen, Jacob Perkins, in drawing out diseases with his metallic tractors, was quite as successful as modern "faith and mind" doctors. The Quakers, whipped at Hampton on one hand and at Salem on the other, went back and forth unmolested in Newbury, for they could make no impression on its iron-clad orthodoxy. Whitefield set the example, since followed by the Salvation Army, of preaching in its streets, and now lies buried under one of its churches with almost the honors of sainthood. William Lloyd Garrison was born in Newbury. The town must be regarded as the Alpha and Omega of anti-slavery agitation, beginning with its abolition deacon and ending with Garrison. Puritanism, here as elsewhere, had a flavor of radicalism; it had its humorous side, and its ministers did not hesitate to use wit and sarcasm, like Elijah before the priests of Baal. As, for instance, the wise and learned clergyman, Puritan of the Puritans, beloved and reverenced by all, who has just laid down the burden of his nearly one hundred years, startled and shamed his brother ministers who were zealously for the enforcement of the Fugitive Slave Law, by preparing for them a form of prayer for use while engaged in catching runaway slaves.

I have, I fear, dwelt too long upon the story and tradition of the old town, which will doubtless be better told by the orator of the day. The theme is to me full of interest. Among the blessings which I would gratefully own is the fact that my lot has been cast in the beautiful valley of the Merrimac, within sight of Newbury steeples, Plum Island, and Crane Neck and Pipe Stave hills.

Let me, in closing, pay something of the debt I have owed from boyhood, by expressing a sentiment in which I trust every son of the ancient town will unite: Joshua Coffin, historian of Newbury, teacher, scholar, and antiquarian, and one of the earliest advocates of slave emancipation. May his memory be kept green, to use the words of Judge Sewall, "so long as Plum island keeps its post and a sturgeon leaps in Merrimac River."

Amesbury, 6th Month, 1885.

SCHOOLDAY REMEMBRANCES

To Rev. Charles Wingate, Hon. James H. Carleton, Thomas B. Garland,

Esq., Committee of Students of Haverhill Academy:

DEAR FRIENDS,—I was most agreeably surprised last evening by receiving your carefully prepared and beautiful Haverhill Academy Album, containing the photographs of a large number of my old friends and schoolmates. I know of nothing which could have given me more pleasure. If the faces represented are not so unlined and ruddy as those which greeted each other at the old academy, on the pleasant summer mornings so long ago, when life was before us, with its boundless horizon of possibilities, yet, as I look over them, I see that, on the whole, Time has not been hard with us, but has touched us gently. The hieroglyphics he has traced upon us may, indeed, reveal something of the cares, trials, and sorrows incident to humanity, but they also tell of generous endeavor, beneficent labor, developed character, and the slow, sure victories of patience and fortitude. I turn to them with the proud satisfaction of feeling that I have been highly favored in my early companions, and that I have not been disappointed in my school friendships. The two years spent at the academy I have always reckoned among the happiest of my life, though I have abundant reason for gratitude that, in the long, intervening years, I have been blessed beyond my deserving.

It has been our privilege to live in an eventful period, and to witness wonderful changes since we conned our lessons together. How little we then dreamed of the steam car, electric telegraph, and telephone! We studied the history and geography of a world only half-explored. Our country was an unsolved mystery. "The Great American Desert" was an awful blank on our school maps. We have since passed through the terrible ordeal of civil war, which has liberated enslaved millions, and made the union of the States an established fact, and no longer a doubtful theory. If life is to be measured not so much by years as by thoughts, emotion, knowledge, action, and its opportunity of a free exercise of all our powers and faculties, we may congratulate ourselves upon really outliving the venerable patriarchs. For myself, I would not exchange a decade of my own life for a century of the Middle Ages, or a "cycle of Cathay."

Let me, gentlemen, return my heartiest thanks to you, and to all who have interested themselves in the preparation of the Academy Album, and assure you of my sincere wishes for your health and happiness.

OAK KNOLL, DANVERS, 12th Month, 25, 1885.

EDWIN PERCY WHIPPLE

I have been pained to learn of the decease of nay friend of many years, Edwin P. Whipple. Death, however expected, is always something of a surprise, and in his case I was not prepared for it by knowing of any serious failure of his health. With the possible exception of Lowell and Matthew Arnold, he was the ablest critical essayist of his time, and the place he has left will not be readily filled.

Scarcely inferior to Macaulay in brilliance of diction and graphic portraiture, he was freer from prejudice and passion, and more loyal to the truth of fact and history. He was a thoroughly honest man. He wrote with conscience always at his elbow, and never sacrificed his real convictions for the sake of epigram and antithesis. He instinctively took the right side of the questions that came before him for decision, even when by so doing he ranked himself with the unpopular minority. He had the manliest hatred of hypocrisy and meanness; but if his language had at times the severity of justice, it was never merciless. He "set down naught in malice."

Never blind to faults, he had a quick and sympathetic eye for any real excellence or evidence of reserved strength in the author under discussion.

He was a modest man, sinking his own personality out of sight, and he always seemed to me more interested in the success of others than in his own. Many of his literary contemporaries have had reason to thank him not only for his cordial recognition and generous praise, but for the firm and yet kindly hand which pointed out deficiencies and errors of taste and judgment. As one of those who have found pleasure and profit in his writings in the past, I would gratefully commend them to the generation which survives him. His *Literature of the Age of Elizabeth* is deservedly popular, but there are none of his Essays which will not repay a careful study. "What works of Mr. Baxter shall I read?" asked Boswell of Dr. Johnson. "Read any of them," was the answer, "for they are all good."

He will have an honored place in the history of American literature. But I cannot now dwell upon his authorship while thinking of him as the beloved member of a literary circle now, alas sadly broken. I recall the wise, genial companion and faithful friend of nearly half a century, the memory of whose words and acts of kindness moistens my eyes as I write.

It is the inevitable sorrow of age that one's companions must drop away on the right hand and the left with increasing frequency, until we are compelled to ask with Wordsworth, —

"Who next shall fall and disappear?"

But in the case of him who has just passed from us, we have the satisfaction of knowing that his life-work has been well and faithfully done, and that he leaves behind him only friends.

DANVERS, 6th Month, 18, 1886.

HISTORICAL PAPERS

DANIEL O'CONNELL

In February, 1839, Henry Clay delivered a speech in the United States Senate, which was intended to smooth away the difficulties which his moderate opposition to the encroachments of slavery had erected in his path to the presidency. His calumniation of O'Connell called out the following summary of the career of the great Irish patriot. It was published originally in the Pennsylvania Freeman of Philadelphia, April 25, 1839.

Perhaps the most unlucky portion of the unlucky speech of Henry Clay on the slavery question is that in which an attempt is made to hold up to scorn and contempt the great Liberator of Ireland. We say an attempt, for who will say it has succeeded? Who feels contempt for O'Connell? Surely not the slaveholder? From Henry Clay, surrounded by his slave-gang at Ashland, to the most miserable and squalid slave-driver and small breeder of human cattle in Virginia and Maryland who can spell the name of O'Connell in his newspaper, these republican brokers in blood fear and hate the eloquent Irishman. But their contempt, forsooth! Talk of the sheep-stealer's contempt for the officer of justice who nails his ears to the pillory, or sets the branding iron on his forehead!

After denouncing the abolitionists for gratuitously republishing the advertisements for runaway slaves, the Kentucky orator says:—

"And like a notorious agitator upon another theatre, they would hunt down and proscribe from the pale of civilized society the inhabitants of that entire section. Allow me, Mr. President, to say that whilst I recognize in the justly wounded feelings of the Minister of the United States at the Court of St. James much to excuse the notice which he was provoked to take of that agitator, in my humble opinion he would better have consulted the dignity of his station and of his country in treating him with contemptuous silence. He would exclude us from European society, he who himself, can only obtain a contraband admission, and is received with scornful repugnance into it! If he be no more desirous of our society than we are of his, he may rest assured that a state of perpetual non- intercourse will exist between us. Yes, sir, I think the American Minister would best have pursued the dictates of true dignity by regarding the language of the member of the British House of Commons as the malignant ravings of the plunderer of his own country, and the libeller of a foreign and kindred people."

The recoil of this attack "followed hard upon" the tones of congratulation and triumph of partisan editors at the consummate skill and dexterity with which their candidate for the presidency had absolved himself from the suspicion of abolitionism, and by a master-stroke of policy secured the confidence of the slaveholding section of the Union. But the late Whig defeat in New York has put an end to these premature rejoicings. "The speech of Mr. Clay in reference to the Irish agitator has been made use of against us with no small success," say the New York papers. "They failed," says the Daily Evening Star, "to convince the Irish voters that Daniel O'Connell was the 'plunderer of his country,' or that there was an excuse for thus denouncing him."

The defeat of the Whigs of New York and the cause of it have excited no small degree of alarm among the adherents of the Kentucky orator. In this city, the delicate *Philadelphia Gazette* comes magnanimously to the aid of Henry Clay, —

"A tom-tit twittering on an eagle's back."

The learned editor gives it as his opinion that Daniel O'Connell is a "political beggar," a "disorganizing apostate;" talks in its pretty way of the man's "impudence" and "falsehoods" and "cowardice," etc.; and finally, with a modesty and gravity which we cannot but admire, assures us that "his weakness of mind is almost beyond calculation!"

We have heard it rumored during the past week, among some of the self- constituted organs of the Clay party in this city, that at a late meeting in Chestnut Street a committee was appointed to collect, collate, and publish the correspondence between Andrew Stevenson and O'Connell, and so much of the latter's speeches and writings as relate to American slavery, for the purpose of convincing the countrymen of O'Connell of the justice, propriety, and, in view of the aggravated circumstances of the case, moderation and forbearance of Henry Clay when speaking of a man who has had the impudence to intermeddle with the "patriarchal institutions" of our country, and with the "domestic relations" of Kentucky and Virginia slave-traders.

We wait impatiently for the fruits of the labors of this sagacious committee. We should like to see those eloquent and thrilling appeals to the sense of shame and justice and honor of America republished. We should like to see if any Irishman, not wholly recreant to the interests and welfare of the Green Island of his birth, will in consequence of this publication give his vote to the slanderer of Ireland's best and noblest champion.

But who is Daniel O'Connell? "A demagogue—a ruffian agitator!" say the Tory journals of Great Britain, quaking meantime with awe and apprehension before the tremendous moral and political power which he is wielding,—a power at this instant mightier than that of any potentate of Europe. "A blackguard"—a fellow who "obtains contraband admission into European society"—a "malignant libeller"—a "plunderer of his country"—a man whose "wind should be stopped," say the American slaveholders, and their apologists, Clay, Stevenson, Hamilton, and the Philadelphia Gazette, and the Democratic Whig Association.

But who is Daniel O'Connell? Ireland now does justice to him, the world will do so hereafter. No individual of the present age has done more for human liberty. His labors to effect the peaceable deliverance of his own oppressed countrymen, and to open to the nations of Europe a new and purer and holier pathway to freedom unstained with blood and unmoistened by tears, and his mighty instrumentality in the abolition of British colonial slavery, have left their impress upon the age. They will be remembered and felt beneficially long after the miserable slanders of Tory envy and malignity at home, and the clamors of slaveholders abroad, detected in their guilt, and writhing in the gaze of Christendom, shall have perished forever,—when the Clays and Calhouns, the Peels and Wellingtons, the opponents of reform in Great Britain and the enemies of slave emancipation in the United States, shall be numbered with those who in all ages, to use the words of the eloquent Lamartine, have "sinned against the Holy Ghost in opposing the improvement of things,—in an egotistical and stupid attempt to draw back the moral and social world which God and nature are urging forward."

The character and services of O'Connell have never been fully appreciated in this country. Engrossed in our own peculiar interests, and in the plenitude of our self-esteem; believing that "we are the people, and that wisdom will perish with us," that all patriotism and liberality of feeling are confined to our own territory, we have not followed the untitled Barrister of Derrynane Abbey, step by step, through the development of one of the noblest experiments ever made for the cause of liberty and the welfare of man.

The revolution which O'Connell has already partially effected in his native land, and which, from the evident signs of cooperation in England and Scotland, seems not far from its entire accomplishment, will form a new era in the history of the civilized world. Heretofore the patriot has relied more upon physical than moral means for the regeneration of his country and its redemption from oppression. His revolutions, however pure in principle, have ended in practical crime. The great truth was yet to be learned that brute force is incompatible with a pure love of freedom, inasmuch as it is in itself an odious species of tyranny—the relic of an age of slavery and barbarism—the common argument of despotism—a game

> "which, were their subjects wise,
>
> Kings would not play at."

But the revolution in which O'Connell is engaged, although directed against the oppression of centuries, relies with just confidence upon the united moral energies of the people: a moral victory of reason over prejudice, of justice over oppression; the triumph of intellectual energy where the brute appeal to arms had miserably failed; the vindication of man's eternal rights, not by the sword fleshed in human hearts, but by weapons tempered in the armory of Heaven with truth and mercy and love.

Nor is it a visionary idea, or the untried theory of an enthusiast, this triumphant reliance upon moral and intellectual power for the reform of political abuses, for the overthrowing of tyranny and the pulling down of the strongholds of arbitrary power. The emancipation of the Catholic of Great Britain from the thrall of a century, in 1829, prepared the way for the bloodless triumph of English reform in 1832. The Catholic Association was the germ of those political unions which compelled, by their mighty yet peaceful influence, the King of England to yield submissively to the supremacy of the people.

> (The celebrated Mr. Attwood has been called the "father of political unions." In a speech delivered by his brother, C. Attwood, Esq., at the Sunderland Reform Meeting, September 10, 1832, I find the following admission: "Gentlemen, the first political union was the Roman Catholic Association of Ireland, and the true founder and father of political unions is Daniel O'Connell.")

Both of these remarkable events, these revolutions shaking nations to their centre, yet polluted with no blood and sullied by no crime, were effected by the salutary agitations of the public mind, first set in motion by the masterspirit of O'Connell, and spreading from around him to every portion of the British empire like the undulations from the disturbed centre of a lake.

The Catholic question has been but imperfectly understood in this country. Many have allowed their just disapprobation of the Catholic religion to degenerate into a most unwarrantable prejudice against its conscientious followers. The cruel persecutions of the dissenters from the Romish Church, the massacre of St. Bartholomew's day, the horrors of the Inquisition, the crusades against the Albigenses and the simple dwellers of the Vaudois valleys, have been regarded as atrocities peculiar to the believers in papal infallibility, and the necessary consequences of their doctrines; and hence they have looked upon the constitutional agitation of the Irish Catholics for relief from grievous disabilities and unjust distinctions as a struggle merely for supremacy or power.

Strange, that the truth to which all history so strongly testifies should thus be overlooked,—the undeniable truth that religious bigotry and intolerance have been confined to no single sect; that the persecuted of one century have been the persecutors of another. In our own country, it would be well for us to remember that at the very time when in New England the Catholic, the Quaker, and the Baptist were banished on pain of death, and where some even suffered that dreadful penalty, in Catholic Maryland, under the Catholic Lord Baltimore, perfect liberty of conscience was established, and Papist and Protestant went quietly through the same streets to their respective altars.

At the commencement of O'Connell's labors for emancipation he found the people of Ireland divided into three great classes,—the Protestant or Church party, the Dissenters, and the Catholics: the Church party constituting about one tenth of the population, yet holding in possession the government and a great proportion of the landed property of Ireland, controlling church and state and law and revenue, the army, navy, magistracy, and corporations, the entire patronage of the country, holding their property and power by the favor of England, and consequently wholly devoted to her interest; the Dissenters, probably twice as numerous as the Church party, mostly engaged in trade and manufactures,—sustained by their own talents and industry, Irish in feeling, partaking in no small degree of the oppression of their Catholic brethren, and among the first to resist that oppression in 1782; the Catholics constituting at least two thirds of the whole population, and almost the entire peasantry of the country, forming a large proportion of the mercantile interest, yet nearly excluded from the possession of landed property by the tyrannous operation of the penal laws. Justly has a celebrated Irish patriot (Theobald Wolfe Tone) spoken of these laws as "an execrable and infamous code, framed with the art and malice of demons to plunder and degrade and brutalize the Catholics of Ireland. There was no disgrace, no injustice, no disqualification, moral, political, or religious, civil or military, which it has not heaped upon them."

The following facts relative to the disabilities under which the Catholics of the United Kingdom labored previous to the emancipation of 1829 will serve to show in some measure the oppressive operation of those laws which placed the foot of one tenth of the population of Ireland upon the necks of the remainder.

A Catholic peer could not sit in the House of Peers, nor a Catholic commoner in the House of Commons. A Catholic could not be Lord Chancellor, or Keeper, or Commissioner of the Great Seal; Master or Keeper of the Rolls; Justice of the King's Bench or of the Common Pleas; Baron of the Exchequer; Attorney or Solicitor General; King's Sergeant at Law; Member of the King's Council; Master in Chancery, nor Chairman of Sessions for the County of Dublin. He could not be the Recorder of a city or town; an advocate in the spiritual courts; Sheriff of a county, city, or town; Sub-Sheriff; Lord Lieutenant, Lord Deputy, or other governor of Ireland; Lord High Treasurer; Governor of a county; Privy Councillor; Postmaster General; Chancellor of the Exchequer or Secretary of State; Vice Treasurer, Cashier of the Exchequer; Keeper of the Privy Seal or Auditor General; Provost or Fellow of Dublin University; nor Lord Mayor or Alderman of a corporate city or town. He could not be a member of a parish vestry, nor bequeath any sum of money or any lands for the maintenance of a clergyman, or for the support of a chapel or a school; and in corporate towns he was excluded from the grand juries.

O'Connell commenced his labors for emancipation with the strong conviction that nothing short of the united exertions of the Irish people could overthrow the power of the existing government, and that a union of action could only be obtained by the establishment of something like equality between the different religious parties. Discarding all other than peaceful means for the accomplishment of his purpose, he placed himself and his followers beyond the cognizance of unjust and oppressive laws. Wherever he poured the oil of his eloquence upon the maddened spirits of his wronged and insulted countrymen, the mercenary soldiery found no longer an excuse for violence; and calm, firm, and united, the Catholic Association remained secure in the moral strength of its pure and peaceful purpose, amid the bayonets of a Tory administration. His influence was felt in all parts of the island. Wherever an unlawful association existed, his great legal knowledge enabled him at once to detect its character, and, by urging its dissolution, to snatch its deluded members from the ready fangs of their enemies. In his presence the Catholic and the Protestant shook hands together, and the wild Irish clansman forgot his feuds. He taught the party in power, and who trembled at the dangers around them, that security and peace could only be obtained by justice and kindness. He entreated his oppressed Catholic brethren to lay aside their weapons, and with pure hearts and naked hands to stand firmly together in the calm but determined energy of men, too humane for deeds of violence, yet too mighty for the patient endurance of wrong.

The spirit of the olden time was awakened, of the day when Flood thundered and Curran lightened; the light which shone for a moment in the darkness of Ireland's century of wrong burned upwards clearly and steadily from all its ancient altars. Shoulder to shoulder gathered around him the patriot spirits of his nation,—men unbribed by the golden spoils of governmental patronage Shiel with his ardent eloquence, O'Dwyer and Walsh, and Grattan and O'Connor, and Steel, the Protestant agitator, wearing around him the emblem of national reconciliation, of the reunion of Catholic and Protestant,—the sash of blended orange and green, soiled and defaced by his patriotic errands, stained with the smoke of cabins, and the night rains and rust of weapons, and the mountain mist, and the droppings of the wild woods of Clare. He united in one mighty and resistless mass the broken and discordant factions, whose desultory struggles against tyranny had hitherto only added strength to its fetters, and infused into that mass his own lofty principles of action, until the solemn tones of expostulation and entreaty, bursting at once from the full heart of Ireland, were caught up by England and echoed back from Scotland, and the language of justice and humanity was wrung from the reluctant lips of the cold and remorseless oppressor of his native land, at once its disgrace and glory,—the conqueror of Napoleon; and, in the words of his own Curran, the chains of the Catholic fell from around him, and he stood forth redeemed and disenthralled by the irresistible genius of Universal Emancipation.

On the passage of the bill for Catholic emancipation, O'Connell took his seat in the British Parliament. The eyes of millions were upon him. Ireland— betrayed so often by those in whom she had placed her confidence; brooding in sorrowful remembrance over the noble names and brilliant reputations sullied by treachery and corruption, the long and dark catalogue of her recreant sons, who, allured by British gold and British patronage, had sacrificed on the altar of their ambition Irish pride and Irish independence, and lifted their parricidal arms against their sorrowing mother, "crownless and voiceless in her woe"—now hung with breathless eagerness over the ordeal to which her last great champion was subjected.

The crisis in O'Connell's destiny had come.

The glitter of the golden bribe was in his eye; the sound of titled magnificence was in his ear; the choice was before him to sit high among the honorable, the titled, and the powerful, or to take his humble seat in the hall of St. Stephen's as the Irish demagogue, the agitator, the Kerry representative. He did not hesitate in his choice. On the first occasion that offered he told the story of Ireland's wrongs, and demanded justice in the name of his suffering constituents. He had put his hand to the plough of reform, and he could not relinquish his hold, for his heart was with it.

Determined to give the Whig administration no excuse for neglecting the redress of Irish grievances, he entered heart and soul into the great measure of English reform, and his zeal, tact, and eloquence contributed not a little to its success. Yet even his friends speak of his first efforts in the House of Commons as failures. The Irish accent; the harsh avowal of purposes smacking of rebellion; the eccentricities and flowery luxuriance of an eloquence nursed in the fervid atmosphere of Ireland suddenly transplanted to the cold and commonplace one of St. Stephen's; the great and illiberal prejudices against him scarcely abated from what they were when, as the member from Clare, he was mobbed on his way to London, for a time opposed a barrier to the influence of his talents and patriotism. But he triumphed at last: the mob-orator of Clare and Kerry, the declaimer in the Dublin Rooms of the Political and Trades' Union, became one of the most attractive and popular speakers of the British Parliament; one whose aid has been courted and whose rebuke has been feared by the ablest of England's representatives. Amid the sneers of derision and the clamor of hate and prejudice he has triumphed, — on that very arena so fatal to Irish eloquence and Irish fame, where even Grattan failed to sustain himself, and the impetuous spirit of Flood was stricken down.

No subject in which Ireland was not directly interested has received a greater share of O'Connell's attention than that of the abolition of colonial slavery. Utterly detesting tyranny of all kinds, he poured forth his eloquent soul in stern reprobation of a system full at once of pride and misery and oppression, and darkened with blood. His speech on the motion of Thomas Fowell Buxton for the immediate emancipation of the slaves gave a new tone to the discussion of the question. He entered into no petty pecuniary details; no miserable computation of the shillings and pence vested in beings fashioned in the image of God. He did not talk of the expediency of continuing the evil because it had grown monstrous. To use his own words, he considered "slavery a crime to be abolished; not merely an evil to be palliated." He left Sir Robert Peel and the Tories to eulogize the characters and defend the interests of the planters, in common with those of a tithe-reaping priesthood, building their houses by oppression and their chambers by wrong, and spoke of the negro's interest, the negro's claim to justice; demanding sympathy for the plundered as well as the plunderers, for the slave as well as his master. He trampled as dust under his feet the blasphemy that obedience to the law of eternal justice is a principle to be acknowledged in theory only, because unsafe in practice. He would, he said, enter into no compromise with slavery. He cared not what cast or creed or color it might assume, whether personal or political, intellectual or spiritual; he was for its total, immediate abolition. He was for justice, — justice in the name of humanity and according to the righteous law of the living God.

Ardently admiring our free institutions, and constantly pointing to our glorious political exaltation as an incentive to the perseverance of his own countrymen in their struggle against oppression, he has yet omitted no opportunity of rebuking our inexcusable slave system. An enthusiastic admirer of Jefferson, he has often regretted that his practice should have so illy accorded with his noble sentiments on the subject of slavery, which so fully coincided with his own. In truth, wherever man has been oppressed by his fellow-man, O'Connell's sympathy has been directed: to Italy, chained above the very grave of her ancient liberties; to the republics of Southern America; to Greece, dashing the foot of the indolent Ottoman from her neck; to France and Belgium; and last, not least, to Poland, driven from her cherished nationality, and dragged, like his own Ireland, bleeding and violated, to the deadly embrace of her oppressor. American slavery but shares in his common denunciation of all tyranny; its victims but partake of his common pity for the oppressed and persecuted and the trodden down.

In this hasty and imperfect sketch we cannot enter into the details of that cruel disregard of Irish rights which was manifested by a Reformed Parliament, convoked, to use the language of William IV., "to ascertain the sense of the people." It is perhaps enough to say that O'Connell's indignant refusal to receive as full justice the measure of reform meted out to Ireland was fully justified by the facts of the case. The Irish Reform Bill gave Ireland, with one third of the entire population of the United Kingdoms, only one sixth of the Parliamentary delegation. It diminished instead of increasing the number of voters; in the towns and cities it created a high and aristocratic franchise; in many boroughs it established so narrow a basis of franchise as to render them liable to corruption and abuse as the rotten boroughs of the old system. It threw no new power into the hands of the people; and with no little justice has O'Connell himself termed it an act to restore to power the Orange ascendancy in Ireland, and to enable a faction to trample with impunity on the friends of reform and constitutional freedom. (Letters to the Reformers of Great Britain, No. 1.)

In May, 1832, O'Connell commenced the publication of his celebrated *Letters to the Reformers of Great Britain*. Like Tallien, before the French convention, he "rent away the veil" which Hume and Atwood had only partially lifted. He held up before the people of Great Britain the new indignities which had been added to the long catalogue of Ireland's wrongs; he appealed to their justice, their honor, their duty, for redress, and cast down before the Whig administration the gauntlet of his country's defiance and scorn. There is a fine burst of indignant Irish feeling in the concluding paragraphs of his fourth letter:—

"I have demonstrated the contumelious injuries inflicted upon us by this Reform Bill. My letters are long before the public. They have been unrefuted, uncontradicted in any of their details. And with this case of atrocious injustice to Ireland placed before the reformers of Great Britain, what assistance, what sympathy, do we receive? Why, I have got some half dozen drivelling letters from political unions and political characters, asking me whether I advise them to petition or bestir themselves in our behalf!

"Reformers of Great Britain! I do not ask you either to petition or be silent. I do not ask you to petition or to do any other act in favor of the Irish. You will consult your own feelings of justice and generosity, unprovoked by any advice or entreaty of mine.

"For my own part, I never despaired of Ireland; I do not, I will not, I cannot, despair of my beloved country. She has, in my view, obtained freedom of conscience for others, as well as for herself. She has shaken off the incubus of tithes while silly legislation was dealing out its folly and its falsehoods. She can, and she will, obtain for herself justice and constitutional freedom; and although she may sigh at British neglect and ingratitude, there is no sound of despair in that sigh, nor any want of moral energy on her part to attain her own rights by peaceable and legal means."

The tithe system, unutterably odious and full of all injustice, had prepared the way for this expression of feeling on the part of the people. Ireland had never, in any period of her history, bowed her neck peaceably to the ecclesiastical yoke. From the Canon of Cashel, prepared by English deputies in the twelfth century, decreeing for the first time that tithes should be paid in Ireland, down to the present moment, the Church in her borders has relied solely upon the strong arm of the law, and literally reaped its tithes with the sword. The decree of the Dublin Synod, under Archbishop Comyn, in 1185, could only be enforced within the pale of the English settlement. The attempts of Henry VIII. also failed. Without the pale all endeavors to collect tithes were met by stern opposition. And although from the time of William III. the tithe system has been established in Ireland, yet at no period has it been regarded otherwise than as a system of legalized robbery by seven eighths of the people. An examination of this system cannot fail to excite our wonder, not that it has been thus regarded, but that it has been so long endured by any people on the face of the earth, least of all by Irishmen. Tithes to the amount of L1,000,000 are annually wrung from impoverished Ireland, in support of a clergy who can only number about one sixteenth of her population as their hearers; and wrung, too, in an undue proportion, from the Catholic counties. (See Dr. Doyle's Evidence before Hon. E. G. Stanley.) In the southern and middle counties, almost entirely inhabited by the Catholic peasantry, every thing they possess is subject to the tithe: the cow is seized in the hovel, the potato in the barrel, the coat even on the poor man's back. (Speech of T. Reynolds, Esq., at an anti- tithe meeting.) The revenues of five of the dignitaries of the Irish Church Establishment are as follows: the Primacy L140,000; Derry L120,000; Kilmore L100,000; Clogher L100,000; Waterford L70,000. Compare these enormous sums with that paid by Scotland for the maintenance of the Church, namely L270,000. Yet that Church has 2,000,000 souls under its care, while that of Ireland has not above 500,000. Nor are these princely livings expended in Ireland by their possessors. The bishoprics of Cloyne and Meath have been long held by absentees,—by men who know no more of their flocks than the non-resident owner of a West India plantation did of the miserable negroes, the fruits of whose thankless labor were annually transmitted to him. Out of 1289 benefited clergymen in Ireland, between five and six hundred are non-residents, spending in Bath and London, or in making the fashionable tour of the Continent, the wealth forced from the Catholic peasant and the Protestant dissenter by the bayonets of the military. Scorching and terrible was the sarcasm of Grattan applied to these locusts of the Church: "A beastly and pompous priesthood, political potentates and Christian pastors, full of false zeal, full of worldly pride, and full of gluttony, empty of the true religion, to their flocks oppressive, to their inferior clergy brutal, to their king abject, and to their God impudent and familiar,—they stand on the altar as a stepping-stone to the throne, glorying in the ear of princes, whom they poison with crooked principles and heated advice; a faction against their king when they are not his slaves,—ever the dirt under his feet or a poniard to his heart."

For the evils of absenteeism, the non-residence of the wealthy landholders, draining from a starving country the very necessaries of life, a remedy is sought in a repeal of the union, and the provisions of a domestic parliament. In O'Connell's view, a restoration of such a parliament can alone afford that adequate protection to the national industry so loudly demanded by thousands of unemployed laborers, starving amid the ruins of deserted manufactories. During the brief period of partial Irish liberty which followed the pacific revolution of '82, the manufactures of the country revived and flourished; and the smile of contented industry was visible all over the land. In 1797 there were 15,000 silk-weavers in the city of Dublin alone. There are now but 400. Such is the practical effect of the Union, of that suicidal act of the Irish Parliament which yielded up in a moment of treachery and terror the dearest interests of the country to the legislation of an English Parliament and the tender mercies of Castlereagh,—of that Castlereagh who, when accused by Grattan of spending L15,000 in purchasing votes for the Union, replied with the rare audacity of high-handed iniquity, "We did spend L15,000, and we would have spent L15,000,000 if necessary to carry the Union; "that Castlereagh who, when 707,000 Irishmen petitioned against the Union and 300,000 for it, maintained that the latter constituted the majority! Well has it been said that the deep vengeance which Ireland owed him was inflicted by the great criminal upon himself. The nation which he sold and plundered saw him make with his own hand the fearful retribution. The great body of the Irish people never assented to the Union. The following extract from a speech of Earl (then Mr.) Grey, in 1800, upon the Union question, will show what means were made use of to drag Ireland, while yet mourning over her slaughtered children, to the marriage altar with England: "If the Parliament of Ireland had been left to itself, untempted and unawed, it would without hesitation have rejected the resolutions. Out of the 300 members, 120 strenuously opposed the measure, 162 voted for it: of these, 116 were placemen; some of them were English generals on the staff, without a foot of ground in Ireland, and completely dependent on government." "Let us reflect upon the arts made use of since the last session of the Irish Parliament to pack a majority, for Union, in the House of Commons. All persons holding offices under government, if they hesitated to vote as directed, were stripped of all their employments. A bill framed for preserving the purity of Parliament was likewise abused, and no less than 63 seats were vacated by their holders having received nominal offices."

The signs of the times are most favorable to the success of the Irish Liberator. The tremendous power of the English political unions is beginning to develop itself in favor of Ireland. A deep sympathy is evinced for her sufferings, and a general determination to espouse her cause. Brute force cannot put down the peaceable and legal agitation of the question of her rights and interests. The spirit of the age forbids it. The agitation will go on, for it is spreading among men who, to use the words of the eloquent Shiel, while looking out upon the ocean, and gazing upon the shore, which Nature has guarded with so many of her bulwarks, can hear the language of Repeal muttered in the dashing of the very waves which separate them from Great Britain by a barrier of God's own creation. Another bloodless victory, we trust, awaits O'Connell,—a victory worthy of his heart and intellect, unstained by one drop of human blood, unmoistened by a solitary tear.

Ireland will be redeemed and disenthralled, not perhaps by a repeal of the Union, but by the accomplishment of such a thorough reform in the government and policy of Great Britain as shall render a repeal unnecessary and impolitic.

The sentiments of O'Connell in regard to the means of effecting his object of political reform are distinctly impressed upon all his appeals to the people. In his letter of December, 1832, to the Dublin Trades Union, he says: "The Repealers must not have our cause stained with blood. Far indeed from it. We can, and ought to, carry the repeal only in the total absence of offence against the laws of man or crime in the sight of God. The best revolution which was ever effected could not be worth one drop of human blood." In his speech at the public dinner given him by—the citizens of Cork, we find a yet more earnest avowal of pacific principles. "It may be stated," said he, "to countervail our efforts, that this struggle will involve the destruction of life and property; that it will overturn the framework of civil society, and give an undue and fearful influence to one rank to the ruin of all others. These are awful considerations, truly, if risked. I am one of those who have always believed that any political change is too dearly purchased by a single drop of blood, and who think that any political superstructure based upon other opinion is like the sand-supported fabric,—beautiful in the brief hour of sunshine, but the moment one drop of rain touches the arid basis melting away in wreck and ruin! I am an accountable being; I have a soul and a God to answer to, in another and better world, for my thoughts and actions in this. I disclaim here any act of mine which would sport with the lives of my fellow-creatures, any amelioration of our social condition which must be purchased by their blood. And here, in the face of God and of our common country, I protest that if I did not sincerely and firmly believe that the amelioration I desire could be effected without violence, without any change in the relative scale of ranks in the present social condition of Ireland, except that change which all must desire, making each better than it was before, and cementing all in one solid irresistible mass, I would at once give up the struggle which I have always kept with tyranny. I would withdraw from the contest which I have hitherto waged with those who would perpetuate our thraldom. I would not for one moment dare to venture for that which in costing one human life would cost infinitely too dear. But it will cost no such price. Have we not had within my memory two great political revolutions? And had we them not without bloodshed or violence to the social compact? Have we not arrived at a period when physical force and military power yield to moral and intellectual energy. Has not the time of 'Cedant arma togae' come for us and the other nations of the earth?"

Let us trust that the prediction of O'Connell will be verified; that reason and intellect are destined, under God, to do that for the nations of the earth which the physical force of centuries and the red sacrifice of a thousand battle-fields have failed to accomplish. Glorious beyond all others will be the day when "nation shall no more rise up against nation;" when, as a necessary consequence of the universal acknowledgment of the rights of man, it shall no longer be in the power of an individual to drag millions into strife, for the unholy gratification of personal prejudice and passion. The reformed governments of Great Britain and France, resting, as they do, upon a popular basis, are already tending to this consummation, for the people have suffered too much from the warlike ambition of their former masters not to have learned that the gains of peaceful industry are better than the wages of human butchery.

Among the great names of Ireland—alike conspicuous, yet widely dissimilar—stand Wellington and O'Connell. The one smote down the modern Alexander upon Waterloo's field of death, but the page of his reputation is dim with the tears of the widow and the orphan, and dark with the stain of blood. The other, armed only with the weapons of truth and reason, has triumphed over the oppression of centuries, and opened a peaceful pathway to the Temple of Freedom, through which its Goddess may be seen, no longer propitiated with human sacrifices, like some foul idol of the East, but clothed in Christian attributes, and smiling in the beauty of holiness upon the pure hearts and peaceful hands of its votaries. The bloodless victories of the latter have all the sublimity with none of the criminality which attaches itself to the triumphs of the former. To thunder high truths in the deafened ear of nations, to rouse the better spirit of the age, to soothe the malignant passions of. assembled and maddened men, to throw open the temple doors of justice to the abused, enslaved, and persecuted, to unravel the mysteries of guilt, and hold up the workers of iniquity in the severe light of truth stripped of their disguise and covered with the confusion of their own vileness,— these are victories more glorious than any which have ever reddened the earth with carnage:—

> "They ask a spirit of more exalted pitch,
> And courage tempered with a holier fire."

Of the more recent efforts of O'Connell we need not speak, for no one can read the English periodicals and papers without perceiving that O'Connell is, at this moment, the leading politician, the master mind of the British empire. Attempts have been made to prejudice the American mind against him by a republication on this side of the water of the false and foul slanders of his Tory enemies, in reference to what is called the "O'Connell rent," a sum placed annually in his hands by a grateful people, and which he has devoted scrupulously to the great object of Ireland's political redemption. He has acquired no riches by his political efforts his heart and soul and mind and strength have been directed to his suffering country and the cause of universal freedom. For this he has deservedly a place in the heart and affections of every son of Ireland. One million of ransomed slaves in the British dependencies will teach their children to repeat the name of O'Connell with that of Wilberforce and Clarkson. And when the stain and caste of slavery shall have passed from our own country, he will be regarded as our friend and benefactor, whose faithful rebukes and warnings and eloquent appeals to our pride of character, borne to us across the Atlantic, touched the guilty sensitiveness of the national conscience, and through shame prepared the way for repentance.

ENGLAND UNDER JAMES II

A review of the first two volumes of Macaulay's History of England
from the Accession of James II.

In accordance with the labor-saving spirit of the age, we have in these volumes an admirable example of history made easy. Had they been published in his time, they might have found favor in the eyes of the poet Gray, who declared that his ideal of happiness was "to lie on a sofa and read eternal new romances."

The style is that which lends such a charm to the author's essays, — brilliant, epigrammatic, vigorous. Indeed, herein lies the fault of the work, when viewed as a mere detail of historical facts. Its sparkling rhetoric is not the safest medium of truth to the simple-minded inquirer. A discriminating and able critic has done the author no injustice in saying that, in attempting to give effect and vividness to his thoughts and diction, he is often overstrained and extravagant, and that his epigrammatic style seems better fitted for the glitter of paradox than the sober guise of truth. The intelligent and well-informed reader of the volume before us will find himself at times compelled to reverse the decisions of the author, and deliver some unfortunate personage, sect, or class from the pillory of his rhetoric and the merciless pelting of his ridicule. There is a want of the repose and quiet which we look for in a narrative of events long passed away; we rise from the perusal of the book pleased and excited, but with not so clear a conception of the actual realities of which it treats as would be desirable. We cannot help feeling that the author has been somewhat over-scrupulous in avoiding the dulness of plain detail, and the dryness of dates, names, and statistics. The freedom, flowing diction, and sweeping generality of the reviewer and essayist are maintained throughout; and, with one remarkable exception, the *History of England* might be divided into papers of magazine length, and published, without any violence to propriety, as a continuation of the author's labors in that department of literature in which he confessedly stands without a rival, — historical review.

That exception is, however, no unimportant one. In our view, it is the crowning excellence of the first volume, — its distinctive feature and principal attraction. We refer to the third chapter of the volume, from page

260 to page 398,—the description of the condition of England at the period of the accession of James II. We know of nothing like it in the entire range of historical literature. The veil is lifted up from the England of a century and a half ago; its geographical, industrial, social, and moral condition is revealed; and, as the panorama passes before us of lonely heaths, fortified farm-houses, bands of robbers, rude country squires doling out the odds and ends of their coarse fare to clerical dependents,—rough roads, serviceable only for horseback travelling,—towns with unlighted streets, reeking with filth and offal, —and prisons, damp, loathsome, infected with disease, and swarming with vermin,—we are filled with wonder at the contrast which it presents to the England of our day. We no longer sigh for "the good old days." The most confirmed grumbler is compelled to admit that, bad as things now are, they were far worse a few generations back. Macaulay, in this elaborate and carefully prepared chapter, has done a good service to humanity in disabusing well-intentioned ignorance of the melancholy notion that the world is growing worse, and in putting to silence the cant of blind, unreasoning conservatism.

In 1685 the entire population of England our author estimates at from five millions to five millions five hundred thousand. Of the eight hundred thousand families at that period, one half had animal food twice a week. The other half ate it not at all, or at most not oftener than once a week. Wheaten, loaves were only seen at the tables of the comparatively wealthy. Rye, barley, and oats were the food of the vast majority. The average wages of workingmen was at least one half less than is paid in England for the same service at the present day. One fifth of the people were paupers, or recipients of parish relief. Clothing and bedding were scarce and dear. Education was almost unknown to the vast majority. The houses and shops were not numbered in the cities, for porters, coachmen, and errand-runners could not read. The shopkeeper distinguished his place of business by painted signs and graven images. Oxford and Cambridge Universities were little better than modern grammar and Latin school in a provincial village. The country magistrate used on the bench language too coarse, brutal, and vulgar for a modern tap-room. Fine gentlemen in London vied with each other in the lowest ribaldry and the grossest profanity. The poets of the time, from Dryden to Durfey, ministered to the popular licentiousness. The most shameless indecency polluted their pages. The theatre and the brothel were in strict unison. The Church winked at the vice which opposed itself to the austere morality or hypocrisy of Puritanism. The superior clergy, with a few noble exceptions, were self-seekers and courtiers; the inferior were idle, ignorant hangerson upon blaspheming squires and knights of the shire. The domestic chaplain, of all men living, held the most unenviable position.

"If he was permitted to dine with the family, he was expected to content himself with the plainest fare. He might fill himself with the corned beef and carrots; but as soon as the tarts and cheese-cakes made their appearance he quitted his seat, and stood aloof till he was summoned to return thanks for the repast, from a great part of which he had been excluded."

Beyond the Trent the country seems at this period to have been in a state of barbarism. The parishes kept bloodhounds for the purpose of hunting freebooters. The farm-houses were fortified and guarded. So dangerous was the country that persons about travelling thither made their wills. Judges and lawyers only ventured therein, escorted by a strong guard of armed men.

The natural resources of the island were undeveloped. The tin mines of Cornwall, which two thousand years before attracted the ships of the merchant princes of Tyre beyond the Pillars of Hercules, were indeed worked to a considerable extent; but the copper mines, which now yield annually fifteen thousand tons, were entirely neglected. Rock salt was known to exist, but was not used to any considerable extent; and only a partial supply of salt by evaporation was obtained. The coal and iron of England are at this time the stable foundations of her industrial and commercial greatness. But in 1685 the great part of the iron used was imported. Only about ten thousand tons were annually cast. Now eight hundred thousand is the average annual production. Equally great has been the increase in coal mining. "Coal," says Macaulay, "though very little used in any species of manufacture, was already the ordinary fuel in some districts which were fortunate enough to possess large beds, and in the capital, which could easily be supplied by water carriage. It seems reasonable to believe that at least one half of the quantity then extracted from the pits was consumed in London. The consumption of London seemed to the writers of that age enormous, and was often mentioned by them as a proof of the greatness of the imperial city. They scarcely hoped to be believed when they affirmed that two hundred and eighty thousand chaldrons—that is to say, about three hundred and fifty thousand tons-were, in the last year of the reign of Charles II., brought to the Thames. At present near three millions and a half of tons are required yearly by the metropolis; and the whole annual produce cannot, on the most moderate computation, be estimated at less than twenty millions of tons."

After thus passing in survey the England of our ancestors five or six generations back, the author closes his chapter with some eloquent remarks upon the progress of society. Contrasting the hardness and coarseness of the age of which he treats with the softer and more humane features of our own, he says: "Nowhere could be found that sensitive and restless compassion which has in our time extended powerful protection to the factory child, the

Hindoo widow, to the negro slave; which pries into the stores and water-casks of every emigrant ship; which winces at every lash laid on the back of a drunken soldier; which will not suffer the thief in the hulks to be ill fed or overworked; and which has repeatedly endeavored to save the life even of the murderer. The more we study the annals of the past, the more shall we rejoice that we live in a merciful age, in an age in which cruelty is abhorred, and in which pain, even when deserved, is inflicted reluctantly and from a sense of duty. Every class, doubtless, has gained largely by this great moral change; but the class which has gained most is the poorest, the most dependent, and the most defenceless."

The history itself properly commences at the close of this chapter. Opening with the deathscene of the dissolute Charles II., it presents a series of brilliant pictures of the events succeeding: The miserable fate of Oates and Dangerfield, the perjured inventors of the Popish Plot; the trial of Baxter by the infamous Jeffreys; the ill-starred attempt of the Duke of Monmouth; the battle of Sedgemoor, and the dreadful atrocities of the king's soldiers, and the horrible perversion of justice by the king's chief judge in the "Bloody Assizes;" the barbarous hunting of the Scotch Dissenters by Claverhouse; the melancholy fate of the brave and noble Duke of Argyle,—are described with graphic power unknown to Smollett or Hume. Personal portraits are sketched with a bold freedom which at times startles us. The "old familiar faces," as we have seen them through the dust of a century and a half, start before us with lifelike distinctness of outline and coloring. Some of them disappoint us; like the ghost of Hamlet's father, they come in a "questionable shape." Thus, for instance, in his sketch of William Penn, the historian takes issue with the world on his character, and labors through many pages of disingenuous innuendoes and distortion of facts to transform the saint of history into a pliant courtier.

The second volume details the follies and misfortunes, the decline and fall, of the last of the Stuarts. All the art of the author's splendid rhetoric is employed in awakening, by turns, the indignation and contempt of the reader in contemplating the character of the wrong-headed king. In portraying that character, he has brought into exercise all those powers of invective and merciless ridicule which give such a savage relish to his delineation of Barrere. To preserve the consistency of this character, he denies the king any credit for whatever was really beneficent and praiseworthy in his government. He holds up the royal delinquent in only two lights: the one representing him as a tyrant towards his people; the other as the abject slave of foreign priests,— a man at once hateful and ludicrous, of whom it is difficult to speak without an execration or a sneer.

The events which preceded the revolution of 1688; the undisguised adherence of the king to the Church of Rome; the partial toleration of the despised Quakers and Anabaptists; the gradual relaxation of the severity of the penal laws against Papists and Dissenters, preparing the way for the royal proclamation of entire liberty of conscience throughout the British realm, allowing the crop-eared Puritan and the Papist priest to build conventicles and mass houses under the very eaves of the palaces of Oxford and Canterbury; the mining and countermining of Jesuits and prelates, are detailed with impartial minuteness. The secret springs of the great movements of the time are laid bare; the mean and paltry instrumentalities are seen at work in the under world of corruption, prejudice, and falsehood. No one, save a blind, unreasoning partisan of Catholicism or Episcopacy, can contemplate this chapter in English history without a feeling of disgust. However it may have been overruled for good by that Providence which takes the wise in their own craftiness, the revolution of 1688, in itself considered, affords just as little cause for self-congratulation on the part of Protestants as the substitution of the supremacy of the crowned Bluebeard, Henry VIII., for that of the Pope, in the English Church. It had little in common with the revolution of 1642. The field of its action was the closet of selfish intrigue,—the stalls of discontented prelates,—the chambers of the wanton and adulteress,—the confessional of a weak prince, whose mind, originally narrow, had been cramped closer still by the strait-jacket of religious bigotry and superstition. The age of nobility and heroism had well-nigh passed away. The pious fervor, the self-denial, and the strict morality of the Puritanism of the days of Cromwell, and the blunt honesty and chivalrous loyalty of the Cavaliers, had both measurably given place to the corrupting influences of the licentious and infidel court of Charles II.; and to the arrogance, intolerance, and shameless self-seeking of a prelacy which, in its day of triumph and revenge, had more than justified the terrible denunciations and scathing gibes of Milton.

Both Catholic and Protestant writers have misrepresented James II. He deserves neither the execrations of the one nor the eulogies of the other. The candid historian must admit that he was, after all, a better man than his brother Charles II. He was a sincere and bigoted Catholic, and was undoubtedly honest in the declaration, which he made in that unlucky letter which Burnet ferreted out on the Continent, that he was prepared to make large steps to build up the Catholic Church in England, and, if necessary, to become a martyr in her cause. He was proud, austere, and self-willed. In the treatment of his enemies he partook of the cruel temper of his time. He was at once ascetic and sensual, alternating between the hair-shirt of penance and the embraces of Catharine Sedley. His situation was one of the most difficult and embarrassing which can be conceived of. He was at once a bigoted Papist and a Protestant pope. He hated the French domination to which his brother had submitted; yet his pride as sovereign was subordinated to his allegiance to Rome and a superstitious veneration for the wily priests with which Louis XIV. surrounded him. As the head of Anglican heretics, he was compelled to submit to conditions galling alike to the sovereign and the man. He found, on his accession, the terrible penal laws against the Papists in full force; the hangman's knife was yet warm with its ghastly butcher-work of quartering and disembowelling suspected Jesuits and victims of the lie of Titus Oates; the Tower of London had scarcely ceased to echo the groans of Catholic confessors stretched on the rack by Protestant inquisitors. He was torn by conflicting interests and spiritual and political contradictions. The prelates of the Established Church must share the responsibility of many of the worst acts of the early part of his reign. Oxford sent up its lawned deputations to mingle the voice of adulation with the groans of tortured Covenanters, and fawning ecclesiastics burned the incense of irreverent flattery under the nostrils of the Lord's anointed, while the blessed air of England was tainted by the carcasses of the ill-fated followers of Monmouth, rotting on a thousand gibbets. While Jeffreys was threatening Baxter and his Presbyterian friends with the pillory and whipping-post; while Quakers and Baptists were only spared from extermination as game preserves for the sport of clerical hunters; while the prisons were thronged with the heads of some fifteen thousand beggared families, and Dissenters of every name and degree were chased from one hiding-place to another, like David among the cliffs of Ziph and the rocks of the wild goats, — the thanksgivings and congratulations of prelacy arose in an unbroken strain of laudation from all the episcopal palaces of England. What mattered it to men, in whose hearts, to use the language of John Milton, "the sour leaven of human traditions, mixed with the poisonous dregs of hypocrisy, lay basking in the sunny warmth of wealth and promotion, hatching Antichrist," that the privileges of Englishmen and the rights secured by the great charter were violated and trodden under foot, so long as usurpation enured to their own benefit? But when King James issued his Declaration of Indulgence, and stretched his prerogative on the side of tolerance and charity, the zeal of the prelates for preserving the integrity of the British constitution and the limiting of the royal power flamed up into rebellion. They forswore themselves without scruple: the disciples of Laud, the asserters of kingly infallibility and divine right, talked of usurped power and English rights in the strain of the very schismatics whom they had persecuted to the death. There is no reason to believe that James supposed that, in issuing his declaration suspending the penal laws, he had transcended the rightful prerogative of his throne. The power which he exercised had been used by his predecessors for far less worthy purposes, and with the approbation of many of the very men who now opposed him. His ostensible object, expressed in language which even those who condemn his policy cannot but admire, was a laudable and noble one. "We trust," said he, "that it will not be vain that we have resolved to use our utmost endeavors to establish liberty of conscience on such just and equal foundations as will render it unalterable, and secure to all people the free exercise of their religion, by which future ages may reap the benefit of what is so undoubtedly the general good of the whole kingdom." Whatever may have been the motive of this declaration,—even admitting the suspicions of his enemies to have been true, that he advocated universal toleration as the only means of restoring Roman Catholics to all the rights and privileges of which the penal laws deprived them,—it would seem that there could have been no very serious objection on the part of real friends of religious toleration to the taking of him at his word and placing Englishmen of every sect on an equality before the law. The Catholics were in a very small minority, scarcely at that time as numerous as the Quakers and Anabaptists. The army, the navy, and nine tenths of the people of England were Protestants. Real danger, therefore, from a simple act of justice towards their Catholic fellow- citizens, the people of England had no ground for apprehending. But the great truth, which is even now but imperfectly recognized throughout Christendom, that religious opinions rest between man and his Maker, and not between man and the magistrate, and that the domain of conscience is sacred, was almost unknown to the statesmen and schoolmen of the seventeenth century. Milton—ultra liberal as he was— excepted the Catholics from his plan of toleration. Locke, yielding to the prejudices of the time, took the same ground. The enlightened latitudinarian ministers of the Established Church—men whose talents and Christian charity redeem in some measure the character of that Church in the day of its greatest power and basest apostasy—stopped short of universal toleration. The Presbyterians excluded Quakers, Baptists, and Papists from the pale of their charity. With the single exception of the sect of which William Penn was a conspicuous member, the idea of complete and impartial toleration was novel and unwelcome to all sects and classes of the English people. Hence it was that the very men whose liberties and estates had been secured by the declaration, and who were thereby permitted to hold their meetings in peace and quietness, used their newly acquired freedom in denouncing the king, because the same key which had opened their prison doors had also liberated the Papists and the Quakers. Baxter's severe and painful spirit could not rejoice in an act which had, indeed, restored him to personal freedom, but which had, in his view, also offended Heaven, and strengthened the powers of Antichrist by extending the same favor to Jesuits and Ranters. Bunyan disliked the Quakers next to the Papists; and it greatly lessened his satisfaction at his release from Bedford jail that it had been brought about by the influence of the former at the court of a Catholic prince. Dissenters forgot the wrongs and persecutions which they had experienced at the hands of the prelacy, and joined the bishops in opposition to the declaration. They almost magnified into Christian confessors the prelates who remonstrated against the indulgence, and actually plotted against the king for restoring them to liberty of person and conscience. The nightmare fear of Popery overcame their love of religious liberty; and they meekly offered their necks to the yoke of prelacy as the only security against the heavier one of Papist supremacy. In a far different manner the cleareyed and plain-spoken John Milton met the claims and demands of the hierarchy in his time. "They entreat us," said he, "that we be not weary of the insupportable grievances that our shoulders have hitherto cracked under; they beseech us that we think them fit to be our justices of peace, our lords, our highest officers of state. They pray us that it would please us to let them still haul us and wrong us with their bandogs and pursuivants; and that it would please the Parliament that they may yet have the whipping, fleecing, and flaying of us in their diabolical courts, to tear the flesh from our bones, and into our wide wounds, instead of balm, to pour in the oil of tartar, vitriol, and mercury. Surely a right, reasonable, innocent, and soft-hearted petition! O the relenting bowels of the fathers!"

Considering the prominent part acted by William Penn in the reign of James II., and his active and influential support of the obnoxious declaration which precipitated the revolution of 1688, it could hardly have been otherwise than that his character should suffer from the unworthy suspicions and prejudices of his contemporaries. His views of religious toleration were too far in advance of the age to be received with favor. They were of necessity misunderstood and misrepresented. All his life he had been urging them with the earnestness of one whose convictions were the result, not so much of human reason as of what he regarded as divine illumination. What the council of James yielded upon grounds of state policy he defended on those of religious obligation. He had suffered in person and estate for the exercise of his religion. He had travelled over Holland and Germany, pleading with those in authority for universal toleration and charity. On a sudden, on the accession of James, the friend of himself and his family, he found himself the most influential untitled citizen in the British realm. He had free access to the royal ear. Asking nothing for himself or his relatives, he demanded only that the good people of England should be no longer despoiled of liberty and estate for their religious opinions. James, as a Catholic, had in some sort a common interest with his dissenting subjects, and the declaration was for their common relief. Penn, conscious of the rectitude of his own motives and thoroughly convinced of the Christian duty of toleration, welcomed that declaration as the precursor of the golden age of liberty and love and good-will to men. He was not the man to distrust the motives of an act so fully in accordance with his lifelong aspirations and prayers. He was charitable to a fault: his faith in his fellow-men was often stronger than a clearer insight of their characters would have justified. He saw the errors of the king, and deplored them; he denounced Jeffreys as a butcher who had been let loose by the priests; and pitied the king, who was, he thought, swayed by evil counsels. He remonstrated against the interference of the king with Magdalen College; and reproved and rebuked the hopes and aims of the more zealous and hot-headed Catholics, advising them to be content with simple toleration. But the constitution of his mind fitted him rather for the commendation of the good than the denunciation of the bad. He had little in common with the bold and austere spirit of the Puritan reformers. He disliked their violence and harshness; while, on the other hand, he was attracted and pleased by the gentle disposition and mild counsels of Locke, and Tillotson, and the latitudinarians of the English Church. He was the intimate personal and political friend of Algernon Sydney; sympathized with his republican theories, and shared his abhorrence of tyranny, civil and ecclesiastical. He found in him a man after his own heart, — genial, generous, and loving; faithful to duty and the instincts of humanity; a true Christian gentleman. His sense of gratitude was strong, and his personal friendships sometimes clouded his judgment. In giving his support to the measures of James in behalf of liberty of conscience, it must be admitted that he acted in consistency with his principles and professions. To have taken ground against them, he must have given the lie to his declarations from his youth upward. He could not disown and deny his own favorite doctrine because it came from the lips of a Catholic king and his Jesuit advisers; and in thus rising above the prejudices of his time, and appealing to the reason and humanity of the people of England in favor of a cordial indorsement on the part of Parliament of the principles of the declaration, he believed that he was subserving the best interests of his beloved country and fulfilling the solemn obligations of religious duty. The downfall of James exposed Penn to peril and obloquy. Perjured informers endeavored to swear away his life; and, although nothing could be proved against him beyond the fact that he had steadily supported the great measure of toleration, he was compelled to live secluded in his private lodgings in London for two or three years, with a proclamation for his arrest hanging over his head. At length, the principal informer against him having been found guilty of perjury, the government warrant was withdrawn; and Lords Sidney, Rochester, and Somers, and the Duke of Buckingham, publicly bore testimony that nothing had been urged against him save by impostors, and that "they had known him, some of them, for thirty years, and had never known him to do an ill thing, but many good offices." It is a matter of regret that one professing to hold the impartial pen of history should have given the sanction of his authority to the slanderous and false imputations of such a man as Burnet, who has never been regarded as an authentic chronicler. The pantheon of history should not be lightly disturbed. A good man's character is the world's common legacy; and humanity is not so rich in models of purity and goodness as to be able to sacrifice such a reputation as that of William Penn to the point of an antithesis or the effect of a paradox.

> *Gilbert Burnet, in liberality as a politician and tolerance as a Churchman, was far in advance of his order and time. It is true that he shut out the Catholics from the pale of his charity and barely tolerated the Dissenters. The idea of entire religious liberty and equality shocked even his moderate degree of sensitiveness. He met Penn at the court of the Prince of Orange, and, after a long and fruitless effort to convince the Dissenter that the penal laws against the Catholics should be enforced, and allegiance to the Established Church continue the condition of qualification for offices of trust and honor, and that he and his friends should rest contented with simple toleration, he became irritated by the inflexible adherence of Penn to the principle of entire religious freedom. One of the most worthy sons of the Episcopal Church, Thomas Clarkson, alluding to this discussion, says "Burnet never mentioned him (Penn) afterwards but coldly or sneeringly, or in a way to lower him in the estimation of the reader, whenever he had occasion to speak of him in his History of his Own Times."*

> *He was a man of strong prejudices; he lived in the midst of revolutions, plots, and intrigues; he saw much of the worst side of human nature; and he candidly admits, in the preface to his great work, that he was inclined to think generally the worst of men and parties, and that the reader should make allowance for this inclination, although he had honestly tried to give the truth. Dr. King, of Oxford, in his Anecdotes of his Own Times, p. 185, says: "I knew Burnet: he was a furious party-man, and easily imposed upon*

by any lying spirit of his faction; but he was a better pastor than any man who is now seated on the bishops' bench." The Tory writers —Swift, Pope, Arbuthnot, and others—have undoubtedly exaggerated the defects of Burnet's narrative; while, on the other hand, his Whig commentators have excused them on the ground of his avowed and

fierce partisanship. Dr. Johnson, in his blunt way, says: "I do not believe Burnet intentionally lied; but he was so much prejudiced that he took no pains to find out the truth." On the contrary, Sir James Mackintosh, in the Edinburgh Review, speaks of the Bishop as an honest writer, seldom substantially erroneous, though often inaccurate in points of detail; and Macaulay, who has quite too closely followed him in his history, defends him as at least quite as accurate as his contemporary writers, and says that, "in his moral character, as in his intellectual, great blemishes were more than compensated by great excellences."

THE BORDER WAR OF 1708

The picturesque site of the now large village of Haverhill, on the Merrimac River, was occupied a century and a half ago by some thirty dwellings, scattered at unequal distances along the two principal roads, one of which, running parallel with the river, intersected the other, which ascended the hill northwardly and lost itself in the dark woods. The log huts of the first settlers had at that time given place to comparatively spacious and commodious habitations, framed and covered with sawed boards, and cloven clapboards, or shingles. They were, many of them, two stories in front, with the roof sloping off behind to a single one; the windows few and small, and frequently so fitted as to be opened with difficulty, and affording but a scanty supply of light and air. Two or three of the best constructed were occupied as garrisons, where, in addition to the family, small companies of soldiers were quartered. On the high grounds rising from the river stood the mansions of the well-defined aristocracy of the little settlement,—larger and more imposing, with projecting upper stories and carved cornices. On the front of one of these, over the elaborately wrought entablature of the doorway, might be seen the armorial bearings of the honored family of Saltonstall. Its hospitable door was now closed; no guests filled its spacious hall or partook of the rich delicacies of its ample larder. Death had been there; its venerable and respected occupant had just been borne by his peers in rank and station to the neighboring graveyard. Learned, affable, intrepid, a sturdy asserter of the rights and liberties of the Province, and so far in advance of his time as to refuse to yield to the terrible witchcraft delusion, vacating his seat on the bench and openly expressing his disapprobation of the violent and sanguinary proceedings of the court, wise in council and prompt in action,—not his own townsmen alone, but the people of the entire Province, had reason to mourn the loss of Nathaniel Saltonstall.

Four years before the events of which we are about to speak, the Indian allies of the French in Canada suddenly made their appearance in the westerly part of the settlement. At the close of a midwinter day six savages rushed into the open gate of a garrison-house owned by one Bradley, who appears to have been absent at the time. A sentinel, stationed in the house, discharged his musket, killing the foremost Indian, and was himself instantly shot down. The mistress of the house, a spirited young woman, was making soap in a large kettle over the fire. —She seized her ladle and dashed the boiling liquid in the faces of the assailants, scalding one of them severely, and was only captured after such a resistance as can scarcely be conceived of by the delicately framed and tenderly nurtured occupants of the places of our great- grandmothers. After plundering the house, the Indians started on their long winter march for Canada. Tradition says that some thirteen persons, probably women and children, were killed outright at the garrison. Goodwife Bradley and four others were spared as prisoners. The ground was covered with deep snow, and the captives were compelled to carry heavy burdens of their plundered household-stuffs; while for many days in succession they had no other sustenance than bits of hide, ground-nuts, the bark of trees, and the roots of wild onions, and lilies. In this situation, in the cold, wintry forest, and unattended, the unhappy young woman gave birth to a child. Its cries irritated the savages, who cruelly treated it and threatened its life. To the entreaties of the mother they replied, that they would spare it on the condition that it should be baptized after their fashion. She gave the little innocent into their hands, when with mock solemnity they made the sign of the cross upon its forehead, by gashing it with their knives, and afterwards barbarously put it to death before the eyes of its mother, seeming to regard the whole matter as an excellent piece of sport. Nothing so strongly excited the risibilities of these grim barbarians as the tears and cries of their victims, extorted by physical or mental agony. Capricious alike in their cruelties and their kindnesses, they treated some of their captives with forbearance and consideration and tormented others apparently without cause. One man, on his way to Canada, was killed because they did not like his looks, "he was so sour;" another, because he was "old and good for nothing." One of their own number, who was suffering greatly from the effects of the scalding soap, was derided and mocked as a "fool who had let a squaw whip him;" while on the other hand the energy and spirit manifested by Goodwife Bradley in her defence was a constant theme of admiration, and gained her so much respect among her captors as to protect her from personal injury or insult. On her arrival in Canada she was sold to a French farmer, by whom she was kindly treated.

In the mean time her husband made every exertion in his power to ascertain her fate, and early in the next year learned that she was a slave in Canada. He immediately set off through the wilderness on foot, accompanied only by his dog, who drew a small sled, upon which he carried some provisions for his sustenance, and a bag of snuff, which the Governor of the Province gave him as a present to the Governor of Canada. After encountering almost incredible hardships and dangers with a perseverance which shows how well he appreciated the good qualities of his stolen helpmate, he reached Montreal and betook himself to the Governor's residence. Travel-worn, ragged, and wasted with cold and hunger, he was ushered into the presence of M. Vaudreuil. The courtly Frenchman civilly received the gift of the bag of snuff, listened to the poor fellow's story, and put him in a way to redeem his wife without difficulty. The joy of the latter on seeing her husband in the strange land of her captivity may well be imagined. They returned by water, landing at Boston early in the summer.

There is a tradition that this was not the goodwife's first experience of Indian captivity. The late Dr. Abiel Abbott, in his manuscript of Judith Whiting's *Recollections of the Indian Wars*, states that she had previously been a prisoner, probably before her marriage. After her return she lived quietly at the garrison-house until the summer of the next year. One bright moonlit-night a party of Indians were seen silently and cautiously approaching. The only occupants of the garrison at that time were Bradley, his wife and children, and a servant. The three adults armed themselves with muskets, and prepared to defend themselves. Goodwife Bradley, supposing the Indians had come with the intention of again capturing her, encouraged her husband to fight to the last, declaring that she had rather die on her own hearth than fall into their hands. The Indians rushed upon the garrison, and assailed the thick oaken door, which they forced partly open, when a well-aimed shot from Goodwife Bradley laid the foremost dead on the threshold. The loss of their leader so disheartened them that they made a hasty retreat.

The year 1707 passed away without any attack upon the exposed frontier settlement. A feeling of comparative security succeeded to the almost sleepless anxiety and terror of the inhabitants; and they were beginning to congratulate each other upon the termination of their long and bitter trials. But the end was not yet.

Early in the spring of 1708, the principal tribes of Indians in alliance with the French held a great council, and agreed to furnish three hundred warriors for an expedition to the English frontier.

They were joined by one hundred French Canadians and several volunteers, consisting of officers of the French army, and younger sons of the nobility, adventurous and unscrupulous. The Sieur de Chaillons, and Hertel de Rouville, distinguished as a partisan in former expeditions, cruel and unsparing as his Indian allies, commanded the French troops; the Indians, marshalled under their several chiefs, obeyed the general orders of La Perriere. A Catholic priest accompanied them. De Ronville, with the French troops and a portion of the Indians, took the route by the River St. Francois about the middle of summer. La Perriere, with the French Mohawks, crossed Lake Champlain. The place of rendezvous was Lake Nickisipigue. On the way a Huron accidentally killed one of his companions; whereupon the tribe insisted on halting and holding a council. It was gravely decided that this accident was an evil omen, and that the expedition would prove disastrous; and, in spite of the endeavors of the French officers, the whole band deserted. Next the Mohawks became dissatisfied, and refused to proceed. To the entreaties and promises of their French allies they replied that an infectious disease had broken out among them, and that, if they remained, it would spread through the whole army. The French partisans were not deceived by a falsehood so transparent; but they were in no condition to enforce obedience; and, with bitter execrations and reproaches, they saw the Mohawks turn back on their warpath. The diminished army pressed on to Nickisipigue, in the expectation of meeting, agreeably to their promise, the Norridgewock and Penobscot Indians. They found the place deserted, and, after waiting for some days, were forced to the conclusion that the Eastern tribes had broken their pledge of cooperation. Under these circumstances a council was held; and the original design of the expedition, namely, the destruction of the whole line of frontier towns, beginning with Portsmouth, was abandoned. They had still a sufficient force for the surprise of a single settlement; and Haverhill, on the Merrimac, was selected for conquest.

In the mean time, intelligence of the expedition, greatly exaggerated in point of numbers and object, had reached Boston, and Governor Dudley had despatched troops to the more exposed out posts of the Provinces of Massachusetts and New Hampshire. Forty men, under the command of Major Turner and Captains Price and Gardner, were stationed at Haverhill in the different garrison-houses. At first a good degree of vigilance was manifested; but, as days and weeks passed without any alarm, the inhabitants relapsed into their old habits; and some even began to believe that the rumored descent of the Indians was only a pretext for quartering upon them two-score of lazy, rollicking soldiers, who certainly seemed more expert in making love to their daughters, and drinking their best ale and cider, than in patrolling the woods or putting the garrisons into a defensible state. The grain and hay harvest ended without disturbance; the men worked in their fields, and the women pursued their household avocations, without any very serious apprehension of danger.

Among the inhabitants of the village was an eccentric, ne'er-do-well fellow, named Keezar, who led a wandering, unsettled life, oscillating, like a crazy pendulum, between Haverhill and Amesbury. He had a smattering of a variety of trades, was a famous wrestler, and for a mug of ale would leap over an ox-cart with the unspilled beverage in his hand. On one occasion, when at supper, his wife complained that she had no tin dishes; and, as there were none to be obtained nearer than Boston, he started on foot in the evening, travelled through the woods to the city, and returned with his ware by sunrise the next morning, passing over a distance of between sixty and seventy miles. The tradition of his strange habits, feats of strength, and wicked practical jokes is still common in his native town. On the morning of the 29th of the eighth month he was engaged in taking home his horse, which, according to his custom, he had turned into his neighbor's rich clover field the evening previous. By the gray light of dawn he saw a long file of men marching silently towards the town. He hurried back to the village and gave the alarm by firing a gun. Previous to this, however, a young man belonging to a neighboring town, who had been spending the night with a young woman of the village, had met the advance of the war-party, and, turning back in extreme terror and confusion, thought only of the safety of his betrothed, and passed silently through a considerable part of the village to her dwelling. After he had effectually concealed her he ran out to give the alarm. But it was too late. Keezar's gun was answered by the terrific yells, whistling, and whooping of the Indians. House after house was assailed and captured. Men, women, and children were massacred. The minister of the town was killed by a shot through his door. Two of his children were saved by the courage and sagacity of his negro slave Hagar. She carried them into the cellar and covered them with tubs, and then crouched behind a barrel of meat just in time to escape the vigilant eyes of the enemy, who entered the cellar and plundered it. She saw them pass and repass the tubs under which the children lay and take meat from the very barrel which concealed herself. Three soldiers were quartered in the house; but they made no defence, and were killed while begging for quarter.

The wife of Thomas Hartshorne, after her husband and three sons had fallen, took her younger children into the cellar, leaving an infant on a bed in the garret, fearful that its cries would betray her place of concealment if she took it with her. The Indians entered the garret and tossed the child out of the window upon a pile of clapboards, where it was afterwards found stunned and insensible. It recovered, nevertheless, and became a man of remarkable strength and stature; and it used to be a standing joke with his friends that he had been stinted by the Indians when they threw him out of the window. Goodwife Swan, armed with a long spit, successfully defended her door against two Indians. While the massacre went on, the priest who accompanied the expedition, with some of the French officers, went into the meeting-house, the walls of which were afterwards found written over with chalk. At sunrise, Major Turner, with a portion of his soldiers, entered the village; and the enemy made a rapid retreat, carrying with them seventeen, prisoners. They were pursued and overtaken just as they were entering the woods; and a severe skirmish took place, in which the rescue of some of the prisoners was effected. Thirty of the enemy were left dead on the field, including the infamous Hertel de Rouville. On the part of the villagers, Captains Ayer and Wainwright and Lieutenant Johnson, with thirteen others, were killed. The intense heat of the weather made it necessary to bury the dead on the same day. They were laid side by side in a long trench in the burial- ground. The body of the venerated and lamented minister, with those of his wife and child, sleep in another part of the burial-ground, where may still be seen a rude monument with its almost llegible inscription:—

"Clauditur hoc tumulo corpus Reverendi pii doctique viri D. Benjamin Rolfe, ecclesiae Christi quae est in Haverhill pastoris fidelissimi; qui domi suae ab hostibus barbare trucidatus. A laboribus suis requievit mane diei sacrae quietis, Aug. XXIX, anno Dom. MDCCVIII. AEtatis suae XLVI."

Of the prisoners taken, some escaped during the skirmish, and two or three were sent back by the French officers, with a message to the English soldiers, that, if they pursued the party on their retreat to Canada, the other prisoners should be put to death. One of them, a soldier stationed in Captain Wainwright's garrison, on his return four years after, published an account of his captivity. He was compelled to carry a heavy pack, and was led by an Indian by a cord round his neck. The whole party suffered terribly from hunger. On reaching Canada the Indians shaved one side of his head, and greased the other, and painted his face. At a fort nine miles from Montreal a council was held in order to decide his fate; and he had the unenviable privilege of listening to a protracted discussion upon the expediency of burning him. The fire was already kindled, and the poor fellow was preparing to meet his doom with firmness, when it was announced to him that his life was spared. This result of the council by no means satisfied the women and boys, who had anticipated rare sport in the roasting of a white man and a heretic. One squaw assailed him with a knife and cut off one of his fingers; another beat him with a pole. The Indians spent the night in dancing and singing, compelling their prisoner to go round the ring with them. In the morning one of their orators made a long speech to him, and formally delivered him over to an old squaw, who took him to her wigwam and treated him kindly. Two or three of the young women who were carried away captive married Frenchmen in Canada and never returned. Instances of this kind were by no means rare during the Indian wars. The simple manners, gayety, and social habits of the French colonists among whom the captives were dispersed seem to have been peculiarly fascinating to the daughters of the grave and severe Puritans.

At the beginning of the present century, Judith Whiting was the solitary survivor of all who witnessed the inroad of the French and Indians in 1708. She was eight years of age at the time of the attack, and her memory of it to the last was distinct and vivid. Upon her old brain, from whence a great portion of the records of the intervening years had been obliterated, that terrible picture, traced with fire and blood, retained its sharp outlines and baleful colors.

THE GREAT IPSWICH FRIGHT

"The Frere into the dark gazed forth;
The sounds went onward towards the north
The murmur of tongues, the tramp and tread
Of a mighty army to battle led."
BALLAD OF THE CID.

Life's tragedy and comedy are never far apart. The ludicrous and the sublime, the grotesque and the pathetic, jostle each other on the stage; the jester, with his cap and bells, struts alongside of the hero; the lord mayor's pageant loses itself in the mob around Punch and Judy; the pomp and circumstance of war become mirth-provoking in a militia muster; and the majesty of the law is ridiculous in the mock dignity of a justice's court. The laughing philosopher of old looked on one side of life and his weeping contemporary on the other; but he who has an eye to both must often experience that contrariety of feeling which Sterne compares to "the contest in the moist eyelids of an April morning, whether to laugh or cry."

The circumstance we are about to relate, may serve as an illustration of the way in which the woof of comedy interweaves with the warp of tragedy. It occurred in the early stages of the American Revolution, and is part and parcel of its history in the northeastern section of Massachusetts.

About midway between Salem and the ancient town of Newburyport, the traveller on the Eastern Railroad sees on the right, between him and the sea, a tall church-spire, rising above a semicircle of brown roofs and venerable elms; to which a long scalloping range of hills, sweeping off to the seaside, forms a green background. This is Ipswich, the ancient Agawam; one of those steady, conservative villages, of which a few are still left in New England, wherein a contemporary of Cotton Mather and Governor Endicott, were he permitted to revisit the scenes of his painful probation, would scarcely feel himself a stranger. Law and Gospel, embodied in an orthodox steeple and a court-house, occupy the steep, rocky eminence in its midst; below runs the small river under its picturesque stone bridge; and beyond is the famous female seminary, where Andover theological students are wont to take unto themselves wives of the daughters of the Puritans. An air of comfort and quiet broods over the whole town. Yellow moss clings to the seaward sides of the roofs; one's eyes are not endangered by the intense glare of painted shingles and clapboards. The smoke of hospitable kitchens curls up through the overshadowing elms from huge-throated chimneys, whose hearth-stones have been worn by the feet of many generations. The tavern was once renowned throughout New England, and it is still a creditable hostelry. During court time it is crowded with jocose lawyers, anxious clients, sleepy jurors, and miscellaneous hangers on; disinterested gentlemen, who have no particular business of their own in court, but who regularly attend its sessions, weighing evidence, deciding upon the merits of a lawyer's plea or a judge's charge, getting up extempore trials upon the piazza or in the bar-room of cases still involved in the glorious uncertainty of the law in the court-house, proffering gratuitous legal advice to irascible plaintiffs and desponding defendants, and in various other ways seeing that the Commonwealth receives no detriment. In the autumn old sportsmen make the tavern their headquarters while scouring the marshes for sea-birds; and slim young gentlemen from the city return thither with empty game-bags, as guiltless in respect to the snipes and wagtails as Winkle was in the matter of the rooks, after his shooting excursion at Dingle Dell. Twice, nay, three times, a year, since third parties have been in fashion, the delegates of the political churches assemble in Ipswich to pass patriotic resolutions, and designate the candidates whom the good people of Essex County, with implicit faith in the wisdom of the selection, are expected to vote for. For the rest there are pleasant walks and drives around the picturesque village. The people are noted for their hospitality; in summer the sea-wind blows cool over its healthy hills, and, take it for all in all, there is not a better preserved or pleasanter specimen of a Puritan town remaining in the ancient Commonwealth.

The 21st of April, 1775, witnessed an awful commotion in the little village of Ipswich. Old men, and boys, (the middle-aged had marched to Lexington some days before) and all the women in the place who were not bedridden or sick, came rushing as with one accord to the green in front of the meeting-house. A rumor, which no one attempted to trace or authenticate, spread from lip to lip that the British regulars had landed on the coast and were marching upon the town. A scene of indescribable terror and confusion followed. Defence was out of the question, as the young and able-bodied men of the entire region round about had marched to Cambridge and Lexington. The news of the battle at the latter place, exaggerated in all its details, had been just received; terrible stories of the atrocities committed by the dreaded "regulars" had been related; and it was believed that nothing short of a general extermination of the patriots—men, women, and children—was contemplated by the British commander.—

Almost simultaneously the people of Beverly, a village a few miles distant, were smitten with the same terror. How the rumor was communicated no one could tell. It was there believed that the enemy had fallen upon Ipswich, and massacred the inhabitants without regard to age or sex.

It was about the middle of the afternoon of this day that the people of Newbury, ten miles farther north, assembled in an informal meeting, at the town-house to hear accounts from the Lexington fight, and to consider what action was necessary in consequence of that event. Parson Carey was about opening the meeting with prayer when hurried hoof-beats sounded up the street, and a messenger, loose-haired and panting for breath, rushed up the staircase. "Turn out, turn out, for God's sake," he cried, "or you will be all killed! The regulars are marching onus; they are at Ipswich now, cutting and slashing all before them!" Universal consternation was the immediate result of this fearful announcement; Parson Carey's prayer died on his lips; the congregation dispersed over the town, carrying to every house the tidings that the regulars had come. Men on horseback went galloping up and down the streets, shouting the alarm. Women and children echoed it from every corner. The panic became irresistible, uncontrollable. Cries were heard that the dreaded invaders had reached Oldtown Bridge, a little distance from the village, and that they were killing all whom they encountered. Flight was resolved upon. All the horses and vehicles in the town were put in requisition; men, women, and children hurried as for life towards the north. Some threw their silver and pewter ware and other valuables into wells. Large numbers crossed the Merrimac, and spent the night in the deserted houses of Salisbury, whose inhabitants, stricken by the strange terror, had fled into New Hampshire, to take up their lodgings in dwellings also abandoned by their owners. A few individuals refused to fly with the multitude; some, unable to move by reason of sickness, were left behind by their relatives. One old gentleman, whose excessive corpulence rendered retreat on his part impossible, made a virtue of necessity; and, seating himself in his doorway with his loaded king's arm, upbraided his more nimble neighbors, advising them to do as he did, and "stop and shoot the devils." Many ludicrous instances of the intensity of the terror might be related. One man got his family into a boat to go to Ram Island for safety. He imagined he was pursued by the enemy through the dusk of the evening, and was annoyed by the crying of an infant in the after part of the boat. "Do throw that squalling brat overboard," he called to his wife, "or we shall be all discovered and killed!" A poor woman ran four or five miles up the river, and stopped to take breath and nurse her child, when she found to her great horror that she had brought off the cat instead of the baby!

All through that memorable night the terror swept onward towards the north with a speed which seems almost miraculous, producing everywhere the same results. At midnight a horseman, clad only in shirt and breeches, dashed by our grandfather's door, in Haverhill, twenty miles up the river. "Turn out! Get a musket! Turn out!" he shouted; "the regulars are landing on Plum Island!" "I'm glad of it," responded the old gentleman from his chamber window; "I wish they were all there, and obliged to stay there." When it is understood that Plum Island is little more than a naked sand-ridge, the benevolence of this wish can be readily appreciated.

All the boats on the river were constantly employed for several hours in conveying across the terrified fugitives. Through "the dead waste and middle of the night" they fled over the border into New Hampshire. Some feared to take the frequented roads, and wandered over wooded hills and through swamps where the snows of the late winter had scarcely melted. They heard the tramp and outcry of those behind them, and fancied that the sounds were made by pursuing enemies. Fast as they fled, the terror, by some unaccountable means, outstripped them. They found houses deserted and streets strewn with household stuffs, abandoned in the hurry of escape. Towards morning, however, the tide partially turned. Grown men began to feel ashamed of their fears. The old Anglo-Saxon hardihood paused and looked the terror in its face. Single or in small parties, armed with such weapons as they found at hand, — among which long poles, sharpened and charred at the end, were conspicuous, — they began to retrace their steps. In the mean time such of the good people of Ipswich as were unable or unwilling to leave their homes became convinced that the terrible rumor which had nearly depopulated their settlement was unfounded.

Among those who had there awaited the onslaught of the regulars was a young man from Exeter, New Hampshire. Becoming satisfied that the whole matter was a delusion, he mounted his horse and followed after the retreating multitude, undeceiving all whom he overtook. Late at night he reached Newburyport, greatly to the relief of its sleepless inhabitants, and hurried across the river, proclaiming as he rode the welcome tidings. The sun rose upon haggard and jaded fugitives, worn with excitement and fatigue, slowly returning homeward, their satisfaction at the absence of danger somewhat moderated by an unpleasant consciousness of the ludicrous scenes of their premature night flitting.

Any inference which might be drawn from the foregoing narrative derogatory to the character of the people of New England at that day, on the score of courage, would be essentially erroneous. It is true, they were not the men to court danger or rashly throw away their lives for the mere glory of the sacrifice. They had always a prudent and wholesome regard to their own comfort and safety; they justly looked upon sound heads and limbs as better than broken ones; life was to them too serious and important, and their hard-gained property too valuable, to be lightly hazarded. They never attempted to cheat themselves by under-estimating the difficulty to be encountered, or shutting their eyes to its probable consequences. Cautious, wary, schooled in the subtle strategy of Indian warfare, where self-preservation is by no means a secondary object, they had little in common with the reckless enthusiasm of their French allies, or the stolid indifference of the fighting machines of the British regular army. When danger could no longer be avoided, they met it with firmness and iron endurance, but with a very vivid appreciation of its magnitude. Indeed, it must be admitted by all who are familiar with the history of our fathers that the element of fear held an important place among their characteristics. It exaggerated all the dangers of their earthly pilgrimage, and peopled the future with shapes of evil. Their fear of Satan invested him with some of the attributes of Omnipotence, and almost reached the point of reverence. The slightest shock of an earthquake filled all hearts with terror. Stout men trembled by their hearths with dread of some paralytic old woman supposed to be a witch. And when they believed themselves called upon to grapple with these terrors and endure the afflictions of their allotment, they brought to the trial a capability of suffering undiminished by the chloroform of modern philosophy. They were heroic in endurance. Panics like the one we have described might bow and sway them like reeds in the wind; but they stood up like the oaks of their own forests beneath the thunder and the hail of actual calamity.

It was certainly lucky for the good people of Essex County that no wicked wag of a Tory undertook to immortalize in rhyme their ridiculous hegira, as Judge Hopkinson did the famous Battle of the Kegs in Philadelphia. Like the more recent Madawaska war in Maine, the great Chepatchet demonstration in Rhode Island, and the "Sauk fuss" of Wisconsin, it remains to this day "unsyllabled, unsung;" and the fast-fading memory of age alone preserves the unwritten history of the great Ipswich fright.

POPE NIGHT

"Lay up the fagots neat and trim;
Pile 'em up higher;
Set 'em afire!
The Pope roasts us, and we 'll roast him!"
Old Song.

The recent attempt of the Romish Church to reestablish its hierarchy in Great Britain, with the new cardinal, Dr. Wiseman, at its head, seems to have revived an old popular custom, a grim piece of Protestant sport, which, since the days of Lord George Gordon and the "No Popery" mob, had very generally fallen into disuse. On the 5th of the eleventh month of this present year all England was traversed by processions and lighted up with bonfires, in commemoration of the detection of the "gunpowder plot" of Guy Fawkes and the Papists in 1605. Popes, bishops, and cardinals, in straw and pasteboard, were paraded through the streets and burned amid the shouts of the populace, a great portion of whom would have doubtless been quite as ready to do the same pleasant little office for the Bishop of Exeter or his Grace of Canterbury, if they could have carted about and burned in effigy a Protestant hierarchy as safely as a Catholic one.

In this country, where every sect takes its own way, undisturbed by legal restrictions, each ecclesiastical tub balancing itself as it best may on its own bottom, and where bishops Catholic and bishops Episcopal, bishops Methodist and bishops Mormon, jostle each other in our thoroughfares, it is not to be expected that we should trouble ourselves with the matter at issue between the rival hierarchies on the other side of the water. It is a very pretty quarrel, however, and good must come out of it, as it cannot fail to attract popular attention to the shallowness of the spiritual pretensions of both parties, and lead to the conclusion that a hierarchy of any sort has very little in common with the fishermen and tent-makers of the New Testament.

Pope Night—the anniversary of the discovery of the Papal incendiary Guy Fawkes, booted and spurred, ready to touch fire to his powder-train under the Parliament House—was celebrated by the early settlers of New England, and doubtless afforded a good deal of relief to the younger plants of grace in the Puritan vineyard. In those solemn old days, the recurrence of the powder-plot anniversary, with its processions, hideous images of the Pope and Guy Fawkes, its liberal potations of strong waters, and its blazing bonfires reddening the wild November hills, must have been looked forward to with no slight degree of pleasure. For one night, at least, the cramped and smothered fun and mischief of the younger generation were permitted to revel in the wild extravagance of a Roman saturnalia or the Christmas holidays of a slave plantation. Bigotry—frowning upon the May-pole, with its flower wreaths and sportive revellers, and counting the steps of the dancers as so many steps towards perdition—recognized in the grim farce of Guy Fawkes's anniversary something of its own lineaments, smiled complacently upon the riotous young actors, and opened its close purse to furnish tar-barrels to roast the Pope, and strong water to moisten the throats of his noisy judges and executioners.

Up to the time of the Revolution the powder plot was duly commemorated throughout New England. At that period the celebration of it was discountenanced, and in many places prohibited, on the ground that it was insulting to our Catholic allies from France. In Coffin's History of Newbury it is stated that, in 1774, the town authorities of Newburyport ordered "that no effigies be carried about or exhibited only in the daytime." The last public celebration in that town was in the following year. Long before the close of the last century the exhibitions of Pope Night had entirely ceased throughout the country, with, as far as we can learn, a solitary exception. The stranger who chances to be travelling on the road between Newburyport and Haverhill, on the night of the 5th of November, may well fancy that an invasion is threatened from the sea, or that an insurrection is going on inland; for from all the high hills overlooking the river tall fires are seen blazing redly against the cold, dark, autumnal sky, surrounded by groups of young men and boys busily engaged in urging them with fresh fuel into intenser activity. To feed these bonfires, everything combustible which could be begged or stolen from the neighboring villages, farm-houses, and fences is put in requisition. Old tar-tubs, purloined from the shipbuilders of the river-side, and flour and lard barrels from the village-traders, are stored away for days, and perhaps weeks, in the woods or in the rain- gullies of the hills, in preparation for Pope Night. From the earliest settlement of the towns of Amesbury and Salisbury, the night of the powder plot has been thus celebrated, with unbroken regularity, down to the present time. The event which it once commemorated is probably now unknown to most of the juvenile actors. The symbol lives on from generation to generation after the significance is lost; and we have seen the children of our Catholic neighbors as busy as their Protestant playmates in collecting, "by hook or by crook," the materials for Pope- Night bonfires. We remember, on one occasion, walking out with a gifted and learned Catholic friend to witness the fine effect of the illumination on the hills, and his hearty appreciation of its picturesque and wild beauty,—the busy groups in the strong relief of the fires, and the play and corruscation of the changeful lights on the bare, brown hills, naked trees, and autumn clouds.

In addition to the bonfires on the hills, there was formerly a procession in the streets, bearing grotesque images of the Pope, his cardinals and friars; and behind them Satan himself, a monster with huge ox-horns on his head, and a long tail, brandishing his pitchfork and goading them onward. The Pope was generally furnished with a movable head, which could be turned round, thrown back, or made to bow, like that of a china- ware mandarin. An aged inhabitant of the neighborhood has furnished us with some fragments of the songs sung on such occasions, probably the same which our British ancestors trolled forth around their bonfires two centuries ago:—

"The fifth of November,
As you well remember,
Was gunpowder treason and plot;
And where is the reason
That gunpowder treason
Should ever be forgot?"

"When James the First the sceptre swayed,
This hellish powder plot was laid;
They placed the powder down below,
All for Old England's overthrow.
Lucky the man, and happy the day,
That caught Guy Fawkes in the middle of his play!"

"Hark! our bell goes jink, jink, jink;
Pray, madam, pray, sir, give us something to drink;
Pray, madam, pray, sir, if you'll something give,
We'll burn the dog, and not let him live.
We'll burn the dog without his head,
And then you'll say the dog is dead."

"Look here! from Rome The Pope has come,
That fiery serpent dire;
Here's the Pope that we have got,
The old promoter of the plot;
We'll stick a pitchfork in his back,
And throw him in the fire!"

There is a slight savor of a Smithfield roasting about these lines, such as regaled the senses of the Virgin Queen or Bloody Mary, which entirely reconciles us to their disuse at the present time.

It should be the fervent prayer of all good men that the evil spirit of religious hatred and intolerance, which on the one hand prompted the gunpowder plot, and which on the other has ever since made it the occasion of reproach and persecution of an entire sect of professing Christians, may be no longer perpetuated. In the matter of exclusiveness and intolerance, none of the older sects can safely reproach each other; and it becomes all to hope and labor for the coming of that day when the hymns of Cowper and the Confessions of Augustine, the humane philosophy of Channing and the devout meditations of Thomas a Kempis, the simple essays of Woolman and the glowing periods of Bossuet, shall be regarded as the offspring of one spirit and one faith,—lights of a common altar, and precious stones in the temple of the one universal Church.

THE BOY CAPTIVES. AN INCIDENT
OF THE INDIAN WAR OF 1695

The township of Haverhill, even as late as the close of the seventeenth century, was a frontier settlement, occupying an advanced position in the great wilderness, which, unbroken by the clearing of a white man, extended from the Merrimac River to the French villages on the St. Francois. A tract of twelve miles on the river and three or four northwardly was occupied by scattered settlers, while in the centre of the town a compact village had grown up. In the immediate vicinity there were but few Indians, and these generally peaceful and inoffensive. On the breaking out of the Narragansett war, the inhabitants had erected fortifications and taken other measures for defence; but, with the possible exception of one man who was found slain in the woods in 1676, none of the inhabitants were molested; and it was not until about the year 1689 that the safety of the settlement was seriously threatened. Three persons were killed in that year. In 1690 six garrisons were established in different parts of the town, with a small company of soldiers attached to each. Two of these houses are still standing. They were built of brick, two stories high, with a single outside door, so small and narrow that but one person could enter at a time; the windows few, and only about two and a half feet long by eighteen inches with thick diamond glass secured with lead, and crossed inside with bars of iron. The basement had but two rooms, and the chamber was entered by a ladder instead of stairs; so that the inmates, if driven thither, could cut off communication with the rooms below. Many private houses were strengthened and fortified. We remember one familiar to our boyhood, — a venerable old building of wood, with brick between the weather boards and ceiling, with a massive balustrade over the door, constructed of oak timber and plank, with holes through the latter for firing upon assailants. The door opened upon a stone-paved hall, or entry, leading into the huge single room of the basement, which was lighted by two small windows, the ceiling black with the smoke of a century and a half; a huge fireplace, calculated for eight-feet wood, occupying one entire side; while, overhead, suspended from the timbers, or on shelves fastened to them, were household stores, farming utensils, fishing-rods, guns, bunches of herbs gathered perhaps a century ago, strings of dried apples and pumpkins, links of mottled sausages, spareribs, and flitches of bacon; the firelight of an evening dimly revealing the checked woollen coverlet of the bed in one far-off corner, while in another "the pewter plates on the dresser Caught and reflected the flame as shields of armies the sunshine."

Tradition has preserved many incidents of life in the garrisons. In times of unusual peril the settlers generally resorted at night to the fortified houses, taking thither their flocks and herds and such household valuables as were most likely to strike the fancy or minister to the comfort or vanity of the heathen marauders. False alarms were frequent. The smoke of a distant fire, the bark of a dog in the deep woods, a stump or bush taking in the uncertain light of stars and moon the appearance of a man, were sufficient to spread alarm through the entire settlement, and to cause the armed men of the garrison to pass whole nights in sleepless watching. It is said that at Haselton's garrison-house the sentinel on duty saw, as he thought, an Indian inside of the paling which surrounded the building, and apparently seeking to gain an entrance. He promptly raised his musket and fired at the intruder, alarming thereby the entire garrison. The women and children left their beds, and the men seized their guns and commenced firing on the suspicious object; but it seemed to bear a charmed life, and remained unharmed. As the morning dawned, however, the mystery was solved by the discovery of a black quilted petticoat hanging on the clothes-line, completely riddled with balls.

As a matter of course, under circumstances of perpetual alarm and frequent peril, the duty of cultivating their fields, and gathering their harvests, and working at their mechanical avocations was dangerous and difficult to the settlers. One instance will serve as an illustration. At the garrison-house of Thomas Dustin, the husband of the far-famed Mary Dustin, (who, while a captive of the Indians, and maddened by the murder of her infant child, killed and scalped, with the assistance of a young boy, the entire band of her captors, ten in number,) the business of brick-making was carried on. The pits where the clay was found were only a few rods from the house; yet no man ventured to bring the clay to the yard within the enclosure without the attendance of a file of soldiers. An anecdote relating to this garrison has been handed down to the present tune. Among its inmates were two young cousins, Joseph and Mary Whittaker; the latter a merry, handsome girl, relieving the tedium of garrison duty with her light-hearted mirthfulness, and

> "Making a sunshine in that shady place."

Joseph, in the intervals of his labors in the double capacity of brick-maker and man-at-arms, was assiduous in his attentions to his fair cousin, who was not inclined to encourage him. Growing desperate, he threatened one evening to throw himself into the garrison well. His threat only called forth the laughter of his mistress; and, bidding her farewell, he proceeded to put it in execution. On reaching the well he stumbled over a log; whereupon, animated by a happy idea, he dropped the wood into the water instead of himself, and, hiding behind the curb, awaited the result. Mary, who had been listening at the door, and who had not believed her lover capable of so rash an act, heard the sudden plunge of the wooden Joseph. She ran to the well, and, leaning over the curb and peering down the dark opening, cried out, in tones of anguish and remorse, "O Joseph, if you're in the land of the living, I 'll have you!" "I'll take ye at your word," answered Joseph, springing up from his hiding-place, and avenging himself for her coyness and coldness by a hearty embrace.

Our own paternal ancestor, owing to religious scruples in the matter of taking arms even for defence of life and property, refused to leave his undefended house and enter the garrison. The Indians frequently came to his house; and the family more than once in the night heard them whispering under the windows, and saw them put their copper faces to the glass to take a view of the apartments. Strange as it may seen, they never offered any injury or insult to the inmates.

In 1695 the township was many times molested by Indians, and several persons were killed and wounded. Early in the fall a small party made their appearance in the northerly part of the town, where, finding two boys at work in an open field, they managed to surprise and capture them, and, without committing further violence, retreated through the woods to their homes on the shore of Lake Winnipesaukee. Isaac Bradley, aged fifteen, was a small but active and vigorous boy; his companion in captivity, Joseph Whittaker, was only eleven, yet quite as large in size, and heavier in his movements. After a hard and painful journey they arrived at the lake, and were placed in an Indian family, consisting of a man and squaw and two or three children. Here they soon acquired a sufficient knowledge of the Indian tongue to enable them to learn from the conversation carried on in their presence that it was designed to take them to Canada in the spring. This discovery was a painful one. Canada, the land of Papist priests and bloody Indians, was the especial terror of the New England settlers, and the anathema maranatha of Puritan pulpits. Thither the Indians usually hurried their captives, where they compelled them to work in their villages or sold them to the French planters. Escape from thence through a deep wilderness, and across lakes and mountains and almost impassable rivers, without food or guide, was regarded as an impossibility. The poor boys, terrified by the prospect of being carried still farther from their home and friends, began to dream of escaping from their masters before they started for Canada. It was now winter; it would have been little short of madness to have chosen for flight that season of bitter cold and deep snows. Owing to exposure and want of proper food and clothing, Isaac, the eldest of the boys, was seized with a violent fever, from which he slowly recovered in the course of the winter. His Indian mistress was as kind to him as her circumstances permitted,—procuring medicinal herbs and roots for her patient, and tenderly watching over him in the long winter nights. Spring came at length; the snows melted; and the ice was broken up on the lake. The Indians began to make preparations for journeying to Canada; and Isaac, who had during his sickness devised a plan of escape, saw that the time of putting it in execution had come. On the evening before he was to make the attempt he for the first time informed his younger companion of his design, and told him, if he intended to accompany him, he must be awake at the time appointed. The boys lay down as usual in the wigwam, in the midst of the family. Joseph soon fell asleep; but Isaac, fully sensible of the danger and difficulty of the enterprise before him, lay awake, watchful for his opportunity. About midnight he rose, cautiously stepping over the sleeping forms of the family, and securing, as he went, his Indian master's flint, steel, and tinder, and a small quantity of dry moose-meat and cornbread. He then carefully awakened his companion, who, starting up, forgetful of the cause of his disturbance, asked aloud, "What do you want?" The savages began to stir; and Isaac, trembling with fear of detection, lay down again and pretended to be asleep. After waiting a while he again rose, satisfied, from the heavy breathing of the Indians, that they were all sleeping; and fearing to awaken Joseph a second time, lest he should again hazard all by his thoughtlessness, he crept softly out of the wigwam. He had proceeded but a few rods when he heard footsteps behind him; and, supposing himself pursued, he hurried into the woods, casting a glance backward. What was his joy to see his young companion running after him! They hastened on in a southerly direction as nearly as they could determine, hoping to reach their distant home. When daylight appeared they found a large hollow log, into which they crept for concealment, wisely judging that they would be hotly pursued by their Indian captors.

Their sagacity was by no means at fault. The Indians, missing their prisoners in the morning, started off in pursuit with their dogs. As the young boys lay in the log they could hear the whistle of the Indians and the barking of dogs upon their track. It was a trying moment; and even the stout heart of the elder boy sank within him as the dogs came up to the log and set up a loud bark of discovery. But his presence of mind saved him. He spoke in a low tone to the dogs, who, recognizing his familiar voice, wagged their tails with delight and ceased barking. He then threw to them the morsel of moose-meat he had taken from the wigwam. While the dogs were thus diverted the Indians made their appearance. The boys heard the light, stealthy sound of their moccasins on the leaves. They passed close to the log; and the dogs, having devoured their moose- meat, trotted after their masters. Through a crevice in the log the boys looked after them and saw them disappear in the thick woods. They remained in their covert until night, when they started again on their long journey, taking a new route to avoid the Indians. At daybreak they again concealed themselves, but travelled the next night and day without resting. By this time they had consumed all the bread which they had taken, and were fainting from hunger and weariness. Just at the close of the third day they were providentially enabled to kill a pigeon and a small tortoise, a part of which they ate raw, not daring to make a fire, which might attract the watchful eyes of savages. On the sixth day they struck upon an old Indian path, and, following it until night, came suddenly upon a camp of the enemy. Deep in the heart of the forest, under the shelter of a ridge of land heavily timbered, a great fire of logs and brushwood was burning; and around it the Indians sat, eating their moose-meat and smoking their pipes.

The poor fugitives, starving, weary, and chilled by the cold spring blasts, gazed down upon the ample fire; and the savory meats which the squaws were cooking by it, but felt no temptation to purchase warmth and food by surrendering themselves to captivity. Death in the forest seemed preferable. They turned and fled back upon their track, expecting every moment to hear the yells of pursuers. The morning found them seated on the bank of a small stream, their feet torn and bleeding, and their bodies emaciated. The elder, as a last effort, made search for roots, and fortunately discovered a few ground-nuts, (glicine apios) which served to refresh in some degree himself and his still weaker companion. As they stood together by the stream, hesitating and almost despairing, it occurred to Isaac that the rivulet might lead to a larger stream of water, and that to the sea and the white settlements near it; and he resolved to follow it. They again began their painful march; the day passed, and the night once more overtook them. When the eighth morning dawned, the younger of the boys found himself unable to rise from his bed of leaves. Isaac endeavored to encourage him, dug roots, and procured water for him; but the poor lad was utterly exhausted. He had no longer heart or hope. The elder boy laid him on leaves and dry grass at the foot of a tree, and with a heavy heart bade him farewell. Alone he slowly and painfully proceeded down the stream, now greatly increased in size by tributary rivulets. On the top of a hill, he climbed with difficulty into a tree, and saw in the distance what seemed to be a clearing and a newly raised frame building. Hopeful and rejoicing, he turned back to his young companion, told him what he had seen, and, after chafing his limbs awhile, got him upon his feet. Sometimes supporting him, and at others carrying him on his back, the heroic boy staggered towards the clearing. On reaching it he found it deserted, and was obliged to continue his journey. Towards night signs of civilization began to appear,—the heavy, continuous roar of water was heard; and, presently emerging from the forest, he saw a great river dashing in white foam down precipitous rocks, and on its bank the gray walls of a huge stone building, with flankers, palisades, and moat, over which the British flag was flying. This was the famous Saco Fort, built by Governor Phips two years before, just below the falls of the Saco River. The soldiers of the garrison gave the poor fellows a kindly welcome. Joseph, who was scarcely alive, lay for a long time sick in the fort; but Isaac soon regained his strength, and set out for his home in Haverhill, which he had the good fortune to arrive at in safety.

Amidst the stirring excitements of the present day, when every thrill of the electric wire conveys a new subject for thought or action to a generation as eager as the ancient Athenians for some new thing, simple legends of the past like that which we have transcribed have undoubtedly lost in a great degree their interest. The lore of the fireside is becoming obsolete, and with the octogenarian few who still linger among us will perish the unwritten history of border life in New England.

THE BLACK MEN IN THE REVOLUTION AND WAR OF 1812

The return of the festival of our national independence has called our attention to a matter which has been very carefully kept out of sight by orators and toast-drinkers. We allude to the participation of colored men in the great struggle for American freedom. It is not in accordance with our taste or our principles to eulogize the shedders of blood even in a cause of acknowledged justice; but when we see a whole nation doing honor to the memories of one class of its defenders to the total neglect of another class, who had the misfortune to be of darker complexion, we cannot forego the satisfaction of inviting notice to certain historical facts which for the last half century have been quietly elbowed aside, as no more deserving of a place in patriotic recollection than the descendants of the men to whom the facts in question relate have to a place in a Fourth of July procession.

Of the services and sufferings of the colored soldiers of the Revolution no attempt has, to our knowledge, been made to preserve a record. They have had no historian. With here and there an exception, they have all passed away; and only some faint tradition of their campaigns under Washington and Greene and Lafayette, and of their cruisings under Decatur and Barry, lingers among their, descendants. Yet enough is known to show that the free colored men of the United States bore their full proportion of the sacrifices and trials of the Revolutionary War.

The late Governor Eustis, of Massachusetts,—the pride and boast of the democracy of the East, himself an active participant in the war, and therefore a most competent witness,—Governor Morrill, of New Hampshire, Judge Hemphill, of Pennsylvania, and other members of Congress, in the debate on the question of admitting Missouri as a slave State into the Union, bore emphatic testimony to the efficiency and heroism of the black troops. Hon. Calvin Goddard, of Connecticut, states that in the little circle of his residence he was instrumental in securing, under the act of 1818, the pensions of nineteen colored soldiers. "I cannot," he says, "refrain from mentioning one aged black man, Primus Babcock, who proudly presented to me an honorable discharge from service during the war, dated at the close of it, wholly in the handwriting of George Washington; nor can I forget the expression of his feelings when informed, after his discharge had been sent to the War Department, that it could not be returned. At his request it was written for, as he seemed inclined to spurn the pension and reclaim the discharge." There is a touching anecdote related of Baron Stenben on the occasion of the disbandment of the American army. A black soldier, with his wounds unhealed, utterly destitute, stood on the wharf just as a vessel bound for his distant home was getting under way. The poor fellow gazed at the vessel with tears in his eyes, and gave himself up to despair. The warm-hearted foreigner witnessed his emotion, and, inquiring into the cause of it, took his last dollar from his purse and gave it to him, with tears of sympathy trickling down his cheeks. Overwhelmed with gratitude, the poor wounded soldier hailed the sloop and was received on board. As it moved out from the wharf, he cried back to his noble friend on shore, "God Almighty bless you, Master Baron!"

"In Rhode Island," says Governor Eustis in his able speech against slavery in Missouri, 12th of twelfth month, 1820, "the blacks formed an entire regiment, and they discharged their duty with zeal and fidelity. The gallant defence of Red Bank, in which the black regiment bore a part, is among the proofs of their valor." In this contest it will be recollected that four hundred men met and repulsed, after a terrible and sanguinary struggle, fifteen hundred Hessian troops, headed by Count Donop. The glory of the defence of Red Bank, which has been pronounced one of the most heroic actions of the war, belongs in reality to black men; yet who now hears them spoken of in connection with it? Among the traits which distinguished the black regiment was devotion to their officers. In the attack made upon the American lines near Croton River on the 13th of the fifth month, 1781, Colonel Greene, the commander of the regiment, was cut down and mortally wounded; but the sabres of the enemy only reached him through the bodies of his faithful guard of blacks, who hovered over him to protect him, every one of whom was killed. The late Dr. Harris, of Dunbarton, New Hampshire, a Revolutionary veteran, stated, in a speech at Francistown, New Hampshire, some years ago, that on one occasion the regiment to which he was attached was commanded to defend an important position, which the enemy thrice assailed, and from which they were as often repulsed. "There was," said the venerable speaker, "a regiment of blacks in the same situation,—a regiment of negroes fighting for our liberty and independence, not a white man among them but the officers,—in the same dangerous and responsible position. Had they been unfaithful or given way before the enemy, all would have been lost. Three times in succession were they attacked with most desperate fury by well- disciplined and veteran troops; and three times did they successfully repel the assault, and thus preserve an army. They fought thus through the war. They were brave and hardy troops."

In the debate in the New York Convention of 1821 for amending the Constitution of the State, on the question of extending the right of suffrage to the blacks, Dr. Clarke, the delegate from Delaware County, and other members, made honorable mention of the services of the colored troops in the Revolutionary army.

The late James Forten, of Philadelphia, well known as a colored man of wealth, intelligence, and philanthropy, enlisted in the American navy under Captain Decatur, of the Royal Louis, was taken prisoner during his second cruise, and, with nineteen other colored men, confined on board the horrible Jersey prison-ship; All the vessels in the American service at that period were partly manned by blacks. The old citizens of Philadelphia to this day remember the fact that, when the troops of the North marched through the city, one or more colored companies were attached to nearly all the regiments.

Governor Eustis, in the speech before quoted, states that the free colored soldiers entered the ranks with the whites. The time of those who were slaves was purchased of their masters, and they were induced to enter the service in consequence of a law of Congress by which, on condition of their serving in the ranks during the war, they were made freemen. This hope of liberty inspired them with courage to oppose their breasts to the Hessian bayonet at Red Bank, and enabled them to endure with fortitude the cold and famine of Valley Forge. The anecdote of the slave of General Sullivan, of New Hampshire, is well known. When his master told him that they were on the point of starting for the army, to fight for liberty, he shrewdly suggested that it would be a great satisfaction to know that he was indeed going to fight for his liberty. Struck with the reasonableness and justice of this suggestion, General Sullivan at once gave him his freedom.

The late Tristam Burgess, of Rhode Island, in a speech in Congress, first month, 1828, said "At the commencement of the Revolutionary War, Rhode Island had a number of slaves. A regiment of them were enlisted into the Continental service, and no braver men met the enemy in battle; but not one of them was permitted to be a soldier until he had first been made a freeman."

The celebrated Charles Pinckney, of South Carolina, in his speech on the Missouri question, and in defence of the slave representation of the South, made the following admissions:—

"They (the colored people) were in numerous instances the pioneers, and in all the laborers, of our armies. To their hands were owing the greatest part of the fortifications raised for the protection of the country. Fort Moultrie gave, at an early period of the inexperienced and untried valor of our citizens, immortality to the American arms; and in the Northern States numerous bodies of them were enrolled, and fought side by side with the whites at the battles of the Revolution."

Let us now look forward thirty or forty years, to the last war with Great Britain, and see whether the whites enjoyed a monopoly of patriotism at that time.

Martindale, of New York, in Congress, 22d of first month, 1828, said: "Slaves, or negroes who had been slaves, were enlisted as soldiers in the war of the Revolution; and I myself saw a battalion of them, as fine, martial-looking men as I ever saw, attached to the Northern army in the last war, on its march from Plattsburg to Sackett's Harbor."

Hon. Charles Miner, of Pennsylvania, in Congress, second month, 7th, 1828, said: "The African race make excellent soldiers. Large numbers of them were with Perry, and helped to gain the brilliant victory of Lake Erie. A whole battalion of them were distinguished for their orderly appearance."

Dr. Clarke, in the convention which revised the Constitution of New York in 1821, speaking of the colored inhabitants of the State, said:—

"In your late war they contributed largely towards some of your most splendid victories. On Lakes Erie and Champlain, where your fleets triumphed over a foe superior in numbers and engines of death, they were manned in a large proportion with men of color. And in this very house, in the fall of 1814, a bill passed, receiving the approbation of all the branches of your government, authorizing the governor to accept the services of a corps of two thousand free people of color. Sir, these were times which tried men's souls. In these times it was no sporting matter to bear arms. These were times when a man who shouldered his musket did not know but he bared his bosom to receive a death-wound from the enemy ere he laid it aside; and in these times these people were found as ready and as willing to volunteer in your service as any other. They were not compelled to go; they were not drafted. No; your pride had placed them beyond your compulsory power. But there was no necessity for its exercise; they were volunteers,—yes, sir, volunteers to defend that very country from the inroads and ravages of a ruthless and vindictive foe which had treated them with insult, degradation, and slavery."

On the capture of Washington by the British forces, it was judged expedient to fortify, without delay, the principal towns and cities exposed to similar attacks. The Vigilance Committee of Philadelphia waited upon three of the principal colored citizens, namely, James Forten, Bishop Allen, and Absalom Jones, soliciting the aid of the people of color in erecting suitable defences for the city. Accordingly, twenty-five hundred colored then assembled in the State-House yard, and from thence marched to Gray's Ferry, where they labored for two days almost without intermission. Their labors were so faithful and efficient that a vote of thanks was tendered them by the committee. A battalion of colored troops was at the same time organized in the city under an officer of the United States army; and they were on the point of marching to the frontier when peace was proclaimed.

General Jackson's proclamations to the free colored inhabitants of Louisiana are well known. In his first, inviting them to take up arms, he said:—

"As sons of freedom, you are now called on to defend our most inestimable blessings. As Americans, your country looks with confidence to her adopted children for a valorous support. As fathers, husbands, and brothers, you are summoned to rally round the standard of the eagle, to defend all which is dear in existence."

The second proclamation is one of the highest compliments ever paid by a military chief to his soldiers:—

"TO THE FREE PEOPLE OF COLOR.

"Soldiers! when on the banks of the Mobile I called you to take up arms, inviting you to partake the perils and glory of your white fellow- citizens, I expected much from you; for I was not ignorant that you possessed qualities most formidable to an invading enemy. I knew with what fortitude you could endure hunger, and thirst, and all the fatigues of a campaign. I knew well how you loved your native country, and that you, as well as ourselves, had to defend what man holds most dear,—his parents, wife, children, and property. You have done more than I expected. In addition to the previous qualities I before knew you to possess, I found among you a noble enthusiasm, which leads to the performance of great things.

"Soldiers! the President of the United States shall hear how praiseworthy was your conduct in the hour of danger, and the Representatives of the American people will give you the praise your exploits entitle you to. Your general anticipates them in applauding your noble ardor."

It will thus be seen that whatever honor belongs to the "heroes of the Revolution" and the volunteers in "the second war for independence" is to be divided between the white and the colored man. We have dwelt upon this subject at length, not because it accords with our principles or feelings, for it is scarcely necessary for us to say that we are one of those who hold that

> "Peace hath her victories
>
> No less renowned than war,"

and certainly far more desirable and useful; but because, in popular estimation, the patriotism which dares and does on the battle-field takes a higher place than the quiet exercise of the duties of peaceful citizenship; and we are willing that colored soldiers, with their descendants, should have the benefit, if possible, of a public sentiment which has so extravagantly lauded their white companions in arms. If pulpits must be desecrated by eulogies of the patriotism of bloodshed, we see no reason why black defenders of their country in the war for liberty should not receive honorable mention as well as white invaders of a neighboring republic who have volunteered in a war for plunder and slavery extension. For the latter class of "heroes" we have very little respect. The patriotism of too many of them forcibly reminds us of Dr. Johnson's definition of that much-abused term "Patriotism, sir! 'T is the last refuge of a scoundrel."

"What right, I demand," said an American orator some years ago, "have the children of Africa to a homestead in the white man's country?" The answer will in part be found in the facts which we have presented. Their right, like that of their white fellow-citizens, dates back to the dread arbitrament of battle. Their bones whiten every stricken field of the Revolution; their feet tracked with blood the snows of Jersey; their toil built up every fortification south of the Potomac; they shared the famine and nakedness of Valley Forge and the pestilential horrors of the old Jersey prisonship. Have they, then, no claim to an equal participation in the blessings which have grown out of the national independence for which they fought? Is it just, is it magnanimous, is it safe, even, to starve the patriotism of such a people, to cast their hearts out of the treasury of the Republic, and to convert them, by political disfranchisement and social oppression, into enemies?

THE SCOTTISH REFORMERS

"The mills of God grind slowly, but they grind exceeding small;
Though with patience He stands waiting, with exactness grinds He
all."

FRIEDRICH VON LOGAU.

The great impulse of the French Revolution was not confined by geographical boundaries. Flashing hope into the dark places of the earth, far down among the poor and long oppressed, or startling the oppressor in his guarded chambers like that mountain of fire which fell into the sea at the sound of the apocalyptic trumpet, it agitated the world.

The arguments of Condorcet, the battle-words of Mirabeau, the fierce zeal of St. Just, the iron energy of Danton, the caustic wit of Camille Desmoulins, and the sweet eloquence of Vergniaud found echoes in all lands, and nowhere more readily than in Great Britain, the ancient foe and rival of France. The celebrated Dr. Price, of London, and the still more distinguished Priestley, of Birmingham, spoke out boldly in defence of the great principles of the Revolution. A London club of reformers, reckoning among its members such men as Sir William Jones, Earl Grey, Samuel Whitbread, and Sir James Mackintosh, was established for the purpose of disseminating liberal appeals and arguments throughout the United Kingdom.

In Scotland an auxiliary society was formed, under the name of Friends of the People. Thomas Muir, young in years, yet an elder in the Scottish kirk, a successful advocate at the bar, talented, affable, eloquent, and distinguished for the purity of his life and his enthusiasm in the cause of freedom, was its principal originator. In the twelfth month of 1792 a convention of reformers was held at Edinburgh. The government became alarmed, and a warrant was issued for the arrest of Muir. He escaped to France; but soon after, venturing to return to his native land, was recognized and imprisoned. He was tried upon the charge of lending books of republican tendency, and reading an address from Theobald Wolfe Tone and the United Irishmen before the society of which he was a member. He defended himself in a long and eloquent address, which concluded in the following manly strain:—

"What, then, has been my crime? Not the lending to a relation a copy of Thomas Paine's works,—not the giving away to another a few numbers of an innocent and constitutional publication; but my crime is, for having dared to be, according to the measure of my feeble abilities, a strenuous and an active advocate for an equal representation of the people in the House of the people,—for having dared to accomplish a measure by legal means which was to diminish the weight of their taxes and to put an end to the profusion of their blood. Gentlemen, from my infancy to this moment I have devoted myself to the cause of the people. It is a good cause: it will ultimately prevail,—it will finally triumph."

He was sentenced to transportation for fourteen years, and was removed to the Edinburgh jail, from thence to the hulks, and lastly to the transport-ship, containing eighty-three convicts, which conveyed him to Botany Bay.

The next victim was Palmer, a learned and highly accomplished Unitarian minister in Dundee. He was greatly beloved and respected as a polished gentleman and sincere friend of the people. He was charged with circulating a republican tract, and was sentenced to seven years' transportation.

But the Friends of the People were not quelled by this summary punishment of two of their devoted leaders. In the tenth month, 1793, delegates were called together from various towns in Scotland, as well as from Birmingham, Sheffield, and other places in England. Gerrald and Margarot were sent up by the London society. After a brief sitting, the convention was dispersed by the public authorities. Its sessions were opened and closed with prayer, and the speeches of its members manifested the pious enthusiasm of the old Cameronians and Parliament-men of the times of Cromwell. Many of the dissenting clergy were present. William Skirving, the most determined of the band, had been educated for the ministry, and was a sincerely religious man. Joseph Gerrald was a young man of brilliant talents and exemplary character. When the sheriff entered the hall to disperse the friends of liberty, Gerrald knelt in prayer. His remarkable words were taken down by a reporter on the spot. There is nothing in modern history to compare with this supplication, unless it be that of Sir Henry Vane, a kindred martyr, at the foot of the scaffold, just before his execution. It is the prayer of universal humanity, which God will yet hear and answer.

"O thou Governor of the universe, we rejoice that, at all times and in all circumstances, we have liberty to approach Thy throne, and that we are assured that no sacrifice is more acceptable to Thee than that which is made for the relief of the oppressed. In this moment of trial and persecution we pray that Thou wouldst be our defender, our counsellor, and our guide. Oh, be Thou a pillar of fire to us, as Thou wast to our fathers of old, to enlighten and direct us; and to our enemies a pillar of cloud, and darkness, and confusion.

"Thou art Thyself the great Patron of liberty. Thy service is perfect freedom. Prosper, we beseech Thee, every endeavor which we make to promote Thy cause; for we consider the cause of truth, or every cause which tends to promote the happiness of Thy creatures, as Thy cause.

"O thou merciful Father of mankind, enable us, for Thy name's sake, to endure persecution with fortitude; and may we believe that all trials and tribulations of life which we endure shall work together for good to them that love Thee; and grant that the greater the evil, and the longer it may be continued, the greater good, in Thy holy and adorable providence, may be produced therefrom. And this we beg, not for our own merits, but through the merits of Him who is hereafter to judge the world in righteousness and mercy."

He ceased, and the sheriff, who had been temporarily overawed by the extraordinary scene, enforced the warrant, and the meeting was broken up. The delegates descended to the street in silence, — Arthur's Seat and Salisbury Crags glooming in the distance and night, — an immense and agitated multitude waiting around, over which tossed the flaring flambeaux of the sheriff's train. Gerrald, who was already under arrest, as he descended, spoke aloud, "Behold the funeral torches of Liberty!"

Skirving and several others were immediately arrested. They were tried in the first month, 1794, and sentenced, as Muir and Palmer had previously been, to transportation. Their conduct throughout was worthy of their great and holy cause. Gerrald's defence was that of freedom rather than his own. Forgetting himself, he spoke out manfully and earnestly for the poor, the oppressed, the overtaxed, and starving millions of his countrymen. That some idea may be formed of this noble plea for liberty, I give an extract from the concluding paragraphs: —

"True religion, like all free governments, appeals to the understanding for its support, and not to the sword. All systems, whether civil or moral, can only be durable in proportion as they are founded on truth and calculated to promote the good of mankind. This will account to us why governments suited to the great energies of man have always outlived the perishable things which despotism has erected. Yes, this will account to us why the stream of Time, which is continually washing away the dissoluble fabrics of superstitions and impostures, passes without injury by the adamant of Christianity.

"Those who are versed in the history of their country, in the history of the human race, must know that rigorous state prosecutions have always preceded the era of convulsion; and this era, I fear, will be accelerated by the folly and madness of our rulers. If the people are discontented, the proper mode of quieting their discontent is, not by instituting rigorous and sanguinary prosecutions, but by redressing their wrongs and conciliating their affections. Courts of justice, indeed, may be called in to the aid of ministerial vengeance; but if once the purity of their proceedings is suspected, they will cease to be objects of reverence to the nation; they will degenerate into empty and expensive pageantry, and become the partial instruments of vexatious oppression. Whatever may become of me, my principles will last forever. Individuals may perish; but truth is eternal. The rude blasts of tyranny may blow from every quarter; but freedom is that hardy plant which will survive the tempest and strike an everlasting root into the most unfavorable soil.

"Gentlemen, I am in your hands. About my life I feel not the slightest anxiety: if it would promote the cause, I would cheerfully make the sacrifice; for if I perish on an occasion like the present, out of my ashes will arise a flame to consume the tyrants and oppressors of my country."

Years have passed, and the generation which knew the persecuted reformers has given place to another. And now, half a century after William Skirving, as he rose to receive his sentence, declared to his judges, "You may condemn us as felons, but your sentence shall yet be reversed by the people," the names of these men are once more familiar to British lips. The sentence has been reversed; the prophecy of Skirving has become history. On the 21st of the eighth month, 1853, the corner-stone of a monument to the memory of the Scottish martyrs—for which subscriptions had been received from such men as Lord Holland, the Dukes of Bedford and Norfolk; and the Earls of Essex and Leicester—was laid with imposing ceremonies in the beautiful burial-place of Calton Hill, Edinburgh, by the veteran reformer and tribune of the people, Joseph Hume, M. P. After delivering an appropriate address, the aged radical closed the impressive scene by reading the prayer of Joseph Gerrald. At the banquet which afterwards took place, and which was presided over by John Dunlop, Esq., addresses were made by the president and Dr. Ritchie, and by William Skirving, of Kirkaldy, son of the martyr. The Complete Suffrage Association of Edinburgh, to the number of five hundred, walked in procession to Calton Hill, and in the open air proclaimed unmolested the very principles for which the martyrs of the past century had suffered.

The account of this tribute to the memory of departed worth cannot fail to awaken in generous hearts emotions of gratitude towards Him who has thus signally vindicated His truth, showing that the triumph of the oppressor is but for a season, and that even in this world a lie cannot live forever. Well and truly did George Fox say in his last days,

"The truth is above all."

Will it be said, however, that this tribute comes too late; that it cannot solace those brave hearts which, slowly broken by the long agony of colonial servitude, are now cold in strange graves? It is, indeed, a striking illustration of the truth that he who would benefit his fellow-man must "walk by faith," sowing his seed in the morning, and in the evening withholding not his hand; knowing only this, that in God's good time the harvest shall spring up and ripen, if not for himself, yet for others, who, as they bind the full sheaves and gather in the heavy clusters, may perchance remember him with gratitude and set up stones of memorial on the fields of his toil and sacrifices. We may regret that in this stage of the spirit's life the sincere and self-denying worker is not always permitted to partake of the fruits of his toil or receive the honors of a benefactor. We hear his good evil spoken of, and his noblest sacrifices counted as naught; we see him not only assailed by the wicked, but discountenanced and shunned by the timidly good, followed on his hot and dusty pathway by the execrations of the hounding mob and the contemptuous pity of the worldly wise and prudent; and when at last the horizon of Time shuts down between him and ourselves, and the places which have known him know him no more forever, we are almost ready to say with the regal voluptuary of old, This also is vanity and a great evil; "for what hath a man of all his labor and of the vexation of his heart wherein he hath labored under the sun?" But is this the end? Has God's universe no wider limits than the circle of the blue wall which shuts in our nestling-place? Has life's infancy only been provided for, and beyond this poor nursery-chamber of Time is there no playground for the soul's youth, no broad fields for its manhood? Perchance, could we but lift the curtains of the narrow pinfold wherein we dwell, we might see that our poor friend and brother whose fate we have thus deplored has by no means lost the reward of his labors, but that in new fields of duty he is cheered even by the tardy recognition of the value of his services in the old. The continuity of life is never broken; the river flows onward and is lost to our sight, but under its new horizon it carries the same waters which it gathered under ours, and its unseen valleys are made glad by the offerings which are borne down to them from the past,—flowers, perchance, the germs of which its own waves had planted on the banks of Time. Who shall say that the mournful and repentant love with which the benefactors of our race are at length regarded may not be to them, in their new condition of being, sweet and grateful as the perfume of long-forgotten flowers, or that our harvest-hymns of rejoicing may not reach the ears of those who in weakness and suffering scattered the seeds of blessing?

The history of the Edinburgh reformers is no new one; it is that of all who seek to benefit their age by rebuking its popular crimes and exposing its cherished errors. The truths which they told were not believed, and for that very reason were the more needed; for it is evermore the case that the right word when first uttered is an unpopular and denied one. Hence he who undertakes to tread the thorny pathway of reform — who, smitten with the love of truth and justice, or indignant in view of wrong and insolent oppression, is rashly inclined to throw himself at once into that great conflict which the Persian seer not untruly represented as a war between light and darkness — would do well to count the cost in the outset. If he can live for Truth alone, and, cut off from the general sympathy, regard her service as its "own exceeding great reward;" if he can bear to be counted a fanatic and crazy visionary; if, in all good nature, he is ready to receive from the very objects of his solicitude abuse and obloquy in return for disinterested and self-sacrificing efforts for their welfare; if, with his purest motives misunderstood and his best actions perverted and distorted into crimes, he can still hold on his way and patiently abide the hour when "the whirligig of Time shall bring about its revenges;" if, on the whole, he is prepared to be looked upon as a sort of moral outlaw or social heretic, under good society's interdict of food and fire; and if he is well assured that he can, through all this, preserve his cheerfulness and faith in man, — let him gird up his loins and go forward in God's name. He is fitted for his vocation; he has watched all night by his armor. Whatever his trial may be, he is prepared; he may even be happily disappointed in respect to it; flowers of unexpected refreshing may overhang the hedges of his strait and narrow way; but it remains to be true that he who serves his contemporaries in faithfulness and sincerity must expect no wages from their gratitude; for, as has been well said, there is, after all, but one way of doing the world good, and unhappily that way the world does not like; for it consists in telling it the very thing which it does not wish to hear.

Unhappily, in the case of the reformer, his most dangerous foes are those of his own household. True, the world's garden has become a desert and needs renovation; but is his own little nook weedless? Sin abounds without; but is his own heart pure? While smiting down the giants and dragons which beset the outward world, are there no evil guests sitting by his own hearth-stone? Ambition, envy, self-righteousness, impatience, dogmatism, and pride of opinion stand at his door-way ready to enter whenever he leaves it unguarded. Then, too, there is no small danger of failing to discriminate between a rational philanthropy, with its adaptation of means to ends, and that spiritual knight-errantry which undertakes the championship of every novel project of reform, scouring the world in search of distressed schemes held in durance by common sense and vagaries happily spellbound by ridicule. He must learn that, although the most needful truth may be unpopular, it does not follow that unpopularity is a proof of the truth of his doctrines or the expediency of his measures. He must have the liberality to admit that it is barely possible for the public on some points to be right and himself wrong, and that the blessing invoked upon those who suffer for righteousness is not available to such as court persecution and invite contempt; for folly has its martyrs as well as wisdom; and he who has nothing better to show of himself than the scars and bruises which the popular foot has left upon him is not even sure of winning the honors of martyrdom as some compensation for the loss of dignity and self-respect involved in the exhibition of its pains. To the reformer, in an especial manner, comes home the truth that whoso ruleth his own spirit is greater than he who taketh a city. Patience, hope, charity, watchfulness unto prayer,—how needful are all these to his success! Without them he is in danger of ingloriously giving up his contest with error and prejudice at the first repulse; or, with that spiteful philanthropy which we sometimes witness, taking a sick world by the nose, like a spoiled child, and endeavoring to force down its throat the long-rejected nostrums prepared for its relief.

What then? Shall we, in view of these things, call back young, generous spirits just entering upon the perilous pathway? God forbid! Welcome, thrice welcome, rather. Let them go forward, not unwarned of the dangers nor unreminded of the pleasures which belong to the service of humanity. Great is the consciousness of right. Sweet is the answer of a good conscience. He who pays his whole-hearted homage to truth and duty, who swears his lifelong fealty on their altars, and rises up a Nazarite consecrated to their holy service, is not without his solace and enjoyment when, to the eyes of others, he seems the most lonely and miserable. He breathes an atmosphere which the multitude know not of; "a serene heaven which they cannot discern rests over him, glorious in its purity and stillness." Nor is he altogether without kindly human sympathies. All generous and earnest hearts which are brought in contact with his own beat evenly with it. All that is good, and truthful, and lovely in man, whenever and wherever it truly recognizes him, must sooner or later acknowledge his claim to love and reverence. His faith overcomes all things. The future unrolls itself before him, with its waving harvest-fields springing up from the seed he is scattering; and he looks forward to the close of life with the calm confidence of one who feels that he has not lived idle and useless, but with hopeful heart and strong arm has labored with God and Nature for the best.

And not in vain. In the economy of God, no effort, however small, put forth for the right cause, fails of its effect. No voice, however feeble, lifted up for truth, ever dies amidst the confused noises of time. Through discords of sin and sorrow, pain and wrong, it rises a deathless melody, whose notes of wailing are hereafter to be changed to those of triumph as they blend with the great harmony of a reconciled universe. The language of a transatlantic reformer to his friends is then as true as it is hopeful and cheering: "Triumph is certain. We have espoused no losing cause. In the body we may not join our shout with the victors; but in spirit we may even now. There is but an interval of time between us and the success at which we aim. In all other respects the links of the chain are complete. Identifying ourselves with immortal and immutable principles, we share both their immortality and immutability. The vow which unites us with truth makes futurity present with us. Our being resolves itself into an everlasting now. It is not so correct to say that we shall be victorious as that we are so. When we will in unison with the supreme Mind, the characteristics of His will become, in some sort, those of ours. What He has willed is virtually done. It may take ages to unfold itself; but the germ of its whole history is wrapped up in His determination. When we make His will ours, which we do when we aim at truth, that upon which we are resolved is done, decided, born. Life is in it. It is; and the future is but the development of its being. Ours, therefore, is a perpetual triumph. Our deeds are, all of them, component elements of success." (Miall's Essays; Nonconformist, Vol. iv.)

THE PILGRIMS OF PLYMOUTH

From a letter on the celebration of the 250th anniversary of the landing of the Pilgrims at Plymouth, December 22, 1870.

No one can appreciate more highly than myself the noble qualities of the men and women of the Mayflower. It is not of them that I, a descendant of the "sect called Quakers," have reason to complain in the matter of persecution. A generation which came after them, with less piety and more bigotry, is especially responsible for the little unpleasantness referred to; and the sufferers from it scarcely need any present championship. They certainly did not wait altogether for the revenges of posterity. If they lost their ears, it is satisfactory to remember that they made those of their mutilators tingle with a rhetoric more sharp than polite.

A worthy New England deacon once described a brother in the church as a very good man Godward, but rather hard man-ward. It cannot be denied that some very satisfactory steps have been taken in the latter direction, at least, since the days of the Pilgrims. Our age is tolerant of creed and dogma, broader in its sympathies, more keenly sensitive to temporal need, and, practically recognizing the brotherhood of the race, wherever a cry of suffering is heard its response is quick and generous. It has abolished slavery, and is lifting woman from world-old degradation to equality with man before the law. Our criminal codes no longer embody the maxim of barbarism, "an eye for an eye, and a tooth for a tooth," but have regard not only for the safety of the community, but to the reform and well-being of the criminal. All the more, however, for this amiable tenderness do we need the counterpoise of a strong sense of justice. With our sympathy for the wrong-doer we need the old Puritan and Quaker hatred of wrongdoing; with our just tolerance of men and opinions a righteous abhorrence of sin. All the more for the sweet humanities and Christian liberalism which, in drawing men nearer to each other, are increasing the sum of social influences for good or evil, we need the bracing atmosphere, healthful, if austere, of the old moralities. Individual and social duties are quite as imperative now as when they were minutely specified in statute-books and enforced by penalties no longer admissible. It is well that stocks, whipping-post, and ducking- stool are now only matters of tradition; but the honest reprobation of vice and crime which they symbolized should by no means perish with them. The true life of a nation is in its personal morality, and no excellence of constitution and laws can avail much if the people lack purity and integrity. Culture, art, refinement, care for our own comfort and that of others, are all well, but truth, honor, reverence, and fidelity to duty are indispensable.

The Pilgrims were right in affirming the paramount authority of the law of God. If they erred in seeking that authoritative law, and passed over the Sermon on the Mount for the stern Hebraisms of Moses; if they hesitated in view of the largeness of Christian liberty; if they seemed unwilling to accept the sweetness and light of the good tidings, let us not forget that it was the mistake of men who feared more than they dared to hope, whose estimate of the exceeding awfulness of sin caused them to dwell upon God's vengeance rather than his compassion; and whose dread of evil was so great that, in shutting their hearts against it, they sometimes shut out the good. It is well for us if we have learned to listen to the sweet persuasion of the Beatitudes; but there are crises in all lives which require also the emphatic "Thou shalt not" or the Decalogue which the founders wrote on the gate-posts of their commonwealth.

Let us then be thankful for the assurances which the last few years have afforded us that:

> "The Pilgrim spirit is not dead,
> But walks in noon's broad light."

We have seen it in the faith and trust which no circumstances could shake, in heroic self-sacrifice, in entire consecration to duty. The fathers have lived in their sons. Have we not all known the Winthrops and Brewsters, the Saltonstalls and Sewalls, of old times, in gubernatorial chairs, in legislative halls, around winter camp-fires, in the slow martyrdoms of prison and hospital? The great struggle through which we have passed has taught us how much we owe to the men and women of the Plymouth Colony,—the noblest ancestry that ever a people looked back to with love and reverence. Honor, then, to the Pilgrims! Let their memory be green forever!

GOVERNOR ENDICOTT

I am sorry that I cannot respond in person to the invitation of the Essex Institute to its commemorative festival on the 18th. I especially regret it, because, though a member of the Society of Friends, and, as such, regarding with abhorrence the severe persecution of the sect under the administration of Governor Endicott, I am not unmindful of the otherwise noble qualities and worthy record of the great Puritan, whose misfortune it was to live in an age which regarded religious toleration as a crime. He was the victim of the merciless logic of his creed. He honestly thought that every convert to Quakerism became by virtue of that conversion a child of perdition; and, as the head of the Commonwealth, responsible for the spiritual as well as temporal welfare of its inhabitants, he felt it his duty to whip, banish, and hang heretics to save his people from perilous heresy.

The extravagance of some of the early Quakers has been grossly exaggerated. Their conduct will compare in this respect favorably with that of the first Anabaptists and Independents; but it must be admitted that many of them manifested a good deal of that wild enthusiasm which has always been the result of persecution and the denial of the rights of conscience and worship. Their pertinacious defiance of laws enacted against them, and their fierce denunciations of priests and magistrates, must have been particularly aggravating to a man as proud and high tempered as John Endicott. He had that free-tongued neighbor of his, Edward Wharton, smartly whipped at the cart-tail about once a month, but it may be questioned whether the governor's ears did not suffer as much under Wharton's biting sarcasm and "free speech" as the latter's back did from the magisterial whip.

Time has proved that the Quakers had the best of the controversy; and their descendants can well afford to forget and forgive an error which the Puritan governor shared with the generation in which he lived.

WEST OSSIPEE, N. H., 14th 9th Month, 1878.

JOHN WINTHROP

On the anniversary of his landing at Salem

I see by the call of the Essex Institute that some probability is suggested that I may furnish a poem for the occasion of its meeting at The Willows on the 22d. I would be glad to make the implied probability a fact, but I find it difficult to put my thoughts into metrical form, and there will be little need of it, as I understand a lady of Essex County, who adds to her modern culture and rare poetical gifts the best spirit of her Puritan ancestry, has lent the interest of her verse to the occasion.

It was a happy thought of the Institute to select for its first meeting of the season the day and the place of the landing of the great and good governor, and permit me to say, as thy father's old friend, that its choice for orator, of the son of him whose genius, statesmanship, and eloquence honored the place of his birth, has been equally happy. As I look over the list of the excellent worthies of the first emigrations, I find no one who, in all respects, occupies a nobler place in the early colonial history of Massachusetts than John Winthrop. Like Vane and Milton, he was a gentleman as well as a Puritan, a cultured and enlightened statesman as well as a God-fearing Christian. It was not under his long and wise chief magistracy that religious bigotry and intolerance hung and tortured their victims, and the terrible delusion of witchcraft darkened the sun at noonday over Essex. If he had not quite reached the point where, to use the words of Sir Thomas More, he could "hear heresies talked and yet let the heretics alone," he was in charity and forbearance far in advance of his generation.

I am sorry that I must miss an occasion of so much interest. I hope you will not lack the presence of the distinguished citizen who inherits the best qualities of his honored ancestor, and who, as a statesman, scholar, and patriot, has added new lustre to the name of Winthrop.

DANVERS, 6th Month, 19, 1880.